Ugandan Agency within China–Africa Relations

Peace, Society, and the State in Africa

Published in collaboration with the African Leadership Centre,
King's College London

Published in association with the Africa Leadership Centre, this original and necessary series interrogates issues at the intersection of security, conflict and development in Africa, focussing in particular on the relationship between the state and the wider society from which it emerges. Guided by the promotion of Africa-led ideas and respect for independent thinking, the series presents cutting-edge research, fieldwork and theoretical insights into the society-based changes impacting the continent today.

The **African Leadership Centre** (ALC) is an internationally renowned academic unit based within King's College London, with a semi-autonomous research and training centre in Nairobi, Kenya. It incorporates a global community of scholars, whose cutting-edge research on peace, leadership, development and security issues aims to inform and influence intellectual debate, teaching and learning as well as policy discourses both in Africa and globally. Over the years the ALC has attracted some of the most influential African and global thought leaders, diplomats, military personnel, politicians and civil society leaders to speak at lectures and debates with its students in London and Nairobi. Although not exclusively African in its coverage or its student intake, the ALC is nevertheless committed to developing the next generation of African scholars, analysts and leaders.

The series editors are founding Director of the ALC, Professor 'Funmi Olonisakin, and Associate Professor at the ALC, Dr Eka Ikpe.

Ugandan Agency within China–Africa Relations

President Museveni and China's Foreign Policy in East Africa

Barney Walsh

BLOOMSBURY ACADEMIC
LONDON • NEW YORK • OXFORD • NEW DELHI • SYDNEY

BLOOMSBURY ACADEMIC
Bloomsbury Publishing Plc
50 Bedford Square, London, WC1B 3DP, UK
1385 Broadway, New York, NY 10018, USA
29 Earlsfort Terrace, Dublin 2, Ireland

BLOOMSBURY, BLOOMSBURY ACADEMIC and the Diana logo are trademarks
of Bloomsbury Publishing Plc

First published in Great Britain 2022

Copyright © Barney Walsh, 2022

Barney Walsh has asserted his right under the Copyright, Designs and Patents Act,
1988, to be identified as Author of this work.

For legal purposes the Acknowledgments on p. xiii constitute an extension
of this copyright page.

Series design by Adriana Brioso
Cover image © REUTERS/Alamy Stock Photo

All rights reserved. No part of this publication may be reproduced or transmitted
in any form or by any means, electronic or mechanical, including photocopying,
recording, or any information storage or retrieval system, without prior permission
in writing from the publishers.

Bloomsbury Publishing Plc does not have any control over, or responsibility for,
any third-party websites referred to or in this book. All internet addresses given
in this book were correct at the time of going to press. The author and publisher
regret any inconvenience caused if addresses have changed or sites have
ceased to exist, but can accept no responsibility for any such changes.

A catalogue record for this book is available from the British Library.

A catalog record for this book is available from the Library of Congress.

ISBN: HB: 978-1-3502-5548-7
        PB: 978-1-3502-5547-0
        ePDF: 978-1-3502-5550-0
        eBook: 978-1-3502-5549-4

Series: Peace, Society, and the State in Africa

Typeset by RefineCatch Limited, Bungay, Suffolk
Printed and bound in Great Britain

To find out more about our authors and books visit www.bloomsbury.com
and sign up for our newsletters.

To Anna. Thank you for all your love and support

Contents

Abbreviations	ix
Acknowledgments	xiii
Introduction: The importance of China and Uganda	1
Introduction	1
History and background	12
1 China–Uganda relations and the regional imperative	27
Background and history: post-independence and the rise of Museveni	28
Modern relations – structural context	34
Lower-level forces – balancing regime players	42
Domestic opposition and regional alternatives?	49
Conclusion: influence, incorporation and resistance	57
2 China and the East African Community: overarching and low-level impacts	61
History of relations – always important	62
East African Community II – a shared agenda?	68
Contemporary relations – China's structural role in East Africa	72
Security trends and challenges – China's impact on dynamics.	84
Conclusion: spaces being opened	100
3 China's role in regional security and the nature of Museveni's methods	105
'Ugandan' terrorism	106
Chinese Small Arms and Light Weapons (SALW) – impacting all levels	114
Museveni's oil	123
The CNOOC and Uganda's development dream	130

Conclusion: necessary reactions enabling regional
security impacts 142

Conclusion: Museveni as agent of Africa? 145

Notes 159
Bibliography 191
Index 207

Abbreviations

ACIRC	African Capacity for Immediate Response to Crises
ADF	Allied Democratic Forces
AGOA	African Growth and Opportunity Act
ALADI	Latin American Integration Association
AMISOM	African Union Mission to Somalia
ANC	African National Congress
APSA	African Peace and Security Architecture
AQIM	Algeria based Al-Qaeda in Islamic Maghreb
ASEAN	Association of Southeast Asian Nations
ASF	African Standby Force
ATT	UN Arms Trade Treaty
AU	African Union
BCEG	Beijing Construction Engineering Group
BRICS	Brazil, Russia, India, China, South Africa
CAR	Central African Republic
CARICOM	Caribbean Community
CCECC	China Civil Engineering Construction Corporation
CCECC	China Civil Engineering Construction Corporation
CCM	Chama Cha Mapinduzi
CDB	China Development Bank
CEN-SAD	Community of Sahel-Saharan States
CEWS	Continental Early Warning System
CHEC	China Harbour and Engineering Corporation
CI	Confucian Institute
CIF	China International Fund
CMI	Chief of Military Intelligence
CNEEC	China National Electrical Engineering Corporation
CNOOC	China National Offshore Oil Corporation
CNPC	China National Petroleum Corporation

CNU	Chadian National Union
COMESA	Common Market for Eastern and Southern Africa
COREMO	Revolutionary Committee of Mozambique
CoW	Coalition of the Willing
CPC	Communist Party of China
CWE	China International Water and Electric Corporation'
DRC	Democratic Republic of Congo
EAC	East African Community
EACJ	East African Court of Justice
EALA	East African Legislative Assembly
ECCAS	Economic Community of Central African States
ECOWAS	Economic Community of West African States
EPA	Economic Partnership Agreements
ESO	External Security Organisation
EU	European Union
EXIM Bank	Export-Import Bank of China
FDC	Forum for Democratic Change
FDLR	Democratic Forces for the Liberation of Rwanda
FNLA	National Liberation Front of Angola
FOCAC	Forum on Africa-China Cooperation
FRELIMO	Mozambique Liberation Front
GLR	Great Lakes Region
GWOT	Global War on Terror
ICC	International Criminal Court
ICG	International Crisis Group
ICGLR	The International Conference of the Great Lakes Region
IDP	Internally Displaced People
IGAD	Intergovernmental Authority on Development
IMF	International Monetary Fund
IOC	International Oil Company
ISO	Internal Security Organisation
ISOs	Internal Security Officers
KACITA	Kampala City Traders Association
LAPSSET	Lamu Port Southern Sudan-Ethiopia Transport
LC	Local Councils

LRA	Lord's Resistance Army
MDC	Movement for Democratic Change
MONUSCO	United Nations Organization Stabilization Mission in the Democratic Republic of the Congo
MoU	Memorandum of Understanding
MP	Member of Parliament
MPLA	People's Movement for the Liberation of Angola
NAFTA	North American Free Trade Agreement
NALU	National Army for the Liberation of Uganda
NGO	Non-Governmental Organization
NOC	National Oil Company
NORINCO	China North Industries Group Corp
NRA	National Resistance Army
NRM	National Resistance Movement
OAU	Organisation of African Unity
ODM	Orange Democratic Movement
P-5	Permanent five member of the UN Security Council
PAC	Pan Africanist Congress
PEPD	Petroleum Exploration and Production Department
PGB	Presidential Guard Brigade
PSA	Production Sharing Agreements
PSC	African Union's Peace and Security Council
REC	Regional Economic Community
RECSA	Regional Centre on Small Arms
RM	Regional Mechanism
RO	Regional Organization
RPF	Rwandan Patriotic Front
SADC	Southern Africa Development Community
SALW	Small Arms and Light Weapons
SAPs	Structural Adjustment Programmes
SGR	Standard Gauge Railway
Sinopec	China Petroleum & Chemical Corporation
SPLA	Sudan People's Liberation Army
SPLA	Sudan People's Liberation Army
UAE	United Arab Emirates

UMA	Arab Maghreb Union
UN	United Nations
UNAMID	United Nations Mission in Darfur
UNITA	National Union for the Total Independence of Angola
UNSC	United Nations Security Council
UPC	Union of the Peoples of Cameroon
UPDF	Ugandan People's Defence Force
US	United States of America
USSR	Union of Soviet Socialist Republics
UWA	Ugandan Wildlife Authority
ZANU	Zimbabwe African National Union
ZANU-PF	Zimbabwe African National Union – Patriotic Front

Acknowledgments

I express wholehearted thanks and appreciation to all friends and colleagues at the African Leadership Centre (ALC), at both the ALC-Nairobi and the ALC-King's College London, for all the support they have given me over many years and for making me feel very much part of the ALC family.

Regarding this book project, I must specifically thank Funmi Olonisakin who was an unwavering support and inspiration throughout the research and writing process; and all members of ALC's Research Cluster 6 on 'African statehood and the international political economy', namely: Eka Ikpe, Kiven Kewir, Leonide Awar and Hubert Kinkoh. This book is an output from under that cluster and their advice and support has been invaluable.

Special thanks also to several organisations and trusts who have kindly provided me with some financial support to assist with undertaking this work, namely: The Carnegie Corporation of New York; The Professionals Aid Council; and Gilchrist Charitable Trust. Extra special thanks goes to Sidney Perry Foundation and the Sir Richard Stapley Trust. Additional special thanks goes to my mother, Charlotte Walsh, without whose support it would not have been possible to undertake the research component of this effort.

I would like to thank the Centre for Basic Research in Uganda, along with every individual who assisted me and partook in my field research in Uganda and East Africa. They are too many to mention by name but I am immensely grateful for all the help and information that you provided. In particular, I must thank personally Charles Kazooba and Frederic Musisi in Uganda; and Charles Kadonya in Tanzania at the East African Legislative Assembly (along with all other staff and people there). Thanks also to all staff who assisted me at the University of Pretoria during my stay.

Last, but of course in no way least, I would like to thank my long-suffering wife Anna, who has been patient and loving during the various stages gone through to finalise this work. We have gone through much ourselves during that time. This work is dedicated to her.

Introduction

The importance of China and Uganda

'You came here to do business, not politics; if you are not willing to co-operate, leave the country.'

President Museveni to the Head of China Civil Engineering and Construction (CCECC) in Uganda[1]

Introduction

This is a story of African agency in the modern world. This agency – the capacity to act or exert power – is often seen to be solely in the hands of the 'Great Powers'. Africa and Africans are assumed to be the downtrodden recipients or, perhaps more aptly, subjects of that assertion of power and influence, historically and within the contemporary world order. But this story paints a more complex picture. It tells of an African President – Yoweri Museveni of Uganda – who has acted and exerted power against his regional rivals, Great Power 'partners' and emerging global actors with impressive, unexpected consistency.

Museveni is well-known in Africa. He has been in power since his 1986 'Bush War' victory which supposedly brought in a new era of democracy and economic progress. But he has steadily come to be perceived as a classic 'good man turned bad' African story. His regular election victories are marred by intimidation, cash handouts and allegations of fraud; and Uganda is never spoken of in the same breath as other states such as Rwanda and Ethiopia as possible providing an 'African developmental state model. Although Uganda has enjoyed relative stability and with a growing economy for many years, poverty, unemployment and corruption are rampant. Museveni's proclamation in 1986 that 'the problem of Africa in general and Uganda in particular is not the people but leaders who want to overstay in power' is seemingly long forgotten.[2]

Museveni has also become increasingly notorious in the West, where to be known for any reason is still generally an unusual occurrence for any African leader. Uganda's anti-homosexuality legislation in 2014 gained significant international media attention. And government crack downs against Bobi Wine and his supporters – the charismatic hip-hop star turned politician who challenged Museveni for the Presidency in 2021 – also killed enough protestors (at least nineteen in total) to gain some more column inches and occasional newsreader references. Museveni's early successes against HIV/AIDs, the mountains of donor aid support received and his pivotal role in the US Global War on Terror are far less well known.

But this work is not intended as a commentary on Museveni the man or his regime: it offers no moral judgements around his longevity, democratic credentials or human rights record. It is a dispassionate analysis of how African agency is manifest in the world generally, Africa in particular, and Uganda and East Africa specifically. This capacity of Africans and African leaders to act or exert power in the world remains under analysed and misunderstood, with Museveni offering an intriguing case study of its occurrence through means and methods not well documented elsewhere. This is the story of an African leader using the rise of a Great Power – China – for the advancement of his personal and country's strategic importance. This is not the African agency of Nigerian traders sourcing Chinese loans and goods, or Angolan elites getting reasonable deals around oil revenues for their personal profit, as undertaken elsewhere.[3] It is serious, high-level, geopolitical agency that utilizes global forces against regional rivals, of spreading power and influence beyond domestic and regional boundaries, and incorporating (richer) nations into institutional arrangements for a leader's own benefits and interests.

This story is centred on the promise that contemporary Africa faces an external threat, challenge and opportunity of epoch-defining significance; at the same time as it undergoes a great internal effort to remake Africa's continental security arrangements in profound ways. Externally, a global power shift sees China rise as the most credible challenger to the Western-led world system from amongst an array of so-called 'emerging powers'. Internally, Africa's security re-arrangement is the African Union's (AU) efforts to create a viable African Peace and Security Architecture (APSA). This networked web of numerous African regional organizations (ROs) and regional mechanisms (RMs) hopes to create 'a new culture of peace and security on the continent.'[4]

This story sought to uncover how Africa's external and internal challenges were related, and search for how African agency existed within this fluctuating context. What threats and opportunities appear for African nations from a rising China and its impacts on a re-imagined African security structure? What is the role for African leaders in remaking and reshaping these African regions and the continent as a whole? Fundamentally, **how and why does China's engagement in Africa impact the continent's security dynamic, and what is the role of African leaders therein?** This work found that within this global and continental context, President Yoweri Museveni of Uganda has appeared as an outstanding example of African agency. He has skilfully manipulated the increasing presence of China in a fashion that helps maintain his domestic rule in Uganda, and utilized Chinese engagement with the East African Community (EAC) – a regional organization within the APSA framework – to centralize his importance within the EAC and within regional security dynamics more generally.

As China's rise appears as the pre-eminent geopolitical issue of the current age, assessing this interplay between external forces, internal efforts and African agency therein should be alluring for anybody concerned with African development in the twenty-first century. Africa's Regional Economic Communities (RECs) are the building blocks to the imagined new, potentially transformative African Peace and Security Architecture. Understanding the effects of China's bilateral and regional engagements on the security role of these RECs is therefore crucial. The book offers a comprehensive account of how China's engagement within a particular region (East Africa) influences inter-state security dynamics and position of a key regional actor (Uganda), which helps to better understand China's impact on African security as a whole. The book offers a more Africa-centric analysis of China–Africa relations by covering in detail security and development challenges in Africa, and then uncovering China's role within them; rather than – as is commonly done elsewhere – by beginning with what China is doing and trying to assess subsequent impacts in Africa.

The book mainly discusses the period from 2000 when China's global power and African incursions began increasing rapidly, up until December 2015 when the Forum on China-Africa Cooperation VI meeting marked the latest new phase in China–Africa relations. In particular, it mostly focuses on a prolonged snapshot in time of particular interest and complexity, circa 2010–16, when an exciting and potentially transformative regional integration initiative was underway within the East African Community, Uganda and East African oil and resource finds were becoming increasingly significant, local security challenges with global implications were prevalent, and the East African Community was on the cusp of expanding to include South Sudan. South Sudan is not discussed as a fully fledged member of the EAC throughout the book, due to its admission occurring more recently and after the main period of focus; but it is discussed in relation to the key security challenges and dynamics of relevance to the study (in which events in South Sudan unquestionably played an important role).

The role of individual leaders in shaping regional security dynamics and relations with China is central to this story. The book shows how Uganda's leader, President Museveni, has utilized Chinese presence in two prominent security issues – 'terrorism' and the 'oil sector' – in order to impact the East African security environment significantly. Museveni has, on occasion, exerted agency against China; but more significant is how he has used the increasing presence of China across the region to exert influence against his East African regional rivals. During this period of interest, this agency has produced more structured regional security dynamics which benefit Uganda and his personal position. Museveni has welcomed Chinese presence in Uganda to make them a valued partner in resisting international and domestic pressure against his regime, whilst also preventing any overbearing influence from China itself. Within EAC, China's contributory role in security issues related to terrorism and the oil sector has allowed Museveni to significantly influence – and centralize his role within – the security dynamics between member states.

This book highlights the power and methods of President Museveni as an African leader in relation to the supposedly more powerful China, showing that Africa is not, as often assumed, simply a passive space where Great Powers can impose their will. Ultimately, China's attempted exploitation of East Africa's various opportunities has seen it become an unwitting accomplice in aiding President Museveni's agenda. The arguments presented here do not overstate the nature and importance of African agency: China does not simply do the bidding of Museveni, consistently be outsmarted by him, or significantly adjust their overarching strategy and intentions based on his presence. Neither do the arguments intend to present Museveni as some kind of regional power-house or agentic superman who acts at will against his passive, subordinate regional counterparts. But the book does showcase how the increased presence of China – which would have occurred regardless of who holds the Presidency in Uganda – is utilized and manipulated by Museveni in shrewd, cunning ways to suit his personal agenda. And it argues that Museveni has done this more successfully and consistently than other regional actors, to a more impressive level than might have been expected by Ugandan material capacity alone, and maintained his regional importance in unique, impressive ways.

No other work has properly explained how the East African Community (or any other African regional organization) development and security dynamics are influenced by Chinese presence, or how African leaders are able to assert agency within that space by utilizing Chinese investment to shift the regional agenda. No study has analysed the pertinence of African leader's nuanced personalities to the security dynamic between states in East Africa, or how personal friendships and rivalries fluctuate under the present climate of increasing Chinese engagement. Neither has there been analysis of how these inter-locking state relations and fluctuating personal relationships coalesce within an EAC institution which has numerous key security components in its own right. Oil finds in the region mean that the EAC security architecture and activities are likely to gain prominence. Understanding the role of Uganda, and President Museveni, in each of these areas is critical to providing a robust assessment of China's role in modern regional relations.

This book proceeds as follows. The remainder of this introduction chapter provides a brief background to China's increasing role in Africa; the East African Community and the Museveni regime in Uganda. It then discusses key trends within modern China–Africa relations, noting in particular in the regional nature of Chinese incursions and its security impacts (which have been under-discussed in other literature). The introduction explains the period of interest for this work, 2010–15, and will briefly reflects on what other authors have already contributed to these subjects of interest.

Chapter One is a discussion of China–Uganda relations, outlining how China interacts with Uganda's political economy. It explains how Museveni has handled Chinese presence in a means that has solidified his position in Uganda. Chapter Two is a discussion of Museveni and China's role within the East African Community, showing how Uganda's regional position has benefitted from the presence of prominent security issues in which China plays a role and from Chinese presence more generally. Chapter Three is a more detailed discussion of these issues in relation to regional security within East Africa. It focuses on terrorism and oil sector-related security issues, and explains how Museveni has asserted his agency by utilizing China's role within each one to situate himself as centrally important in defining and reacting against these threats. Finally, the conclusion explains that China has encountered a unique African leader in Uganda with the capacity and inclination to successfully manipulate Chinese presence so as to maintain and improve his domestic and regional position, providing a clear indication of African agency not necessarily attuning entirely with Chinese interests. It also justifies the relevance of the case study's conclusions for wider Africa, acknowledges the limitations of the study and identifies areas which warrant further investigation.

China's surge and the impact on African security

The history and fate of Africa have for centuries been linked to the interests of great powers. Global forces have shaken the continent; just as Africa and Africans have influenced the world and adjusted to changing world orders. China is the latest power to engage Africa with, what China claims to be, a beneficial agenda. Through innovative initiatives like the Forum on Africa-China Cooperation (FOCAC) – 'bonanza(s) of developmental assistance projects and loans' that alternate every three years since 2000 between China and African locations[5] – China presents itself as an alternative to the post-colonial Western partnerships through a rhetoric of mutual respect and 'win-win' deals. The continent formed a significant part of Beijing's foreign policy plan by after 2000, by: becoming a 'centrepiece of China's overseas energy strategy';[6] offering a large consumer market for its manufactured goods; and providing state allies to back Chinese positions within international forums – most notably at the UN.[7] China has become Africa's biggest trading partner, and Chinese oil investments are argued to be 'the greatest inflow of money into Africa in history'.[8] In the early 2010s it was estimated China imported 31 per cent of its oil from the continent, although that later dipped to 18 per cent in 2020 through further diversification of supplies (still its most significant region after the Middle East).[9] In late 2013, President Xi Jinping announced China's 'One Belt One Road' initiative and the complementary Maritime Silk road, which has African projects as centrally important. In late 2015, Chinese Foreign Minister Wang Yi reiterated that Africa is 'the foundation of the foundation' in Chinese diplomacy and that 'China will not follow the beaten track of past major powers and will not sacrifice Africa's environment and long-term interests'.[10]

China's forays have increased Africa's prominence within international politics, and helped fuel the beneficial rise in oil prices prior to the price crash in 2014.[11] The block support that Africa can offer at the UN and elsewhere makes it increasingly important in other state's calculations; and talk of the continents 'rise' or 'Africa's century' has gained ground (despite misgivings about how accurate that positive scenario actually is). Brautigam and Xiaoyang argue that 'an economic renaissance' is occurring in Africa largely due to Chinese demands,[12] and the then Senegalese President Wade stated: 'China's approach is simply better adapted to our needs than the slow and slightly patronizing approach (of Europe).'[13]

These points all emphasize that Africa has become increasingly important to China; but China's importance to Africa is even more striking. No other power in recent history has so dramatically altered the political economy of the continent. If you travel to Africa – and truly this means almost any country in Africa – you can *see* the Chinese presence. The Chinese roads, buildings, signage, restaurants, shopping malls and people, are a striking feature in a way that they were not ten or twenty years previously. An understanding of how Africa can, does and should use this Chinese engagement is slowly emerging but still very much in its infancy. A new phase of China–Africa relations began in the second half of 2010s which highlighted the evolving nature of relations: the 2014 commodity price crash; China moving towards a consumer-based economy and experiencing its own economic problems; and the comparative advantage of working in conflict environments becoming increasingly problematic, all altered the context in which relations occurred.[14] But arguments around Chinese presence remain firmly entrenched: on one side, China is seen to be supporting and entrenching authoritarian rule through its policy of non-interference with domestic affairs, or as just another exploiting foreign power focused overwhelmingly on resource extraction; on the other, China is seen as something of a saviour, by finally offering trading partner who is a viable alternative to Western donor aid.

Understanding the *security* aspect of the new Sino–Africa relations is a glaring gap within academia, policy circles and amongst the general citizenry (as is an understanding of how African states are actively adapting to and shaping the changing environment). Regional organizations are integral to the current AU development agenda generally and specific effort to build the African Peace and Security Architecture, which make them interesting focus points for a security-centric analysis. The APSA currently being forged is headed by the AU's Peace and Security Council (PSC), which overseas its interconnected pillars. The 'Panel of the Wise' comprises five highly respected African persons who can advise on African peace and security issues. The proposed 'African Standby Force' (ASF) consists of five rapid reaction regional security forces.[15] The 'Continental Early Warning System' (CEWS) has an observation and monitoring centre at the AU, being fed information from the regional early warning systems within RECs. And the 'Peace Fund' is supposed to provide required finances to peace support operations. 'Regional mechanisms' are the final pillar, but necessarily feed into each of the others.[16]

The successful functioning of this APSA will rely primarily on functional RECs and RMs, which help enable the other pillars to operate. Indeed, 'to some extent, RECs are filling the capacity gap left by the AU'.[17] RECs also compliment the 'African Solutions to African Problems' discourse that has re-emerged since the turn of the millennium and are increasingly seen as credible tools for controlling APSA's Standby Forces. Yet despite a memorandum of understanding (MoU) existing between the AU and RECs, the practical division of labour between them has not been well established. This means that whatever system, structures and relations that currently exist within APSA and RECs are changeable and can be influenced; and understanding likely sources of that

Introduction   9

influence is critical to anyone seeking to study Africa's contemporary security environment.

The EAC – progress or conflict?

Greater East Africa and the Great Lakes Region comprise one of, if not the, most complex and troubled regions in Africa. The false ethnic and geographical map of the region, population density and resultant resource pressure, and high numbers of refugees existing in each country[18] have each contributed to the genocide, inter-continental warfare, government-sponsored proxy forces, brutal civil wars and secessionist movements witnessed over the last twenty years. It also interlocks the Horn of Africa, which has produced devastating 'collapsed states', civil and inter-state war, piracy, terrorism, drought, famine and general underdevelopment. This bleak history, however, is tempered with the notable economic development, regional integration and cooperative security operations that have also taken place.

The paradox in the region can be summarized by two publications in 2012: the United Nations Economic Commission for Africa focused on how countries have made 'impressive progress in economic and financial sector reforms',[19] whilst the *American Foreign Policy Interests* journal cautioned that another genocide in Rwanda 'cannot be ruled out'.[20] And as the source of the Nile River, on the Indian Ocean which facilitates 45 per cent of global trade transits, and now containing several countries with substantive oil and gas finds, it is clear that 'few, if any, sub-regions of Africa command as much strategic significance as Greater East Africa'.[21] China's impact in this volatile, exciting region, therefore, is of compelling importance.

The East African Community (EAC) is a relatively advanced and functional body compared to other African RECs. Since its modern inception in 2001, it has made steady progress towards integration with a Common Market in 2005 and Customs Union in 2010. Each member state has a government Ministry dedicated to regional integration issues, EAC passports allow citizens easier travel and work within the community, and a Protocol on the establishment of an EAC Monetary Union was signed in November 2013. Progress should not be overstated, however. Its proposal for a common currency and fast-tracked political union by 2012 and 2015, respectively, did not materialize, and general functioning of the Market and Union is somewhat questionable.[22]

Nonetheless, the EAC's end-goal of political federation remains in place and make it the most ambitious REC in Africa. It is discussed alongside the Economic Community of West African States (ECOWAS) and Southern Africa Development Community (SADC) as noticeably more successful and advanced than other African RECs. The Intergovernmental Authority on Development (IGAD), also operating within our region of interest, has seen perpetual disagreement between member states, including proxy and full-scale war, and is anyway more a mediation forum rather than institutionalized, integrating politico-economic-security arrangement. The EAC Protocol on Co-operation in Defence Affairs and the EAC Protocol on Peace and Security were signed in April 2012 and February 2013, respectively. These aimed to institutionalize the cooperation on Defence and Security affairs already taking place between member states.[23] Interestingly, in November 2011 China signed a Framework Agreement directly with the EAC aiming to boost Chinese trade and investment in the region: the first agreement of its kind between China and an African REC.[24]

The significance of Uganda

So what of our hero Museveni? How does Uganda fit into this fluctuating era of a rising China, African-led security re-structuring, and East African integration agenda? Uganda's relationship with China has followed a similar path to the rest of Africa: trade and investment has steadily risen since 2000. In 2009/10, China became Uganda's largest trading partner (this had been the UK for the previous ten years) and has remained in the top three ever since.[25] Multi-million dollar 'gifts' included construction or refurbishments of State House, Prime Minister Offices and Parliament, and multi-billion dollar deals have been signed in the oil, transport and energy sectors. Chinese Premiers, leading Chinese officials and Uganda's President Museveni have been outspoken in their praise and adulation around a mutually beneficial partnership.

These arrangements are not unique: increased Chinese investment has occurred in each EAC member country. Yet the role and actions of Museveni have mean that Uganda is unique in combining a number of attributes that make it a compelling case study. Firstly, President Museveni has been extremely skilled in his comprehensive approach to courting substantial Western support, which he has enjoyed ever since being labelled part of the 'new breed' of African leader in the early 1990s. Second, Uganda's military has been particularly active in Greater East Africa. Museveni's adventurism has seen (amongst others): Uganda People's Defence Force (UPDF) in conflict with Congolese and Rwandan forces during hostilities in the Congo; a bloody twenty-year civil war against the LRA in Northern Uganda and then pursued in the Central African Republic (CAR); sponsoring and assistance to the Sudan People's Liberation Army (SPLA) during its secessionist war against Khartoum; and substantial UPDF troops committed to Somalia. Third, and linked to the above points, is that Uganda has been a staunch ally in the US-led Global War on Terror (GWOT), rhetorically and practically. Museveni was one of only five African leaders to publicly support the 2003 US invasion of Iraq, and the Uganda' launch of the African Union Mission to Somalia (AMISOM) against Al-Shabaab has ensured American military training, supplies, equipment and support to UPDF, alongside its donor aid package. Fourth, Uganda has a rare geographical African presence: it borders East Africa, Central Africa and the Horn, as well as attaching to North Africa by being source of the River Nile. And, geo-politically, Museveni has: ensured that Uganda has 'punched above its weight' in terms of continental presence in ways such as leading the Burundi civil war 1993–2005 peace process alongside Nelson Mandela; been publicly outspoken against UN positions on Cote d'Ivoire; mocked Nigeria's handling of the Boko Haram crisis in West Africa; and successfully battled Libya's Colonel Gadhafi at the AU over the proposed pace of African integration. Fifth, oil was discovered in Lake Albert in 2006 and be refined and exported by Uganda by 2021 (although this keeps being delayed). Uganda, alongside Kenya and possibly Somalia, is 'now significant in global calculations' concerning oil access. Sixth and finally, even before he became President, Museveni has been vocal and active in championing greater East African integration. He promoted the inclusion of Rwanda and Burundi in 2007, which was initially opposed by Kenya and Tanzania. He is the region's elder statesman whose longevity in power carries significant clout within the region and against global powers.

Uganda is therefore a unique in the providing these different areas of interest and examples of Chinese engagement, which can teach lessons to wider Africa about the impacts of Beijing's increasing presence. This book shows how Museveni has been able to manipulate and utilize the presence of China in a similar but distinct way to how he has done with the West. China's involvement in Uganda indicates that Museveni is able to prolong his Presidency and maintain his militaristic interventions. Uganda's relations with the US and role in the GWOT is propagated and reinforced by Chinese relations. In addition, China's engagement with EAC and Uganda encourages a narrative that promotes Africa's own security and development efforts generally; and specifically aiding Museveni's own Pan-African ambitions by supporting his domestic regime. China's role in Uganda's oil sector showcases Museveni's impressive ability to balance Chinese presence with other domestic, regional, and international forces, and ultimately helps enhance his regional position within the EAC arrangement.

History and background

China and Africa share a deep interwoven history. Trade has occurred for almost two millennia between them, yet confrontation and conflict has also been more prevalent than is now publicized by current leaders. African states from independence onwards remains trapped in a paradox, which China feeds into and even entrenches further. African states enjoy 'judicial sovereignty', whereby the international community recognizes their existence and engages them as states within the international system (each has a seat at the UN, for example). African leaders, however, have struggled to create 'empirical sovereignty', meaning real-life, practical control over their state territories (such as control over borders and a fully functional tax collection system). Empirical sovereignty has simply not been achieved in most African states.

During Africa's early independence years, China actively sought to influence African state's empirical sovereignty: China supported armed groups against incumbent leaders when these rebels were thought to serve Chinese interests. Modern China from 2000 onwards, however, now promotes judicial sovereignty as the defining feature of any of its relationships regardless of the empirical

Introduction

reality of that country. For African leaders, talk of 'non-interference', 'south-south cooperation' and 'win-win scenarios' has offered a seductive alternative to the traditional Western donor–client relationship, whereas there has been more contestation from local African who also engage China for their own purposes.

There are five significant periods that have shaped China–Africa relations: the pre-colonial sea voyages of Zheng He; the 1954 agreement between China and India and the Bandung Conference of 1955; Chairman Mao's support for anti-colonial liberation struggles during the 1960s and 1970s; the 1980s' and 1990s' 'lost decades'; and the post-2000 era. Throughout these eras, Africa lacked any kind of coordinated, collective approach to China (an issue which persists to this day), meaning the nature of relations was largely shaped by Beijing.

Chinese Admiral Zheng He undertook several large trade missions to Africa in 1418–33. According to legend, Zheng He did not steal or conquer land from the locals: a crucial point that is persistently emphasized by modern officials who promote the idea of an ever-lasting friendship between China and Africa. The 1954 agreement between China and India and the 1955 Bandung Conference established the Five Principles of cooperation between China and the developing world: mutual respect for each other's territorial integrity and sovereignty; mutual non-aggression; mutual non-interference in each other's internal affairs; equality and mutual benefit and peaceful co-existence.[26] Bandung gave China the opportunity to interact with officials from independent Egypt, Ethiopia, Liberia and Libya, and soon to be independent Sudan and Ghana (observers from several liberation movements were also present). Mao and his representatives immediately realized that the anti-colonial struggles of the African-Arab world fit neatly with their own disruptive, revolutionary agenda.[27]

By the early 1960s, Afro-Asian solidarity was a crucial pillar of China's foreign policy. Zhou Enlai reaffirmed a commitment to non-interference during a historic ten-country visit to Africa in 1963–4. Yet China's support for various armed groups and newly independent states was driven by an ideological revolutionary zeal and a desire for international allies. Non-interference did not apply to colonial states, or, more significantly, to independent countries when there were opposition forces who were judged to better serve Beijing's interests. During the insanity of the Cultural Revolution (most severe between 1966 and 1969 but only fully over after Mao's death in 1976), Africa and Latin America were seen as key ideological battlefields; but China's meddling meant that several African regimes expelled Chinese officials from their countries, and intensely complex African affairs were viewed through a rather simplistic Marxist-soaked lens.[28] The bulk of African states, nonetheless, backed the 1971 UN vote that gave Beijing the seat on the UN Security Council at the expense of Taipei: undoubtedly China's crowning global achievement of the era which would not have occurred without the support of African governments.

Deng Xiaoping's subsequent reformist era meant a far more pragmatic approach towards China's African engagement, with less involvement in armed struggle and instead more diplomatic aid-provision measures.[29] Even amidst a perceived disengagement from Africa in the 1980s when China's policy shifted to one of peace and development rather than war and revolution, the continent retained special significance for China. Aid continued to flow despite China remaining in the bottom twenty least developed countries in the word: Africa received more than 57 per cent of China's overseas aid from 1986 to 1995 when Asia's share diminished. China also began realizing that many of the African projects set up in the 1960s and 1970s were now failing after they had been handed over to locals. China's non-interference policy was, again, adjusted somewhat: Chinese management of foreign projects did not impinge on sovereignty.

The fall-out from Tiananmen Square in 1989 also necessitated China to immediately court African states once more, most of whom had no inclination to criticize China over events (unlike the West). Then in 1993 a seismic event took place, the magnitude of which was not appreciated at the time: China went from net exporter to net importer of oil, whilst demand for other minerals also shot up. Trade and investment steadily went up for the remaining 1990s, but would ultimately pale in comparison to the exponential increase in financial flows about to occur.

The current era – post-2000 explosion

These previous events are distinct from the West's relationship with Africa: they form the base of a different kind of modern relationship as a result, as well as a public narrative that is exploited by current leaders. The shared anti-colonial history 'functions as a discursive field through which current foreign policy is legitimised'.[30] China's presence in Africa has become expansive and far reaching, with deals of varying importance increasing in almost every state. Beijing's respect for sovereignty and non-interference doctrine has evolved to include a commitment to 'peaceful rise', which emphasizes the need to respect a diverse range of cultures and practices within the international and UN system.[31]

Throughout the 2000s, China–Africa trade enjoyed a year-on-year growth of 19.3 per cent and in 2013 surpassed $200 billion.[32] Although China's reliance on Africa can be overstated, from the African side the new finance certainly marks a specific historical period. It is estimated that 48 per cent of China's imports from Africa is crude oil, and 'the vast African continent has emerged as the centrepiece of China's overseas energy strategy'.[33] Oil is central to the relationship, but China differentiates itself from the West by investing more fully across all sectors, rather than concentrating only on a country's oil industry. Economic, political and environmental concerns are capable of creating and exacerbating conflict. China also has a global role as both arms supplier and peacekeeper. As oil prices fall, the resource-backed loans which characterized the post-2000 era become less appealing to both sides, meaning that 'we are seeing more normal business behaviour' by Chinese firms seeking finance.[34] In addition to oil, energy resources and raw materials, however, Africa provides China with expanding foreign markets for its goods and – very importantly – international allies at the UN: the 'One-China' policy of not recognizing Taiwan remains central.

China has sought to curry favour with the AU in order to gain bloc continental support for Chinese foreign policy and to gain access to Africa's strategic mineral resources. The construction of the AU headquarters is the most symbolic, and some say demeaning, example of China–AU relations.[35] China and the AU have shared a paradoxical kinship in relation to the respect for sovereignty and non-interference norm. The original Organisation of African Unity (OAU) had non-interference enshrined in its charter. The decision to respect colonial borders had far-reaching ramifications on post-independent Africa's security issues. Ironically, it was during these early independence years that China undertook the most explicit violations of its respect for sovereignty principle in Africa. Then, the more recent revamped AU incorporated a 'non-indifference doctrine' to allow African states' to intervene in another in times of particular crisis.[36]

This more post-modern, Pan-Africanist, integrationary mind-set that creates a cooperative continental security architecture under APSA are problematic for China, and African leaders within the AU also do not necessarily have such desires or ambitions. At this time of African states supposedly, therefore, moving away from a blanket non-interference agenda, China has emerged in Africa championing respect for sovereignty louder than ever. This has been warmly welcomed by a good many African leaders, and China has not yet violated that doctrine in the same crude manner it had done in previous eras. But China is still seeking ways to protect of its own interests and stable bilateral relations within this credible and principled narrative.

A regional portrait

China works with various regime types in Africa showing no particular preference over whether they are democratic or authoritarian, or whether they have stable control over their territories. This is a defining feature of their 'non-interference' policy and China publicly reiterates that Beijing only deals with sitting governments.[37] But China is certainly impacting security dynamics and regional relations across Africa, whether it intends to or not; and it has trodden in a slower, more improvised and adaptable way than is often assumed. China has also become entangled within the *regional* aspects of African states' insecurity, which is manifest in the way domestic issues often spill over into – and are likewise exacerbated by – issues in neighbouring states and the surrounding region. Regional inter-state rivalries and geo-political concerns are also present in Africa's regions. China often engages with influential states and 'regional powerhouses' in ways that can shift and shape these rivalries, with the African leaders that China encounters utilizing their presence in different ways and to varying degrees of success.[38]

In the intensely unstable Horn, China has actually seen progressive cordial relations with all states. This is rather impressive, considering the severity of the Horn's instability, and the fact that China has and does, indeed, play a role within the region's security dynamics. How regional leaders use Chinese

Introduction   17

finance, military support, and mega-infrastructure will determine whether opportunities are taken, or whether serious dangers are realized in the coming decades. Shifting international alliances and problematic regional relations in the 1970s and 1980s eventually became chaos in the 1990s. Relations with Sudan have had a major impacts on regional security issues and the Darfur crisis – or genocide – ensured that President Bashir became the 'poster child' for the argument that China supports tyrants and the relationship damaged Beijing's image in Africa immensely.[39] Ethiopia, Sudan's major regional rival, has showcased a different style of African leader who has utilized China effectively. Meles Zenawi's developmental state model saw China and Chinese companies heavily involved in the major economic progress that Ethiopia has achieved over the last decade.[40] Such developments have the potential to make Khartoum and Addis regional collaborators, but alternatively they can sustain their dangerous rivalry. Meanwhile, South Sudan's civil conflict between President Kiir and Vice-President Machar from 2013 onwards significantly disrupted oil flows.[41] China's 2014 commitment of combat troops to the UNIMISS forces there was the first of its kind. Piracy, one of the Horn's most publicized security issues, means that China's navy has been heavily involved in anti-Somali piracy efforts off the Gulf of Aden (China has also signed oil exploration contracts with Somalia's transitional government).[42] Beijing has also constructed some kind of naval base in Djibouti, ostensibly to assist with those anti-piracy efforts.[43]

Central Africa's abundant riches have created serious instability. China has experienced inescapable difficulties and a lack of genuine penetration, although DRCs looming dominance mirrors Chinese focus there from the Mobutu era onwards. Colonial and newly independent Central Africa posed problems for China, due to a muddled set of policies that included blatant breaches of non-interference. Cameroon was the first African country in which Beijing backed the rebel overthrow of the sitting independent government, and China helped train and equip various insurrectionary groups until Mobutu Sese Seko's 1965 ascendency in then-named Zaire. Such interventions meant that Central African Republic's Bokassa justified his 1966 military coup (unconvincingly) as a pre-emptive strike against China's subversive efforts to depose President Dacko.[44] Post-independence meddling from China is being replaced by a rather obvious resource extraction agenda, which is largely in-line with all great power's engagement in the region. Ultimately, corrupt and long-standing Presidents have incorporated China into their agenda fairly comfortably, without becoming overly dependent on them. It was somewhat inevitable that the DRC behemoth has become China's key regional partner. China supplied aid, military supplies, debt relief, high-level visits and technical cooperation to the conservative tyrant President Mobutu throughout the 1980s, partly due to Chinese rivalry with the Soviet Union. After Joseph Kabila (or Kabila II) became President in 2001, relations grew significantly. Nearly 50 per cent of DRC exports now go to China, including around 90 per cent of the richly endowed Katanga province's mineral exports.[45] In 2007, President Kabila's state of the union address apparently angered Western ambassadors due to his praise for China rescuing DRC.[46] The so-called 'deal of the century' offered a US$9 billion infrastructure loan, reduced to $6 billion following complaints by the International Monetary Fund (IMF), but has largely failed to deliver due to funding withdrawal from EXIM Bank and ongoing re-evaluations into the viability and fairness of various other projects.[47] A Chinese consortium may work with US companies to fund part of the colossal Grand Inga Dam project – the largest in the world if accomplished – which would potentially transform Central and Southern Africa's energy supply.[48]

In a more stable region where economic and political rivalry now shape dynamics more than security threats, Southern Africa is arguably China's most important pin in its post-2000 Africa strategy, giving its leader's potential degrees of agency. Racist Apartheid South Africa and China had no interest in relations, yet now South Africa as regional hegemon is a crucial partner for China, for business reasons but also for its continental and global political agenda. Beijing pushed other members for their inclusion into the BRICS alignment in 2010 after Pretoria assessed the original BRIC group and put forward their case for joining.[49] Angola, however, is both a *major* strategic resource provider and the hallmark example of modern China–Africa relations, despite historic difficulties. In the Angolan civil war, Beijing's interference in Africa was exposed as entirely self-interested, when it supported an FNLA/UNITA 1975 offensive that was not only defeated by the USSR-backed MPLA but also being supplied by Apartheid South Africa. Despite the substantial historic difficulties, however, shared interests post-2000 saw

Angolan relations flourish. The so-called 'Angola Model' of oil exports exchanged for Chinese-funded infrastructure projects has become the trademark of modern Sino–Africa relations.[50] Along with its diamonds, oil and strong army, investment from China and various nations means that Angola's 'potential as a regional power is clear... [it] could become a future rival to South Africa in Southern Africa'.[51] Elsewhere, Mugabe in Zimbabwe caused considerable annoyance for China but ultimately they navigated this troubled space fairly well – where they had, in fact, backed the liberation war victor (China became Zimbabwe's main arms supplier following international embargoes).[52] In Zambia, home to the first Chinese built Special Economic Zone in Africa (the benefits of which remain exceedingly dubious) the Chinese ambassador's threat to leave the country if Sata won the 2006 election whilst running on an anti-Chinese ticket, however, was less exceptional than has been made out when considering Sata had stated he would recognize Taiwan if he won.[53]

In a similar fashion to Central Africa, China's early support for various rebel groups and meddling in domestic affairs caused significant difficulties in gaining West African trust. In modern times, Ghana and Cote d'Ivoire's oil finds see them competing over regional influence in balancing against Nigeria, but they remain thoroughly in its shadow. Nigeria's hegemony is seemingly insurmountable and significant Chinese investment there could potentially create a Sino-leaning region. But the ending of military rule in Nigeria coinciding with China's post-2000 big push has ultimately seen a series of Nigerian leaders unable to fully cement Chinese ties or to utilize them for tangible regional advantage. Unlike other regions, and similarly to Central Africa, China does not have any historical ally and has had issues penetrating the dominant power: trying to replicate the successful Angolan model, they found a far more contested domestic political space within Nigeria's energy industry and had many more problems gaining ground.[54] Chinese activity is frenetic and varied nonetheless, with apparently $7 billion FDI as of 2013 and presence felt in all sectors (under the caveat of it being difficult to ascertain which projects get implemented following announcements).[55] But problems are continuous. Lamido Sanusi, Governor of the Central Bank of Nigeria from 2009 until 2014, wrote a scathing attack on China's presence in 2013, comparing its efforts to colonialism and as contributing to African 'deindustrialisation and underdevelopment'.[56] Nigerian militants in the Niger Delta oil region have kidnapped Chinese workers and held them to ransom. In September 2009, the Movement for the Emancipation of the Niger Delta (MEND) publicly threatened China for investing in the troubled region. Chinese workers have also been killed and kidnapped by Boko Haram in north-east Nigeria and neighbouring Cameron. In addition, there are serious tensions between local market traders due to Chinese competition devastating much of Nigeria's textile and consumer product industry, meaning 'all the danger signs are there, it could become a flash point'.[57]

North Africa's proximity to the Middle East makes its security dynamics entwined much more closely to its global position rather than its continental role in Africa. Terrorism, despot rivalry and the Arab Spring have shaped regional security dynamics, which China must understand and react to in order to pursue North Africa's consumer markets, manufacturing potential and links to Europe. Western oil actors are much more entrenched and competitive. Al-Qaeda and other Islamists loathe the region's leaders, meaning China and its businesses are under threat of militant attacks which have already occurred on energy infrastructure projects.[58] China's long-term interests and relations have not been affected significantly by the Arab Spring due to careful responses from Beijing, but US and Western influence there mean that China is affected by regional security dynamics to a greater extent than it is able to affect them.

Egypt and other powers are far less interested in China's post-2000 incursions than other areas of Africa. China's embassy in Egypt, the first African state to recognize Mao's People's Republic of China in 1956, was essentially a 'field headquarters' for developing diplomatic relations with countries such as Yemen, Somalia and Sudan. Their relationship was based on a more equal footing and Egypt's continued regional importance and strong relationship with the US means that a degree of equality within China relations remains. Egypt's regional power is better balanced than elsewhere in Africa, and the strength of those other regional actors means they also enjoy more autonomy from Chinese influence. They also provide serious security risks to Chinese interests. In Libya, Gadhafi and the Foreign Minister, Musa Kusa, openly warned against a new era of Chinese imperialism in the 2000s.[59]

Security entanglements

The political paradox, on both the African and Chinese side, of claiming to support continental empowerment whilst focusing more attention on cementing bilateral interests, is further exemplified by China's engagement with the AUs African Peace and Security Architecture. Even though China wants to avoid becoming entangled in African security issues, the reality makes it difficult to avoid. Personal safety is a primary concern of individual Chinese in Africa. According to Chinese founder of an NGO in East Africa which assists independent Chinese businesses set up in Africa, 'the other wider, complex issues they might have a bit of knowledge on, but really it is about their own personal safety'.[60] Alden labels this 'citizens' security' – where Chinese living in Africa are in danger – as a key concern for government too. Alden also sees Chinese government being concerned about 'reputational security', where dealings with unsavoury regimes paint China in a bad light, and its 'firm-level security' of business interests being directly threatened.[61] China's vocal preference for multilateral intervention and a role for the UN Security Council in security matters – where 60 per cent of discussions are African issues – means it cannot avoid noting, reacting to and engaging with Africa's security architecture more than it would perhaps like to.

China views peace and security issues primarily through an economic lens: Xi Jinping declared 'poverty is the root cause of chaos whilst peace is the guarantee for development. Development holds the key to solving all problems'.[62] This makes sustained support to security operations problematic. China provided $1.8 to the African predecessor of UNAMID in Sudan, a mission estimated to have cost $466 million a year in 2006. It gave $4.5 million worth of equipment and materials to AMISOM, whose operating costs are thought to be $2 million per day.[63] In contrast, in 2014 the US-Africa summit announced $110 million per year for three to five years to upgrade militaries for rapid peacekeeper deployment capability, to Senegal, Ghana, Ethiopia, Rwanda, Tanzania and Uganda.[64] The FOCAC V launch of the Initiative on China–Africa Cooperative Partnership for Peace and Security also heralded African capacity building, APSA and peacekeeping as key. It is unclear, however, whether FOCAC VI's 'implementation' of the Peace and Security plan furthered this progression in the way that was somewhat expected. Certainly no obvious paradigm shift in ideology or methodology was readily apparent.

The AU tends to play catch-up with developments that are already underway, rather than as an initiating force. Its Agenda 2063 presents infrastructure as the catalyst for wider development, with China seen as crucial by both sides to its realization. In January 2015, an MoU was signed between AU and China to institutionalize the many projects already underway. Hailed as 'the document of the century', by the Chinese Vice-Minister for Foreign Affairs, the agreement aims to link major African cities in all regions by high speed rail, road or new international airports, which is a specific ambition of Agenda 2063.[65] But 'the document of the century' was only a general commitment mostly initiated by China, without any concrete agreements signed or evidence of African initiation.[66]

Major infrastructure projects afford China substantive interregional and continental influence. Serious infrastructural developments have far-reaching ramifications on the geopolitical landscape of the continent, especially regarding border countries linking to other regions. Shifting key energy and transport supply routes re-shapes the flexible and unstable geopolitical structure of Africa. For example, with technical and financial assistance from China, the Benguela Railway reopened in August 2014. This links the DRC's mineral-rich Katanga province to the impressive new Angolan Port of Lobito 2,000 km away, which was built with the help of the China Harbour Engineering Company. This route 'could become a game-changer for the southern African mining industry', as currently all minerals are shipped from Richard's Bay in South Africa, 8,000 km away.[67] This increases efficiency of DRC industry but also leaves it at the mercy of whoever controls Angola's infrastructure: this is currently a murky mix of a Swiss commodity giant, politically connected Angola companies and the increasingly notorious and shadowy China International Fund (CIF, also known as the Queensway Group), with uncertain payment arrangements between them and the Angola and Chinese governments.[68]

Chinese-funded infrastructure projects in Ethiopia and Sudan, as well as Uganda, have far-reaching ramifications on Nile water flows and Egyptian security. The Nile River Basin Cooperative Framework agreement between non-Egyptian riparian states seeks to alter and update the colonial-era Nile

Introduction   23

treaty which favours Egypt. It is a major regional, continental and geo-politically contentious issue. This could undoubtedly spark warfare if not resolved amicably and China will struggle not to take sides at some point.[69] China is already underwriting certain equipment required for constructing the Grand Ethiopian Renaissance Dam, for which Egypt has expressed distaste.[70]

The paradoxical kinship around non-interference has continued in the modern era. It now sees Chinese and African rhetoric conflicting with observable reality. The AU's Pan-African institutional ambition is thwarted by hostility to what this agenda would mean to the position of domestic elites and leaders of member states. Likewise, China gives rhetorical support for south–south cooperation, mutually beneficial partnerships and to African-solutions and African capacity building. But ultimately China sees its bilateral relations, non-interference principle and its own domestic requirements as most important.

Final opening reflections

Since the new post-2000 period of China's engagement with Africa, there have been phases of academic and policy discourse surrounding events. Initially, especially from Western policy makers, there was clearly a period of mistrust, apprehension and condemnation with proclamations such as 'Chinese investment in Africa is potentially the most destabilising force that there is'.[71] This was followed by more mature but still limited analyses seeking to dispel certain myths about China, appreciating the long history of China–Africa relations and non-unitary nature of the Chinese state and engagement.[72] Throughout this second period, there were distinct calls from scholars that more research was needed in order to understand fully the complex dynamics that were unfolding. A steady stream of more sophisticated and nuanced analysis is subsequently slowly emerging – something of a 'Third wave' – of which this book should be seen as part.

Many now call for greater analysis of more micro events, such as the role of the Chinese locals on the ground in Africa,[73] or investigating Chinese scholarship programs and Malaria health treatment centres.[74] China–Africa relations contribution to the *theory* of International Relations and societal interactions is also highlighted,[75] and there is an emerging literature on the African diaspora now living in China.[76] But there are still not enough detailed case studies of specific African countries, especially those with less obvious or scandalous interest than those commonly cited such as Sudan, Angola or the DRC. Little attention has been paid to how China affects Africa's security dynamics. And, perhaps most importantly, centralizing and understanding the role of African agency has not been done enough, and many China–Africa authors 'still tend to attribute the power to China at the expense of Africa'.[77]

What should be clear, in fact, is that Chinese strategy has been improvised much more than is sometimes assumed. The contested and fluctuating relationship requires Chinese reaction to African activity. Parliamentary and civil society interrogation has occurred in certain places such as Ghana, along with state agency resisting Chinese omnipotence in Chad and Angola's oil sectors. China returning to work with Sonangol in Angola, adjusting tactics and entry points in Nigeria, or acknowledging civil society in Ghana, undermine any assumption that a Chinese Great Power is able to penetrate Africa at will. Deng Xiaoping's famous domestic reforms shifted to a changing world; they were not implemented in a continual linear process in the way that history now likes to portray.[78] Similarly, China's African policy is presented as a continuous arch from Zheng He's friendly encounters, through anti-colonial support, to the mutually beneficial current relationship, when in fact decades of interference, trouble, retreat and reaction have been the hallmarks of engagement.

Chinese engagement and influence on Africa's security dynamic has therefore shifted over time, with key partner countries now emerging as a means of protecting wider interests. Non-interference is thought by some to be already changing. Yet it took near or actual genocide in Darfur before China acted subtly behind the scenes. Although China is the P-5's largest supplier and has combat troops now in South Sudan, it remains the only UNSC member never to have committed national troops to an intrastate war. Al-Qaeda and Boko Haram have already impacted on China which resulted in rescuing of nationals, not reactive interference with government.

China is yet to have any tangible impact on the development or trajectory of an REC. China shows interest in ones well-established and capable of supporting its agenda but not in bolstering the less able ones. On occasion

China has supported the use of ROs for managing security matters, as they allow Beijing to take an interest in African security whilst maintaining the seductive non-interference policy. A UN framework remains key, however, as was the case in Sudan and Somalia. But possible polarity shifts are resulting in changes to regional security dynamics. Angola, for example, has been able to balance South Africa to some extent. China could also shape regional security issues within the continent, through both alliances and infrastructure mega-projects – often backed by oil revenues – which link new sections of a country and create regional changes if new routes are established. Engagement with key actors – countries and leaders – inevitably affects the likelihood of such shifts.

Each African region displays unique characteristics which have affected China's relations. Various African leaders have incorporated China's involvement domestically, which has affected regional security dynamics to some extent. And there are security implications from arms supply and resource extraction, as well as from the large infrastructure construction projects underway. A case study analysis allows for more detailed understanding of how African agency occurs within this context, and how African leaders assert influence across their regional environment and in relation to the so-called Great Powers. The next chapter assesses the domestic scene in Uganda, outlining China's historical role and the present relationship with President Museveni. It is a detailed interrogation of Uganda–China relations that provides insight into China's specific engagement with Uganda and Museveni, and the regional reverberations of that relationship. It shows how this important African leader utilizes the presence of China for their own purpose.

1

China–Uganda relations and the regional imperative

'The Chinese they are not concerned about the stability, the future stability of the country. They are simply concerned with finding those people there to help them get as much as they can get.'

Ugandan Opposition MP[1]

President Museveni has greatly enhanced Uganda's international reputation, for good and bad. He has always sought to avoid unwelcome Great Power domination, and now successfully utilizes Chinese engagement to retain his primary goal: the maintenance of his power and position in Uganda. Towards that end, he has also seen regional integration and regional intervention as imperative; an effort in which China has now inevitably played a role. Chinese presence opens space for Museveni to pursue his regional security policies, by helping Museveni shield himself against creeping Western interference at the same time as he protects Western security concerns. China has not altered its non-interference principle significantly but does influence, or tries to influence, a range of domestic players in Uganda's political economy, which also have regional repercussions. Whilst this attempted influence helps China to obtain its regional ambitions to some degree, Museveni's agency has meant that his own regional priorities are furthered to an even more notable extent.

This chapter is divided into four main sections. The first section, 'Background and history: post-independence and the rise of Museveni' outlines the history of China–Uganda relations. It shows how relations have steadily progressed at the same time as continual regional integration efforts and a militarized Ugandan political system. The next section, 'Modern relations – structural context', assesses China's *structural role* in a global battle for influence against the West, and also explains how Chinese overarching presence feeds shadowy patronage networks in Uganda that inevitably impact the region. The third section, 'Lower-level forces – balancing regime players', outlines China's *local-level role* in important constituencies in Uganda's political economy that Museveni must balance to maintain authority: Museveni's inner loyalists; the National Resistance Movement (NRM) party; and army, and the regional implications of this engagement. The final section, 'Domestic opposition and regional alternatives?', continues the discussion on the local political economy, but instead focuses on the direct threats to Museveni's continued rule: parliament and opposition parties; the judiciary; Kingdoms and local citizens. A brief conclusion then follows, explaining that China's direct and indirect interactions with Uganda's domestic regime help foster conditions whereby Museveni's continuation in power is made more likely. This also furthers his regional ambitions by pushing towards regional intervention and cooperation, particularly within the security sector.

Background and history: post-independence and the rise of Museveni

Obote and regional failure

Mao's revolutionary China almost immediately recognized independent Uganda in 1962, but Prime Minister Obote was committed to the non-aligned movement. Obote denounced China's attack on India in 1962 even after receiving a $3 million grant, $12 million loan, some small arms and military assistance from Mao, and he actively prevented Beijing's efforts to gain a revolutionary foothold in the country. Uganda did help facilitate a transfer of Chinese arms to nationalist forces fighting in the Belgian Congo, but this was 'clearly a case of convergence of interests rather than ideological affinity', as both sides hoped for more independent African states.[2] By 1969, China was the fourth largest loan provider to Uganda (behind the UK, the World Bank and the Soviet Union) whilst Uganda exported mostly cotton to Beijing. But Uganda always pursued its own policies and development objectives: foreign influence, from the West and East, has always been checked and resisted when it could be.[3]

Obote was part of the first East African Community formed in 1967, but was overthrown by Idi Amin in a 1971 coup. Amin sought closer links with UK, South Africa and Israel, and falsely accused China of involvement in Ugandan skirmishes with Tanzania. Uganda backed Beijing's restoration to the UN Security Council in October 1971, however, and the Kibimba Rice Scheme established by China in 1973 is still operational. Knowing that the USSR did not want Kampala to turn towards Beijing during the Sino–Soviet split, Amin quite skilfully resisted Russian pressure to support the MPLA in the Angolan Civil War despite USSR being Uganda's main arms supplier.[4] Again, Uganda pursued its own agenda and aimed to resist Great Power influence.

The regional schisms causing the 1977 collapse of EAC I ultimately culminated in Tanzania's overthrow of Amin two years later. Amin alleged that China had been complicit in his downfall, which was never proven; but Beijing did play an indirect role through its significant arms supply and military training to Tanzania at the time. The restoration of Obote again saw a smooth continuation of small but steady China–Uganda relations unfurl. The first Chinese medical teams arrived, cultural exchanges took place and biogas units were constructed.[5] But under Obote II's 1980s rule, Yoweri Museveni now formed an indelible mark on proceedings.

Early China–NRM relations and revived regionalism

The China–Museveni narrative began in the 1970s. In exile during the Amin era, Museveni and many other future NRM actors resided in Beijing-friendly Tanzania whilst it was a bastion of revolutionary ideas and activity. Kizza Besigye, who would later become Uganda's most famous opposition candidate and contest four Presidential elections against Museveni, was an ally during the NRM struggle. He explains:

> I think without any doubt many of our leaders, I must say including myself, were quite inspired by the Chinese revolution, the struggle of the Chinese people and how they overcame all the challenges they had and eventually took over power using guerrilla tactics. That was quite inspirational to us.[6]

China did not supply any arms during the Bush War years of 1980–6 (although Tanzania did, at a time when Beijing was their main supplier).[7]

Immediately after Museveni's 1986 victory, however, the then leftist tendencies of the NRM meant that China 'was our source of supplies, almost exclusively, and also offered training to our officers', whilst the British and Americans still in the country were viewed suspiciously.[8] The economic and geo-political realities of the late 1980s and early 1990s, however, saw the new government adopt a more liberal economic restructuring. In Western eyes Museveni became seen as a 'new-breed' of African leader: He was perceived and presented a neo-liberal 'donor-darling' democratic role model, with elections held in 1996 and open-market economic reforms.

Schlichte has argued that Uganda's 'internationalised rule' means that it cannot be termed a genuinely sovereign state in any meaningful sense.[9] Even where Uganda has enjoyed some leeway from interference, such as in the security sector, donors 'do set the overall policy framework within which security policy, like all other policies, must operate'.[10] Others recognize, however, that Uganda's economic compliance with the Western agenda actually 'allowed for relative independence in some policy areas',[11] and in particular allowed for a more autocratic style of government to develop.[12]

Ultimately, the West's belief that Uganda was 'one of theirs' early on in his rule was a severe misreading of the fact that Museveni was a staunch pragmatist rather than any kind of ideologue. The Bush War origins of Museveni and the NRM were always far more influential on shaping ideas, interests and actions than any Western economic doctrine or Pan-African agenda. The efforts of Western donors to pressure Museveni to open democratic spaces should be seen as an arrogant misjudgement of their role in the country. The return to multi-party politics for the 2006 election obviously resulted from Western donor influence (the NRM's 'no-party movement' had outlawed all political parties until then), but Museveni cleverly compromised: when legalizing parties he simultaneously scrapped Presidential term limits, which would prove far more consequential to the fate of Uganda. Witnessing Kenya move to a post-Moi democratic model, Museveni recognized the need to keep donors on board rather than favour the now more liberal Kenyan neighbour; but also made him realize his National Resistance Movement (NRM) would still win multi-party elections.[13]

The personality and presence of Museveni has been centrally important to Uganda's domestic politics and international relations. The Chinese government is clearly very image-conscious, and the rhetoric of 'win-win' and 'south-south cooperation' forms an important aspect of their engagement in Africa. In similar fashion, the Museveni regime has used discourse and symbolism to present an image of the President that helps maintain order (alongside traditional military intimidation). Kagoro argues that the Ugandan population at large has grown to associate military strength with political power, illustrating how Museveni has gained a significant amount of 'symbolic capital' through his use of discourse around the history of his Bush War struggle and professing his own military prowess and warrior persona.[14] Rhetoric has also formed a prominent part in Museveni's dealings with the West, with his outspoken criticism such as: 'I have a real problem with this paternalistic arrangement of the so-called "donor" and "beggar" relationship.'[15]

But reliance on a narrowing ethnic core is increasing resentment from excluded groups, including parliament and his inner-circle. Uganda's restored traditional Kingdoms and use of Local Councils (LCs) are now becoming more fertile ground for genuine opposition. And reliance on patronage has eventually created widespread corruption and economic failings. The state-coffer money required for funding Museveni's 2011 election campaign, for example, is understood to have caused significant fiscal problems which encouraged dramatic and sustained protests in Kampala.[16]

This has remained in essence a military government. The renamed Uganda People's Defence Force (UPDF) expelled the Lord's Resistance Army (LRA) into neighbouring territories in the late 2000s who were the last troublesome violent force opposed to NRM rule (the rest of the country had been pacified and stabilized many years previously). Museveni constantly reminds any audience of the sacrifice he made to gain power. Speaking at State House in November 2014 to local government NRM representatives, he is reported to have said:

> I did not spend five years in the bush for nothing ... even a fool knows that the NRM government is built on the foundation of the army ... It is, therefore, not acceptable at all for anybody to play around with this unity that we have built.[17]

Alongside the professionalization of the UPDF, the Police during the 2010s have also become much more militarized. The Presidential Guard Brigade (PGB), Internal Security Organisation (ISO), and Chief of Military Intelligence (CMI), as well as state-sponsored thugs such as the Black Mambas and various street gang militias have also all quelled hostility to the NRM regime when required, including through violence.[18] Museveni's concessions in creating Local Councils (LCs), restoring the traditional Kingdoms as cultural institutions, and creating a quota system within Parliament for women, military and youth MPs cleverly pacified key constituents and has steadily extended NRM's reach. Following Kenya's 2007/8 post-election violence, Museveni apparently felt the need to create a 'more tolerant and competition-friendly form of authoritarianism' with cash bribes replacing intimidation during his 2011 re-election.[19] Museveni has thus steadily created a 'patronage empire' of reliant subordinates to keep this NRM model in place. Conroy-Krutz and Logan rightly note that 'this mix of carrot and stick has made Museveni one of the most durable rulers in post-independence Africa'.[20]

A regional agenda

Of additional importance is that Uganda's inherent landlockedness, the NRM's espoused Pan-Africanism and intensely unstable regional security environment have all meant Uganda under Museveni has played a key role in regional relations and integration. Even as a student in Dar es Salaam, Museveni practised and preached Pan-Africanism by organizing students to actively support liberation struggles in Mozambique and Southern Africa.[21] Once in power he almost immediately began pushing at reviving EAC integration. It is hard to underestimate the personal role he has played in subsequent developments. Museveni's problematic relations with his contemporaries shaped different eras of integration. These never created grudges that hindered progress, nor enough trust to enable political federation. In 1987, there had been military build-up and border tension between Museveni and Kenya under Moi,[22] but their rapprochement led to a steady flow of regional agreements and further progress which culminated in the 2001 re-launch of the East African Community between Uganda, Tanzania and Kenya.

Crucially, the EAC II Treaty lacked technical detail around implementing the customs union, common market and political federation. This meant that regional geo-politics, personal ambition and security issues remained crucial to progress, as leaders were not tied to specific actions or timetables. Museveni also continuously pressured for Rwanda and Burundi to be included. In 1998, this expansion debate had even risked scuppering the EAC revival due to Kenya and Tanzania's hostility to the idea.[23] But Museveni's effort never dwindled, even amidst intense personal animosity between him and Rwanda's Kagame, until Rwanda's and Burundi's admittance to the EAC occurred in 2007. A secure and friendly region means domestic threats to his rule can be more easily tackled, whereas regional instability and hostility would undoubtedly help flame those local reactions. Days before the 2016 election, Museveni proclaimed that he would remain in power until East Africa was united. He stated:

> If you want to survive, you blacks, you must work for African unity and for Pan-Africanism. How will you survive against Britain, China and India? … that's why I am here to see whether I can help you and escort you.[24]

The then leader of the opposition in Parliament sums up Museveni's ambition perfectly during an interview with the author: 'in his own estimation Uganda is too small for him. Although he is getting old and is in his evening hours, he thinks Uganda is too small and he would have wanted to be the leader of East Africa.'[25] But EAC partners' awareness of this has arguably stalled any grand ambition to unite federally. Tanzania has been hesitant over a political federation Fast-Tracking agenda from 2005 onwards at least partly from Museveni's personal role in pushing it.[26] It is certain that Museveni would have accepted any forthcoming opportunity to be President of East Africa. But in the same was as he was willing to sacrifice his potentially progressive, African-born no-party democratic model in exchange for him remaining as President indefinitely; it is certain that Museveni would not be willing to step down as President in exchange for an East African political federation of which he was not part.

Yet despite reservations and suspicions over his personal ambitions, and many arguing political federation is an unrealistic step in the near future, Museveni has always managed to keep the possibility of federation on the EAC agenda. In November 2014, EAC leaders failed to adopt proposals for a federated union as championed by Uganda, but at the March 2015 Northern Corridor Infrastructure Projects initiative Museveni again sought to kick-start the fast-tracking process amongst leaders (especially amongst the Northern Corridor countries Kenya, Uganda and Rwanda, discussed further in later chapters). South Sudan's ascension to EAC in March 2016 is something of a crowning geo-political achievement for Museveni, it being Uganda's leading export market and an intense security issue. The expansion of EAC II is a marked example of Museveni's agency, as leader of Uganda, by him actively linking his own security interests to other new and existing member states. With four landlocked neighbours now balancing the sea-facing Kenya and Tanzania, Museveni has unequivocally stamped his mark on EAC II's history and current structure.

But what role has a post-2000 China played in these domestic and regional developments? Has Museveni been able to incorporate them into his agenda, or are Chinese interest and influence threatening those ambitions? Scholarship on Ugandan security has always debated the roles of, and interactions between, the domestic and global in determining the country's security concerns and general development trajectory. Museveni's explicit and coherent non-alignment in international relations has been as consistent as this pragmatism. During the time of supposedly Western-inspired economic reforms, the first major Chinese construction occurred between 1993 and 1997: Uganda's National Sports Stadium was a noteworthy precursor to the high-visibility mega-projects which would help define China–Africa relations in later years. But trade levels remained under $10 million until 1999.[27] Notably, however, in 1996 and 1997 Uganda supported China's position during sessions of the UN Human Rights Commission, and in 2000 backed the Chinese UN motion to maintain and observe the Anti-Ballistic Missile Treaty.[28] This made Uganda a worthy beneficiary of China's post-2000 big push into Africa. Chinese investment in Uganda inevitably means it is now relying less on traditional donor finance, whilst remaining wary of becoming unduly reliant on and influenced by Beijing.

Modern relations – structural context

Competing global actors

Uganda's ongoing stability, meaning stable government without serious threat of internal conflict, depends on Museveni's ability to retain control himself over the various moveable power-centres within the country; or on his successfully handing over power. The Ugandan 'succession question' is of central importance to domestic and regional developments. Balancing important, powerful people and institutions in Uganda is an ongoing, complex task. 'You really have a distinct absence of hierarchy there,' says a well-known Ugandan journalist, consultant and oil expert, 'so it's difficult to say in what direction things are going to go, because you do have many moving parts.'[29] And as noted by a Western British Defence Attaché, 'controlling this country is not about controlling 40 million people, it's about controlling 5000'.[30]

For pragmatic and ideological reasons, Museveni and NRM 'have no interests in benefactors that control them'. Museveni has employed what the journalist terms the 'Global Mix' where Ugandan foreign policy 'is just a patchwork of strange bedfellows'.[31] Museveni is rightly seen as protecting Western security interests whilst also engaging with North Korea, and has strong ties with Israel whilst also being vocal within the Organisation of Islamic Conference, for example. In the post-2000 era, Chinese presence is clearly increasing rapidly across Africa and East Africa specifically. Museveni has also been mindful of the US possibly drifting away from him strategically. Rationally, therefore, he must incorporate China into his domestic and regional ambitions, as 'the repercussions of not doing so is to be bashed by the whips of the West'.[32]

As noted in the Introduction, China's ideology sees it championing judicial sovereignty of African states by promoting mutually respectful state-to-state relationships. However, China's engagement with Uganda – whether intentionally or not – interacts the different arms of government, state, party and society significantly, either directly or indirectly. This is not a straightforward financial injection. China's construction of the pillars of nation-building – sports stadium, the State House, the Prime Minister's Office and the Ministry of Foreign Affairs – directly stamp their presence on youths, politics and foreign relations. As noted by a security sector specialist and NRM MP, this is entirely different from the UK and Western agenda of promoting democracy and market forces:

> The Chinese have systematically and carefully done it ... if the President is sleeping in a State House, staring at a ceiling built by Chinese, he will think twice before he acts against them. I tell you that's *huge* influence ... the whole

thing is to capture the psyche of the higher political thinking of African leaders, and make them think or look at China as an alternative friendly power.[33]

China's engagement with Uganda and Africa is inherently more appealing than that of the West. During the 2000s, Museveni skilfully courted Western support – donor aid made up to 50 per cent of the national budget up until the early 2010 – at the same time as relations with China expanded.[34] China's emergence surely played a role in Museveni's more vocal criticism of the West after relations became problematic following the 2006 removal of term limits. Donors themselves note the significance of 2006, saying, 'That's what the Ugandan government would cite as the moment when things became a bit more strained ... governance sort of crept into the dialogue more and more', which led to increasing resentment.[35] That same year, the Chinese were giving grants of more than $30 million to expand Uganda's Parliament Chambers and build new Offices for the Prime Minster and President, writing off $17 million worth of debt, and providing a $106 million loan to build a fibre optic internet network.[36] According to the Uganda Minister of State for International Affairs, 'the Chinese intervention has strengthened what we have already been telling the West: that we are fed up of lectures.'[37] Chinese in Uganda also appreciate Museveni's ability to deflect US attention from governance issues, and hope that it continues. Zhang Ho, the largest Chinese employer of Ugandans in the country and Chairman of the Uganda Overseas China Association, states:

> I don't want to say too much about the Americans, the whole world has Americans. So America will try to do something different, they will try to put in something different. Like Iraq, Egypt, all of those countries. Of course Uganda also has similar things, like Museveni has been controlling this country for a very long time. So that is the kind of thing America doesn't want. So that is what I am worried about.[38]

The recent trend of diminishing donor aid due to increasing governance and human rights concerns less problematic due to the emergence of China.[39] The British High Commission, in fact, began unofficially courting Chinese businesses with informal meet-and-greet networking events from at least 2014.[40]

Incorporating China into his domestic and regional agendas, therefore, helps Museveni insulate himself against pressure from the West to reform his governance structures. Museveni thus utilizes China to shape Uganda into an image very much of his own making, whilst also remaining indispensable in protecting Western security interests. A Western Defence attaché bluntly points out that 'China's involvement stops us being subconsciously imperialistic, which we are ... it forces us to treat these countries as sovereign countries as opposed to still inferior in some way.'[41] China's engagement allows Museveni to concentrate on Uganda's regional security role, which he has always known to be the West's primary concern. The attaché states on the West's relationship:

> Underlying, its excellent. Despite our ups and downs on occasional individual issues ... the reality is you have a disaster zone in Eastern Congo, Southern Sudan with a whole lot of history ... now Uganda because of its history and the current regime, is going to intervene for a variety of reasons.[42]

Tactically allowing China into Uganda's complex political economy, however, risks losing the long-term strategy of avoiding undue foreign influence. If incursions continue at the present rate, Uganda could reach a 'point of no return' whereby indebtedness to China financially and politically becomes constraining. According to the security sector specialist, 'it needs a lot of courage and resource if you want to sort that out'.[43] Chinese presence helps shape the global structural environment in which Museveni's must operate within, as well as in to Uganda's political economy at the local level.

Museveni's role in steady expansion

Museveni never shied publicly or privately from criticizing Western presence in Uganda as being neo-colonial and the relationship as inherently imbalanced. China has received no such similar treatment from the President or other prominent officials. China's narrative around respecting sovereignty and entrusting the developing world to work together is entirely in tune with Museveni's expressed world view. Publicly he has undiluted praise for China in line with Beijing's own discourse, such as 'our relationship is always based on equality and mutual respect for each other'.[44]

A cursory overview of the post-2000 relationship shows a steadily expanding trade and diplomatic relationship, coinciding with the revived EAC. High-level regular visits from Museveni, Chinese Premiers and Ministers from both sides have occurred regularly over the last decade. Museveni personally attended FOCAC II, III, IV, VI and VII, and the first major deals and subsequent flourishing of the relationship occurred after FOCAC II in 2003.[45] Fang Min, owner of the Fang Fang Group, is a prominent Chinese business lady in Uganda who 'is a friend to so many people in government, top quality, top brass . . . she was the first Chinese to really build a bridge between the Chinese and our government'.[46] Fang Min emphasizes the role of Museveni in easing foreign investors' potential to make money which the Chinese have seized upon:

> The President is good, he has been here a long time and he makes it easy to visit here. It's so easy for China to come here, easy to make money, easy to come and go . . . I came here 25 years ago and everything was different . . . Kenya and Tanzania is not so easy, it's much easier to come here and make money.[47]

Each year since 2009/2010, China has been the biggest foreign direct investment contributor in Uganda, and in 2014, Museveni angered private Western investors when he publicly criticized their lack of effort as compared to the Chinese.[48] Most Chinese finance is project based and comes as non-concessional loans and tied aid. It appears across all sectors in Uganda, from offering debt relief and building infrastructure to donating farm seeds and sports equipment. Funds or donations have been provided by a diverse range of actors, including the well-known China EXIM Bank, China Development Bank, China–Africa Development Fund, Xinhua News Agency and Huawei Technologies, as well as groups like the Association of Student Sports of China and the Red Cross Society of China.[49] According to the Bank of Uganda, exports to China went from approximately $1 million in 2002 to $57 in 2015 (down from $65 in 2014). Imports from China went from $45 million to $701 million over the same period.[50] China is now Uganda's biggest trading partner, accounting for at least 30 per cent of all its foreign trade.[51] Zhang Ho explains that Chinese business people associate Museveni with stability and many have close personal relationships with the President. He states:

> You know all of our people like Museveni. Because when we come here he is the one controlling the country, and actually he is the one building the foundation in this country. So of course every person likes him. Especially the business people who have come from outside . . . When I came here in

1999 up until now it is very much different, from this government being in control.[52]

The most high-profile and significant funds are now within the oil, energy and transport infrastructure sectors. Stand out projects include multi-billion dollar oil investment by the China National Offshore Oil Corporation (CNOOC), the construction of the Kampala-Entebbe highway partly funded with a $350 million EXIM Bank loan, construction of the $6 billion Standard Gauge Railway Line (SGR) and the $1.7 billion 600 MW Karuma Dam. Chinese finance was also used for the smaller but significant hydro-power facility at Isimba, and is earmarked for the massive 840 MW Ayago Dam.[53] A Chinese consortium is reviving the Kilembe copper and cobalt mine.[54] This larger-scale oil, energy and infrastructure development and their regional implications will be discussed in detail in Chapters Three and Four.

Shadowy domestic networks

Uganda is a comparative economic success with a slowly and steadily expanding economy, health and educational improvements, and attainment of the first Millennium Development Goal on poverty reduction. This has been an important component of NRM remaining a credible ruling party, and in finance being available for the NRM patronage networks. The unemployment crisis is severe, however, as is the infrastructure deficit and poor health care system. Most Ugandan's remain poor peasants within a neglected agricultural sector and the NRM cannot lay any serious claim to be labelled a developmental state model. Flavia Kabahandra, NRM MP and Chairperson of Parliamentary Committee on Tourism, Trade and Industry, states that Chinese private companies and SMEs have had 'a very great impact here' in job creation, but the overall effects have been negligible due to the scale of Uganda's unemployment crisis. Chinese SMEs have also mentored and trained Ugandan local industries, with the intention those local players will eventually supply the larger-scale heavy Chinese investors that are now increasing in numbers.[55] But Uganda has not taken full advantage of the private investment available from China. A successful Chinese entrepreneur with large shoe-making factories in Rwanda, Ethiopia and Kenya says she has not been asked to invest in Uganda. She states that 'it's up to the leadership in each country to approach me and other entrepreneurs with their ideas and ambitions, I haven't had time to visit all the different places myself'.[56] Another Chinese researcher explains that Chinese agricultural investors in Uganda have mostly been frustrated with the sector's stagnancy.[57]

Regarding the patronage networks that are a hallmark of Uganda's political economy, Chinese companies have become increasingly successful in winning construction contracts by fair means or foul. 'Their pricing by our standards is suicidal,' according to a consultant who arranges tenders for private Chinese companies, who is unsure how shortfalls in bidding prices are made up. They are also far more willing to take on risk than Western companies and do business for a much lower rate of return, and there are accusations of ignoring or not understanding costly regulations which were agreed to (such as environmental policies).[58] A former Secretary General of the Uganda Overseas China Association explains that for Chinese businesses entering Uganda:

> Most of them don't know people here very well so they must find a way to short cut. And if you are trying to find a short cut, you do something abnormal or illegal things, so you can quickly reach the space. This is happening, it doesn't matter if it's Chinese private or government enterprise.[59]

Chinese SMEs or state owned/linked companies engage the Ugandan system of local 'fixers' being required to help package deals. This small group of rich businessmen or well-connected locals take a cut in exchange for bringing project proposals to Museveni or whichever relevant government Minister will decide on who gets the contract. This system was not created by Chinese companies, but they seemingly embrace the model more effectively than others as a means of entering the Ugandan economy, and are now actively sought out by the local networks. Speaking in a private capacity, a spokesperson for the Ministry of Finance states:

> There is an increasing crop of businessmen who have seen the opportunity and the might of the Chinese currency. And therefore when they identify an opportunity they look out for a Chinese company that can take up this opportunity. And these Ugandans are known, unfortunately the crop is not big, the few of them they are known.[60]

Larger businesses get help and assistance from Chinese on the ground, who can access the China-centric layer of business people and contacts with access to government if required. Chinese players like Fang Min and Zhang Ho help businesses and take a cut, along with others.[61] Fang Min is particularly well-known amongst Chinese and her role is somewhat resented, as she is seen to exploit her position and benefits from other businesses relying on her networks.[62] So Chinese finance is not creating or necessarily driving the patron-client system of awarding government tenders, but it is certainly engaged with them in a somewhat mutually reinforcing manner. A Chinese researcher who has investigated infrastructure projects notes, however, 'that shadiness in getting deals and projects started does not prevent success from occurring.'[63]

Regional implications – central to integration

China's role and interest in Uganda therefore creates an overarching presence whereby a Great Power ally has appeared whose methods are more closely aligned with Museveni's own pragmatic, anti-interference outlook. It also impacts tangibly at a local-level whereby any kind of economic development is beneficial to Museveni retaining credibility with domestic citizens, and money for patronage networks keeps on-board key players in the political economy. This inevitably creates significant regional consequences. A functional Ugandan economy is crucial to any integrated East African market. Each of the major Chinese infrastructure projects also has specific regional impacts. When discussing the Karuma Dam, for example, a hydro-power expert and Ugandan government advisor explains that 'the regional aspect is always our concern, it's always our concern. When you are looking at this power plant, you look at the market, where is it going to sell electricity to.'[64]

Museveni's role in formulating and implementing such initiatives therefore becomes of central importance to the EAC's development agenda as a whole. If Uganda–Chinese business practices delay projects, the entire regional process is shifted. 'The weaknesses you have on the domestic front, impact on and also reflect at the regional-level,' notes former Forum for Democratic Change (FDC) party President and ex-Commander of the UPDF, Major General (Retired) Muntu. 'You cannot have corrupt regimes at the domestic-level and not expect that is going to be reflected at the regional-level. Very difficult to do that.'[65] Muntu, who was an NRM East African Legislative Assembly (EALA) representative when EAC II was launched in 2001, recognizes how prioritizing domestic control in Uganda inevitably shapes the regional integration process:

> If a Chinese company comes in to do business around the region and they find corrupt actors in three partner states, and none of them are willing to say these are the terms and the terms are transparent, if there is not care for good governance systems being established in the domestic front. I can tell you that it won't matter if it is a Chinese company or Portuguese, Spanish, American, British. If it's a company that is willing to go along, that is what will determine how that project is done.[66]

In a regional context where Museveni's domestic methods of engaging China are unlikely to be criticized or challenged by EAC partner states, Museveni's hand is strengthened by Ugandan projects inevitably impacting on the wider development agenda. But as well as this overarching role, China is also impacting on the domestic institutions being balanced by Museveni within the Ugandan state.

Lower-level forces – balancing regime players

The most serious domestic challenge to Museveni staying President actually comes from his NRM colleagues and Bush War veterans who retain control over different arms of government and the economy.[67] A local journalist explains that these are 'the big corrupt people who are surrounding him, they call them the king makers, they do so many things'.[68] Despite being a cohort of strong long-term allies, they are becoming increasingly difficult to control: public spats, expulsions and defections have appeared through the NRM era and steadily increased. China influences certain aspects of these relations, either consciously or subconsciously, through their interactions with Uganda.

The Inner Circle: significant impacts amidst personal relationships

During the period which this work is focused on, Museveni's strongest internal challenger was former Prime Minister Amama Mbabazi, an NRM stalwart and

Secretary General of the party. He had been extremely public in his praise for China and was central to establishing the current relationship.[69] Mbabazi was sacked as Prime Minster in October 2014, due to Museveni's belief he was steadily acquiring funds and allies to support his bid for the Presidency at the 2016 election. Although Mbabazi eventually polled badly in the 2016 election, he was clearly a powerful well-connected NRM figure thought to have sympathizers in the army.

Elsewhere in Africa and around the world, China has courted potential successors to incumbent rulers as part of its long-term strategy for securing its investments. Its non-interference principle remains in place and is distinct from Western practice in both theory and practice; but this apparently does not mean that China acts as a mere passive observer to domestic affairs. A Chair of the Parliamentary Committee on Foreign Affairs in Uganda explains that China analyses its partnerships carefully and thoughtfully, and certainly pays attention to goings-on within the NRM:

> With Uganda they have told me openly that they want a close and long relationship with the government. So they are going to make sure that even the government that is likely to come in the future, they know their position or they know the possible leaders of government and they are in [the] good books of Chinese. They are very clear about that. Because they know any group of leaders is not going to last forever.[70]

In Uganda, Mbabazi was clearly earmarked as the potential next leader. During a meeting involving Mbabazi, Museveni and the high-ranking Chinese visitor Zhang Dejiang in September 2013, Dejiang thanked Museveni for choosing Mbabazi as his successor. This faux pas was a red flag to Museveni, who realized that Prime Minister Mbabazi had been selling himself to the Chinese as the inevitable next-in-line for the Presidency.[71] A very well-connected source, who helped break the newspaper story which exposed the incident, states 'they understood that, the Chinese thought Mbabazi was going to take over. I heard it from a very good authority . . . That definitely happened, you can take it from me that conversation with Dejiang happened.'[72]

This made Museveni realize that 'he needed to clarify his position with the Chinese', who subsequently accepted that Mbabazi was moved out of the picture and Museveni remains at the helm.[73] The networks that Chinese companies had developed in order to gain contracts were disrupted as 'most of them were fished by Mbabazi ... if there is any change it shakes them'.[74] The Daily Monitor reported that 'Chinese investors began trooping to State House confessing their loyalty to government and not Mr Mbabazi. Some made confessions about their dealings with Mr Mbabazi.'[75] Museveni has apparently remained cautious of Chinese support for his rival, nonetheless. He courted South Korean finance in October 2015 in order to diversify further foreign investment sources, amidst concern that Beijing still backed Mbabazi in some way.[76]

This example shows how China – whether intentionally or not – plays a new role within Ugandan domestic networks and political wrangling's. It is not the case that China definitively preferred Mbabazi and were cynically moving against the President, but their presence and – potentially manipulated – expectations certainly played a role. Potential successors in Uganda, along with Museveni and the Chinese themselves, now need to be well-attuned to China's role and perspectives alongside the repercussions of any fall-out between the domestic players involved. In the case, the wealth, power and prestige that Mbabazi was building up with China and other domestic and international partners was recognized and swiftly acted against by Museveni: he immediately and successfully sought to reassert his authority. The removal of Mbabazi will be further referenced in subsequent chapters.

The NRM party: direct engagement

Museveni's would clear prefer an NRM dominant system in Uganda, somewhat akin to the Communist Party of China (CPC). Several UPDF officers interviewed were explicit that they and many colleagues condemned multi-partyism, one stating that 'we made a mistake accepting a multi-party system in this country',[77] and another that 'a lot of people have nostalgia for the non-party Movement, they wish they could go back to that'.[78] Both the NRM and CPC promote a nationalist rhetoric, prefer a centralized political system, and are sceptical of Western models and interference, whilst they both have shown a pragmatic approach in choosing an open capitalist economy which heavily engages the West and foreign partners. The Parliamentary Chair regularly works with the Chinese and says that 'our people in the (NRM) party admire that, they feel this is something that can fit our society'. Even though they ceded to Western pressure on multi-partyism, 'we still believe that the Chinese model would be best for us, yes. There is that kind of link I think in ideology that brings the two together.'[79]

The NRM and CPC have friendship, ideology and strategy exchanges, which include women, youth and leadership group delegations meeting in China and Uganda annually.[80] 'Quite a good number of delegates from the NRM have actually gone to China to study the party structures and ideology,' says a Ministry counsellor and spokesperson for Ministry of Foreign Affairs.[81] Politicized youths of the NRM are also given direct opportunities to visit China and engage with the CPC government. A National Vice Chairman of Youth League of NRM Kampala region, and member of the National Executive Council, has been part of such delegations on numerous occasions. He explains:

> They only work with youth leaders in the ruling parties, period ... they take you to the Great Wall of China, they take you to the Forbidden City, they take you to different party schools like the Beijing Administrative College, they just take you there for ideological orientation.[82]

This representative believes political youths in Uganda have generally brought the idea that China is a powerful ally worth engaging.[83] The National Youth Chairman of NRM, who also travels regularly to China, explains that many political youths are also businessmen who see financial opportunities available with China.[84] Therefore, although Chinese non-interference policy is officially willing to work with any ruling party in any country, it clearly prefers stability and continuation of the regime in Uganda, with NRM rule presently seeing as being in China's best long-term interests. The Parliamentary Chair says:

> What I know is that they still have a very deep trust in the party, and they want this party to continue. And they have invested all their trust, commitment, and also I think agreements in this party ... They talk about that. The party talks about it with Chinese, they talk about it openly.[85]

So, as well as monitoring specific influential players within NRM, China also interacts with Uganda's ruling party as a whole. Museveni has to keep the party members onside in order to continue his project and avoid internal discord: the CPC now seems to be both an ally and inspiration in this regard.

UPDF: increasingly warm relations

Uganda is a country that has never had a peaceful transition of regimes. In Uganda, to wield political power, 'you have to be in full control of the military', and the UPDF has, in general, been a core supporter of Museveni.[86] It has always produced defectors and critics, however, whose numbers have steadily increased. This has helped produce a 'weak dominant party' system where the NRM maintains power but only with a shrinking inner core of Museveni loyalists.[87] In 2014, alleged efforts by Museveni to anoint his son, Brigadier Muhoozi, as his successor received a massive backlash. General Sejusa, Senior Presidential Adviser and Coordinator of Intelligence, publicly denounced Museveni, the NRM, and his own part in the increasingly corrupt, authoritarian regime. Former Internal Security Organisation (ISO) head of discipline, Lieutenant Kabahena, defected to the opposition in February 2015, exclaiming that he was tired of stealing votes for Museveni. Lower down the ranks, low pay and poor conditions see regular desertions from UPDF, including from the elite Presidential Guard Brigade (although precise figures on defections are hard to discern). Ex-military, some with arms, are an increasing phenomenon in Uganda and stolen UPDF weapons make a notable contribution to the small arms and light weapons proliferation issues to be discussed in later chapters. Therefore, although the personal historical links between Museveni and the UPDF are clearly important, he still has to relate to UPDF with an awareness of it being one of the powerful, fluctuating centres of influence within Uganda's political economy. It must be managed and engaged with, not simply ordered around and coerced.

China pledged to promote military ties with Uganda in 2007, and has subsequently donated military equipment such as trucks, has helped renovate barracks and UPDF headquarters, and provided training to UPDF officers.[88] Arms supply is discussed in later chapters. UPDF training sessions with China are not exceptional: various Western and non-Western nations offer similar opportunities, and most training outside of Uganda takes place within East Africa.[89] China appears, however, to be making an increasing number of training slots available to UPDF, a source saying that 'there are more people going than previously, there are increased numbers now'. He estimates about 200 staff went to China between 2011 and 2014, and whereas most other countries take two or three staff at a time, 'I think the biggest China have taken in one go is 45. That's big, that's very big.'[90] A UPDF Colonel confirms it is numbers rather than content which differentiates the Chinese, saying that the 'Chinese have been giving us slots of training in the region of 100 (per year), no Western country has ever given us that number of vacancies.'[91]

UPDF-China relations, in fact, exemplify Uganda's Global Mix foreign policy referred to above. UPDF is effectively a British/Western modelled army, with whom they retain good military relations; but UPDF also deals regularly with other partners when value is offered and circumstances allow. According to a UPDF Brigadier:

> With China we are doing a lot of military relations with them. I think that the biggest is through or via military training; we do a lot of training with them. We have some military platforms we buy from them, we don't buy from the West because they are very expensive and they have a lot of issues if you are to buy arms from them. Trucks, medium sized weapons. But basically we buy from the East, if it's not Russia it will be China, North Korea, former Russian republics. And we have always stood our ground on that to say we will go for the fairest prices and we will go for what we think suits our demands at that time.[92]

So Museveni has certainly helped enable China to become a notable partner within UPDF's training and exchange catalogue, with increasing numbers of interactions taking place between personnel.

Supporting the regional agenda

Museveni's regional credibility is an important component of his rule, discussed further in the next chapter. China's engagement with the power-centres who traditionally support him in Uganda – the inner circle, NRM party and UPDF – help this regional position. Museveni's indelible mark on regional affairs means that the nature of Ugandan succession, or lack thereof, will create significant repercussions across East Africa. EAC integration remains mostly an elite-driven process, whereby a weak private sector and lack of genuine civil society involvement make the political role of Museveni and other leaders crucial to the efforts underway.[93] China's assumption of Mbabazi as pending successor, for example, was swiftly reacted to by Museveni: any preference China may or may not have had for a successor they felt they could influence was successfully resisted. Museveni therefore remains very well positioned to continue impacting on regional dynamics.

Uganda's regional strategy is enshrined in the 1995 Ugandan constitution set up by NRM. Its list of Foreign Policy objectives includes 'Uganda shall actively participate in international and regional organisations' and 'the State shall promote regional and Pan-African cultural, economic and political cooperation and integration'.[94] No other EAC member's constitution contains any such clauses. Likewise, the NRM party itself has a constitution with strategic objectives to 'pursue economic and political integration of East Africa', and 'pursue a policy of Pan-Africanism, promotion of a common African market and pursue the realisation of African Union'.[95] A Ugandan representative at EALA remarks:

> Uganda is looking at security as a strategic imperative to enhance our development agenda ... Uganda believes that when we create a stable and viable entity called 'East Africa' then we will be able to also deal with our security threats.[96]

Uganda's regional interests and incursions will therefore continue whilst the NRM regime remains in place – certainly whilst under the current Bush War generation. China's engagement with Uganda opens regional opportunities for Museveni by ultimately supporting and solidifying his NRM's position, which holds regional integration as a strategic imperative.

This is made even more clear by Chinese relations with UPDF, which has remained central to regional intervention and integration. The Chief Political Commissar in the UPDF states unequivocally:

> We see ourselves as an East African force. Because we believe we can't survive on our own as a country, we are too small to survive in this competitive world ... the purpose of my work is to touch the brain of the soldier. That yes we have discipline, you have been trained, you have laws, but you must also be a conscious solider of what your country is, of what your region is, where we are coming from and where we want to go.[97]

Beyond the rhetoric, since the expulsion of the LRA the UPDF has been active in Somalia, Central African Republic and South Sudan (to be discussed further in later chapters). Uganda has always presented quite a credible narrative of tying national security issues within a moral framework that holds regional stability as paramount. Uganda's intervention in December 2013's inter-elite hostilities between Machar and Kiir in South Sudan, which then became ethnic-based violence amongst communities, was essentially a realist action to ensure an outcome that favoured Uganda. Yet UPDF and NRM politicians interviewed persistently championed the moral dimension, insisting that 'we ensured it did not degenerate into genocide'[98] and 'we staved off genocide, a Rwanda type genocide'.[99]

We do not know how the China–UPDF relationship will fully evolve, but we do know that the UPDF clearly and consistently stamps an indelible mark on the East African region through joint training and interventions. By engaging UPDF, through supplies and training, China increases the army's capacity whilst also helping to ensure undue influence from the West can continue to be resisted through the Global Mix framework. China's increased interactions with UPDF are interactions with a force that Museveni ensures is active and capable in East Africa, the Great Lakes Region and perhaps beyond. At the UN in 2015, Museveni spoke openly and forcefully about the need to empower African regional organizations (ROs), support the African Capacity for Immediate Response to Crises (ACIRC), and for the UN to allow quicker action through ROs.[100] China supports each of these as a means to protect its own security interests within its non-interference principle, thereby strengthening Museveni's positioning of UPDF as a regional intervention force.

Museveni's ability to act on his regional environment is thus aided by Chinese presence. These core constituencies within the NRM regime all see some kind of Chinese engagement. This engagement with other actors is not automatically or intentionally oppositional to Museveni, but it has been utilized or resisted by the President to his own advantage in Uganda and the region. Museveni is also forced, however, to acknowledge other troublesome actors and institutions that have influence within Uganda outside of the NRM. Again, each of these has seen Chinese engagement.

Domestic opposition and regional alternatives?

The NRM is no monolith, and opposition to Museveni appears from institutions and actors that might be thought of as supportive. These combine with the form of direct opposition which Museveni has also been compelled to allow. These opponents contribute further to the complexity of Museveni maintaining control and therefore also to the complexity of assessing China's growing impact, whose non-interference does not prevent engagement with such forces.

Parliament and judiciary: direct and indirect engagements

Although dominated by NRM since 1986, Uganda's parliament does still try to hold the government to account to some extent; and it can produce significant, influential political players. Younger members in particular are becoming outspoken and hostile to certain government practices. The speaker of parliament, Rebecca Kadaga, has an increasingly public profile and is capable of organizing discontent. This author was told that a backroom deal was done between herself and Museveni in August 2014, where she agreed not to run for the Presidency in exchange for him stopping undermining her in public.[101] And the four so-called 'rebel MPs' became a troublesome thorn in the side of Museveni during our period of interest, by constantly highlighting corruption allegations and calling for commissions of enquiry. After his split with Mbabazi, Museveni was forced to bring these young rebels back into the NRM fold in order to prevent them becoming overly problematic.[102] The official main opposition, the Forum for Democratic Change (FDC), is essentially an NRM splinter group formed by disgruntled Bush War veterans and former allies. It proved a constant nuisance to Museveni for more than a decade, but a continued lack of unity means that the FDC 'are internally weak and structurally flawed', and unable to form a convincing programme beyond the removal of Museveni.[103] Bobi Wine – known as the Ghetto President – would later emerge as part of a new generation of activists and political opponents who gained some global attention circa 2020.[104] But Bobi Wine's emergence (potentially) marks a new era: for the area of study, and up until Bobi Wine, the most credible challenges and political threats to Museveni had come from within the NRM part or the groups who had split from it.

China actively courts Ugandan MPs as part of its Africa strategy. NRM and opposition MPs are regularly invited to sessions at the Academy for International Business Officials in Beijing at the full expense of CPC, to attend training, education and cultural exposure lessons. They also tour military installations, power projects and factories. One MP states:

> We spent three weeks there and traversed something like seven states or provinces of China. They wanted to expose China to the participants ... it was promoting China and cementing that relationship, and trying to tell developing countries that China was your best ally.[105]

An Independent MP believes that he and colleagues are being prepared for the increasing numbers of Chinese companies in Uganda, and that these MPs will be the ones vetting and approving China's larger-scale investments.[106] As the patronage system of Ugandan politics spreads beyond the executive, MPs are becoming increasingly indebted as they seek re-election by satisfying constituents. Personal costs of re-election can be vast. The vetting of the large government deals tempts MPs to 'shake down serious other ones for money', rather than to undertake proper oversight.[107] In July 2013, a Parliamentary Commission struck a deal with an unnamed Chinese firm with finance from a Chinese bank to buy off MPs' debt and allow them to pay back at a lower rate.[108] This move was blocked by Museveni, as he became wary of China gaining too many avenues of influence into particular power centres: MPs should be in debt to the NRM, not China. Kizza Besigye feels his work as an opposition figure has 'without any shadow of a doubt' been hindered by the emergence of China. Museveni's increasingly vocal disdain for the West occurs 'with the knowledge that the Chinese can come and invest ... definitely it has had an impact on governance'.[109]

Along with parliament, the judiciary is another arm of government with which Museveni must wrestle. Whilst Western donors have invested in supporting legal frameworks and institutions in Uganda, China does not seem to have any direct role. A Minster for Justice and Major General notes, however, that 'like anybody else, when they invest substantial amounts in the country they want a legal regime that will protect that investment, that's natural'.[110] The Ugandan judiciary exemplifies the complexity of the shifting power struggles within Museveni's state-building. Justice Kanyeihamba, a retired Supreme Court Judge, says that any constitutional obstacles to Museveni's ambitions can simply be ignored or amended.[111] However, credible legal and constitutional frameworks legitimize the NRM regime alongside the more militaristic tendencies. This means that the judiciary is 'not always controlled by Museveni, there is a real power dynamic . . . the judiciary is not independent, but it does protect its own turf'.[112] In 2007, for example, the judiciary went on strike after the High Court was besieged by armed forces after it bailed treason suspects. In August 2014, the constitutional court ruled that Museveni could not appoint a Chief Justice without following proper procedure involving a Judicial Service Commission. It does, nonetheless, 'kowtow to the Executive' on matters centrally important to the larger NRM project, such as declaring that elections do not have to be re-run or that rebel MPs can be expelled from Parliament.[113]

Kingdoms and locals: welcoming and resisting

Museveni's policy of reinstating Uganda's Kingdoms as cultural institutions consolidated NRMs position after taking power, but he has then guarded against their potentially increasing prominence. He has skilfully played and ceded to them as required. Their inability or unwillingness to ever form a united front against NRM means collectively the Kingdoms have never posed a serious challenge to the state-building underway, but they are nonetheless an integral part of Uganda's political landscape. The Rwenzururu Kingdom witnessed a bloody exchange in July 2014, when military barracks were attacked in a coordinated effort to seize arms and ammunitions, and 100 people were killed. Motivations were unclear, but this was a general reminder of the Kingdoms' continued relevance and potentially destabilizing presence.[114]

Buganda has always been the most prominent and capable Kingdom: it is a political problem for NRM. Buganda youths rioted in Kampala in 2009, for example, when their King was not allowed to attend a rally, killing twenty people and injuring fifty. In 2013, Buganda signed an MoU with the government which agreed to return some properties to the Kingdom and improved the relationship after years of friction.[115] Buganda is now actively courting Chinese investment and was consciously aware of the opportunity that Chinese finance provided when updating its strategic economic objectives. The Buganda Kingdom Minister for Investments, Planning and Development says that 'naturally these days, the people who are liquid are Chinese, they are aggressive, sometimes they offer quite interesting propositions'. Buganda has an MoU with a Chinese company to develop real estate, and they are looking at farming opportunities.

Outside Chinese government and SME investment, Chinese local traders are also now a feature at Ugandan markets. Approximately 8,000 to 10,000 Chinese now live in Uganda, with about 2,000 to 4,000 present at any one time due to shop owners travelling back and forth from China at different parts of the year.[116] As is the case elsewhere in Africa, there has been hostility against the Chinese. A May 2009 local market trader strike was, however, only partly against the rising influx of Chinese competitors, and a much larger 2011 two-day protest was against currency inflation issues as much as the Chinese migrants.[117] Besigye states that the FDC has not seen a mobilization opportunity around anti-Chinese sentiment, in part because so many locals are benefitting personally from importing Chinese goods.[118] Increasing numbers of Ugandan traders are travelling directly to China in order to source goods due to easier visa regulations than elsewhere. According to Flavia Kabahandra, 'the US and EU look at everything, they are perfectionists, . . . to access the American visa is a myth, it's a great myth so that discouraged our traders from going to such partner states and China came in'.[119]

Nonetheless, the Kampala City Traders Association (KACITA) is extremely concerned about the Chinese migrants, saying that 'right now there is cold blood especially those who are doing petty trade'.[120] KACITA are resentful of how easy it seems to be for Chinese traders to come to Uganda and of the tax incentives the Chinese government gives them, stating that 'it's a very very big issue here in Uganda'.[121] China and the Chinese have reacted to the potential insecurity this resentment can bring. The Ugandan Overseas China Association began in the early 2000s after Chinese migrants kept being robbed by Ugandan locals due to their propensity for carrying cash (at least three Chinese were killed). That association still operates today, along with six other private organizations and one Chinese government initiative.[122] Zhang Ho also created the private security firm Hash Security in 2006 as part of his increasingly large business portfolio. According to Zhang Ho, this was not for profit but 'just for protection for ourselves . . . we don't want extra clients, we want to stay in the sites we have. This one is for protection of the Chinese, for our companies, for ourselves, and for Chinese'.[123]

From the Uganda side, there have been changes in tax and work permit laws that Zhang Ho and others have lobbied against, and the China Africa Friendship

Association of Uganda (CAFAU) are pressuring the government to make a law that foreign companies have to employ at least 75 per cent local staff.[124] The secretary to the consular at the Chinese Embassy in Kampala has publicly explained they have had dialogue with Ugandan government regarding anti-Chinese sentiment, but admitted that 'we cannot control all of them'.[125]

Risks to regional positioning

Parliament and MPs are players in Uganda's political economy, but they are greatly constrained as to what influence they have in overseeing government dealings with a China who is actively courting their attention. The East African Legislative Assembly is concerned with the corruption taking place in national executives and parliaments. A Kenyan representative introduced an EAC Freedom of Information Bill, Integrity and Anti-corruption Bill, Procurement Bill, and Whistle-blower Bill, as measures aimed against large government contracts in particular. He states:

> All these are efforts we are trying to make to increase the levels of integrity in the community and in the partner states . . . So there is not one answer. We must do these things comprehensibly, both at partner states level and at regional-level. But using many different ways, we can't leave it to one arm of government.[126]

But EALA remains one step removed from exerting authority over such deals. Ugandan MPs and their actions have notable regional implications, but the impact of regional laws on their behaviour is limited.

China deliberately tries to seduce Ugandan MPs into a pro-Beijing mind-set through its immersion visits, whilst offering them finance to help retain their position. This finance appears either deliberately and directly in the case of the Chinese banks offering of debt relief, and indirectly through Chinese projects providing opportunities to fleece more powerful Ministers for kickbacks. Museveni resisted MPs becoming personally indebted to Chinese banks, thereby retaining MP reliance on his own and NRM's networks. Their exposure visits to China plus their continued need for financial support make them more likely to allow big Chinese deals to go ahead, on which those Museveni-NRM networks increasingly rely. The implication of this Chinese influence on the region is that EALA's prevention efforts are unlikely to be strong enough to break this structural corruption.

Regionally, then-FDC party President Muntu admits their preoccupation is 'to build our capacity to take power in Uganda', rather than influencing regional integration or working with opposition parties in partner states.[127] Besigye believes that 'in EAC the attitude towards opposition parties, and not just in Uganda but generally in the region, is one of being treated as inherently subversive'. He explains that on occasions when he has tried to organize meetings with other partner state representatives, 'none would accept meeting because they will tell me you know that will cause problems with Museveni . . . links of opposition parties with the member states are very limited'.[128] And because local media 'can spend a week without writing anything about EAC, or even bother to explain it', civil society engagement is also lacking.[129]

China impacts upon the Ugandan opposition indirectly, therefore, through general bolstering of NRM's position rather than deliberately preventing opposition activities. That said, examples of more direct impacts have occurred: one day before the 2011 election, and one month before the 2016 election, a consignment of Chinese 'anti-riot' equipment including pepper sprayers, water cannons and armoured tear-gas vehicles was delivered to Ugandan police. These were used against protestors during the subsequent inflation riots in 2011, and on opposition supporters in the build-up to and aftermath of the 2016 election.[130] At the time of writing, it is unclear if Chinese equipment was used during 2021 violent election crackdowns (although it does seem clear that China is willing to move further into Uganda as Western donors become increasingly disillusioned with such violence).[131] But these all remain one step removed from China's purposeful involvement in opposition affairs. Museveni is able to suppress opposition through his continued role in Uganda's political economy writ large, rather than utilizing China directly to this end.

The East African Court of Justice (EACJ) is seen as one of the most functional and well-respected organs of EAC. The journalist-consultant expects more disputes to be taken there, due to the perception that plaintiffs have more chance of winning and that multi-national disputes involving increasingly common cross-border projects will need a neutral court.[132] China's regional impact here is a rare example of where Museveni's position could, at least potentially, be undermined. China – or their local fronts – have already sought recourse to EACJ, after whistle-blower complaints alleged impropriety in the open tender bidding process over the Karuma dam project. China International Water and Electric Corporation's (CWE) had their MoU cancelled by Museveni and then awarded to rival Sinohydro. The case was taken to the EACJ due to CWE representatives being frustrated by Ugandan court judgements (the EACJ eventually ruled in the Ugandan government's favour).[133] Further frustrations with Uganda's legal system may help bolster EACJ's importance and Chinese interest in it. Museveni requires a credible legal framework to encourage foreign investment. He does then have some influence over court outcomes in Uganda (although not dictatorial control), but less so when cases move to the EACJ. Further examples of Chinese companies using the justice system will be discussed in later chapters.

Likewise, the Kingdoms pose something of a regional risk to Museveni. Kingdoms retain an indelible role within Museveni's Uganda and are one of the moving and conflictual parts that need managing if domestic stability is to remain, and if further regional integration is to occur. Buganda remains hesitant and sceptical of the NRM's EAC integration agenda due to the lack of dialogue space for the Kingdoms.[134] NRM is aware that the Kingdoms are a problem for their EAC agenda. A UPDF Officer who in 2008 authored a document highlighting East African ethnic and cultural groups who may oppose integration says that 'if the Kingdoms are reluctant to enter the EAC or any other union they would be pulling back the dictates of modern globalisation and the benefits that accrue'.[135] Thus far, Museveni has not seemingly prevented interactions between China and the Kingdoms, and is likely satisfied that China is able to deal with Kingdoms in an amicable, unthreatening manner. Longer term, however, if stronger Kingdoms were able to utilize Chinese finance effectively, they could limit Museveni's regional position due to domestic tensions around the pace and nature of EAC integration.

Finally, at the very lowest level, Museveni's relationship with China necessarily includes a Chinese influx of local traders. Despite the issues discussed, thus far he has managed them well and they were not any kind of election issue in 2016 or 2021. This aspect of relations seems less likely to imprint on regional affairs. The Chinese usually choose to start a business in Uganda due to already knowing someone there. Chinese petty traders 'are thinking Uganda is Uganda, they don't think in part of regions. The region for them is too far.'[136] Thus, although similar local tensions occur in other EAC member countries, these will not likely be exacerbated by events in Uganda.

Conclusion: influence, incorporation and resistance

This chapter investigated China's global so-called 'Great Power' role in a domestic space in Africa. It showcased how China engages Uganda, and whether this engagement aids or restricts Museveni domestically (it also began to look at the regional implications of that engagement). China has not appeared as an obvious enemy of Uganda – in the way the West's outspoken (even if hypocritical) human rights agenda could be perceived to be. Yet any Great Power with potentially transformative economic might is a possible danger to, indeed, any regime; but the African context is clearly at particular risk of being overwhelmed or subdued by any such power. China is normatively in line with Uganda to a much greater extent than the West, and materially China is engaged with and subtly influencing a greater array of actors. Museveni reacts to this by incorporating China into his state-building project when it suits his agenda, but has been able to resist Chinese incursions when it does not. Chinese presence in the shifting tectonic plates that require balancing under the NRM means that the challenges faced by Museveni have not become increasingly prominent. In the same way he has done with Western donors and other powers in previous years, Museveni as leader shows clear agency by incorporating, utilizing and resisting Chinese incursions in order to stabilize the current regime.

Structurally, China–Uganda elite relations share an ideological convergence and shared narrative arc, and China's investments offer development finance and procurement opportunities for key local players. Museveni's capacity to intervene in regional security issues and centralize Uganda's role in the regional development agenda increases through Chinese presence. Locally, elite inner circle disruptions have been resisted, there are clear and definite efforts to engage the wider NRM ruling party, and UPDF training with PLA is increasing. Insulated from Western nagging by a China supportive of these key constituents, this increases Uganda's capacity and willingness to actively influence East African security issues.

These pillars of NRM state-building – the elite circle, patronage networks, party and army – see China engaging in a way that helps stabilize and maintain the status quo, as intended by Museveni. Yet China is also subtly impacting on other forces outside of the NRM but a key feature of Uganda's political economy. MPs are courted by China and the FDC opposition remains weak, encouraging an NRM-dominated EALA agenda. Uganda's judiciary is required for protecting Chinese business interests which, in the long term, may increase the importance of the East African Court of Justice. The Kingdoms (or Buganda, at least) are interacting directly with China itself, which could also halt regional integration efforts. The locals or general populace are so far the most active anti-China players but also utilize Chinese wealth generating opportunities. They have prompted reaction by China and Chinese in Uganda, but are yet to have serious regional implications.

Crude and active pressure of the Western donor kind is not taking place and China's non-interference principle remains key to stable relations. This does not mean, however, that influence is not sought or gained. It is, in fact, the size and scope of Chinese interactions that mark them apart. The conscious and subconscious imperialist beliefs of Uganda's traditional partners occur alongside the globalization of Western culture and the promotion of human rights and democracy. But Western ideology has never found comfortable homes in the minds of Ugandan elites and a range of politicians, and they have never hosted hundreds of MPs and educated them on their achievements. The West are not capable of training record numbers of UPDF, being seen as a readily available source of investment by the Kingdoms, being a cheap source of market-trader goods, or readily and without consequence engaging the shadowy business arrangements required to win deals in Uganda. China may not 'interfere', but it currently engages more actors, levels and sectors than its Western rivals do. Museveni has therefore needed to balance and incorporate them into Uganda's political economy to a degree that suits his agenda.

Regionally, a stable Uganda may ultimately benefit China's regional aspirations also; their agendas are not in direct opposition to one another, but arguably a greater number of tangible benefits accrue to Museveni than Beijing. Museveni and the NRM have always seen regional stability as a pre-requisite for Ugandan development and their own continued rule. Within the security sector, Uganda has been clear, consistent and capable in enacting a regional security policy and shaping the future direction of the EAC. Uganda has been at the forefront of EAC rejuvenation by pushing for the later inclusion of Rwanda and Burundi, being the leading proponent of political union, and the most active military power in intervening outside EAC borders. China is also active within EAC and outside its borders, but whether it consciously sees Uganda as the leading proponent of its regional strategy is unclear. What is clear, however, is that Uganda and Museveni's position within EAC means that Chinese incursions into the state-building project underway inevitably creates regional reverberations.

2

China and the East African Community: overarching and low-level impacts

'There are no 'natural' or 'given' regions, but these are constructed, deconstructed and reconstructed – intentionally or unintentionally – in the process of global transformation, by collective human action and identity formation.'[1]

Prof Joram Mukama Biswaro, Author and Tanzanian Permanent Representative to the African Union and United Nations Economic Commission for Africa

China and East Africa have undergone very distinct, separate development journeys, yet their stories have remained very much connected in different ways across historical eras. The 2001 reincarnation of the East African Community (EAC) sees a unique, expanding role for China within the EAC's integration agenda and security dynamics between member states. This has ultimately benefitted President Museveni of Uganda. This chapter outlines China's relationship with the EAC institution and in each member state. It shows that China's global influence clearly affects the EAC's regional progress, whilst simultaneously impacting local security issues. The chapter explains how China has become a key partner in shaping the EAC's development agenda by providing significant funds for projects deemed essential to integration, and is a notable player in specific regional security threats related to terrorism and the oil sector.

It also discusses Uganda's shifting position within these relationships. The chapter explains that China – whether it intends to or not – contributes significantly to problematic, troublesome impacts in the EAC which provide operating space for Uganda. It does not argue that the Chinese presence is entirely negative and destabilizing, but it does argue that China's role has contributed to significant, direct detrimental impacts, and that these have allowed Museveni the opportunity to increase his standing and status within EAC. It also does not argue that other leaders in East Africa have not influenced the issues and processes discussed, or exercised agency against China and/or Museveni. But it does argue that Museveni has been uniquely influential and is worthy of particular focus. In order to understand Museveni's agency within the East African regional context whilst China's global rise becomes increasingly influential, we must interrogate China's role within the security issues that dominate regional geo-politics and within which Museveni is an active player.

This chapter is divided into four main sections. The first, 'History of relations – always important', builds on the brief historical portrait outlined in the Introduction but with a focus on East Africa, giving a historical overview of China–East African relations from pre-colonial to present time. The second section, 'East African Community II – a shared agenda?', outlines key features of the revived East African Community, emphasizing the importance of personalities of incumbent leaders and the increasing focus on security issues within the partnership. The third section, 'Contemporary relations – China's structural role in East Africa', focuses on China's modern relationship and structural role with East Africa. It explains how China has limited direct involvement with EAC as an institution and provides a summary of its bilateral relations with member states other than Uganda. The final section, 'Security trends and challenges – China's impact on dynamics', explains China's regional role in the leading local security threats currently facing the region and Uganda. It explains how Small Arms and Light Weapons (SALW) proliferation and the ivory trade enmesh China into the terrorism threat, whilst Chinese infrastructure construction related to the oil sector – notably the Standard Gauge Railway project – has clear security implications. It then ends with a brief conclusion summarizing the nature of China's presence and the impact on Museveni's regional role.

History of relations – always important

The long-shared history between China and Africa that is promoted by current leaders is in fact, the story of Greater East Africa. All the major time periods

Pre-colonial links and destruction of Empire

African ivory was imported by China from the second century AD, most likely from the Aksum Empire (modern-day Eritrea and Northern Ethiopia).[2] Trade, using Arab and South East Asian middlemen, increased greatly from the AD 600s onwards, during a time where Europe remained almost entirely ignorant of Africa's riches.[3] Then Zheng He's famous sea voyages in the 1400s sailed to Mogadishu and Brava in modern-day Somalia, then Malindi and Mombasa in Kenya.[4] But when Emperor Yung-Lo died in 1424 (who had sanctioned He's global voyages in defiance of tradition), China reverted to its isolationism and banned the construction of sea-fairing ships. Europe and Africa were considered too far from Chinese borders to be of concern, and Confucian culture viewed the Indian Ocean as a *mare liberum*. Portuguese pirates subsequently conquered it unopposed: peaceful trade ended and the European conquest of Africa slowly began.[5] The industrializing West would now dominate global processes into the twenty-first century. This rise of the West had dramatic ramifications for both China and East Africa, who underwent separate but parallel transformations at the hands of Europeans.

Europe's Westphalian state system with principles of sovereignty rights and state interactions taking place on an equal basis had no meaning in China who viewed itself as so culturally superior that it never engaged countries on an equal basis, including the distant West. Britain's victory in the Opium Wars (1839–42; 1856–60), however, changed dynamics dramatically. China completely misjudged (or did not even have the language to comprehend) the seismic global shift that had occurred when Britain became an Industrial Superpower. This began China's self-perceived 'Century of Humiliation': Britain enforcing free trade utterly undermined China's world view. British military power allowed it to 'construct an imperialistic relationship that would subject China to British economic will for a century'.[6]

Imperialism's violent pursuit of new markets linked East Africa and China, albeit indirectly. China and Asia's relative power meant that Europe's aggressive force concentrated more on Africa. The infamous 'scramble for Africa' became

64   *Ugandan Agency within China–Africa Relations*

central to European competition as industrial countries battled to catch up with the British super power. European powers redrew and remade the Africa's local processes. Direct China–East Africa relations at this time were limited, but Chinese workers were brought to German Tanganyika in 1906 to build the country's first railway and elsewhere in Britain's colonies.[7]

Post-Independence – perceived unity but divergent interests

The subjugation of China and East Africa soon shifted to see their destinies more directly intertwined: almost simultaneous revolutions occurred, each of which saw a clash between idealism and realpolitik. Nationalist realpolitik eventually won in both East Africa and China: the ideals of Pan-Africanism and a pan-continental solidarity movement were ultimately defeated. Mao Tse-Tung's 1949 communist victory over Chiang Kei Sheik in China's civil war completed and consolidated the centralization of the Chinese state, which Sheik had begun from 1928 in an effort to match Chinese state-building to the new industrial era.[8] Meanwhile, East Africa's future leaders promoted ideas of self-rule, sovereignty and socialism into their Pan-Africanist ideology as they agitated for independence.

This meant that the first EAC was a confused mix of revised colonial regional structures fused with a Pan-African agenda trying to break from the imperial past. As nationalism swept Africa and the region, Tanganyika's Julius Nyerere famously argued in 1960 that Uganda, Kenya and Tanganyika's shared history and cultural links meant they should unite after independence.[9] Almost immediately, however, nationalist agenda's created rivalries amongst them that began hindering integration even before the official creation of the first East African Community in 1967, which went ahead nonetheless.

China during this time with Mao's revolutionary objectives and interventionist ideology, saw East Africa as a prime location to inject and support socialist revolution. Uganda's Milton Obote had visited China pre-independence and met Mao during a June 1965 tour. Kenya's Mau Mau uprising had erupted just three years after Mao's 1949 peasant victory and 'betrayed at least a certain awareness of the Chinese model'. In 1964, independent Kenya was the first African country to congratulate Beijing formally for its successful nuclear bomb test. Tanganyika, soon to become

Tanzania when it merged with the island of Zanzibar, enjoyed extremely strong China relations under the Afro-Socialist Nyerere. Beijing also had strong links with the radical Zanzibarian Marxist agitator Abdulrahman Mohamed Babu, who became Minister of External Affairs following the 1964 overthrow of the Sultan of Zanzibar.[10]

This was a glaring misreading from Mao, however: these leaders were East African nationalists, not revolutionary Marxists seeking a grand alliance with China. Mao's quite aggressive diplomacy was ultimately resisted. Nyerere was committed to non-alignment and weary of Great Power interference. The union of Zanzibar and Tanganyika almost immediately after the Zanzibar revolution was in line with Nyerere's Pan-Africanism. But also, in part, it was a means of containing its revolutionary zeal (Zanzibar also sparked fear in Uganda and Kenya of copycat mutinies). Despite his visits to China, Obote had always been weary of being associated with communism both before and after independence.[11] And Kenya's President Jomo Kenyatta was even more hostile to Beijing relations, especially after he fell out with the more pro-China Vice President Odinga, who resigned in 1966 meaning that China in fact supported the Kenyan opposition. In May 1965, a forty-lorry convoy of Chinese arms coming from Tanzania was halted in Western Kenya, apparently on its way to Uganda. The destination for the Chinese arms was likely the Congo, but Obote rushed to reassure Kenyatta that the arms were not meant for Odinga and his supporters, such was the tension and mistrust swilling around the region![12]

Rwanda and Burundi remained in the background to these events, never being part of the original East African cooperative efforts. China again misread their contexts, never fully understanding the complexities of their ethnic issues. China's support for the minority Tutsi government in Burundi led to mistrust during bitter 1960s ethnic rivalry. In Rwanda, China supported the disposed Tutsi King with funds, ammunition and training of refugees in neighbouring countries against the 1962 majority Hutu anti-communist government. Chinese relations with Burundi and Rwanda were not normalized until after 1971.[13]

These issues meant that towards the end of the 1960s as EAC I was formed, Beijing disengaged from East Africa. China remained close to Tanzania, however, thereby retaining East Africa's central importance in the China–Africa narrative. The TAZARA railway linking Tanzania and Zambia was built between 1970 and 1975 and 'still dwarfs other infrastructure projects to date in China's current wave of economic engagement in Africa'.[14] In return, Tanzania played a key role in China's pursuit of the seat at the UN Security Council. According to Charles Nyerere – the son of Julius Nyerere – Tanzanian diplomat Dr Salim Salim was sent to the UN in 1970 to promote the idea that World War III might occur if Beijing was not made a Permanent-5 member of the UNSC, which then occurred amidst strong African support.[15] Chinese citizens have never forgotten Africa's role in this seismic event.[16]

EAC I and 1980s – collapse and retreat

EAC I was characterized by mistrust and personal dislike amongst leaders, as well as economic inequality between states. All member states (as well as Burundi and Rwanda) increased military expenditure and army size dramatically: this regional arms race increased the militarization of society and politics throughout the region.[17] China in no way directly caused the eventual collapse of EAC I in 1977; however, China was indirectly involved some of the key factors.

Lack of private sector and civil society involvement meant that EAC I was an entirely elitist creation, and international foreign influence was felt most strongly through bilateral relations rather than regional programmes. China was no exception to this, giving no direct support to EAC as an institution.[18] Kenya's economic clout, and the ideological divergence between a capitalist Kenya, African socialist Tanzania, and mixed economy Uganda, greatly hindered integration. Rivalry was further exacerbated by Chinese presence, to a degree. The TAZARA railway created resentment due to Tanzania's better terms of trade with China, risked splitting EAC along a north-south axis and an east-west one, and arguably contributed to less Tanzania–Kenya integration. China had an obvious preference for Tanzania's economic model over Kenya, and resentment within EAC was compounded by Nyerere's pre-occupation with the Southern African liberation movements that China also supported. Dissatisfaction with EAC led to a Tanzanian 'southward drift' that would have ramifications for EAC II, discussed throughout remaining sections and chapters.[19]

The 1960s and 1970s, therefore, saw the failure of two interacting ideals. East Africa's post-colonial Pan-African dream of regional unification gave way to nationalist nation-state models. The leaders of that nation-state model subsequently squandered the chance to develop their countries. China, meanwhile, was the exporter of an ideologically driven communist dream which was resisted in East Africa. China's subsequent retrenchment to the insanity of the Cultural Revolution also led to its severe economic decline. By the end of the 1970s, both China and East Africa appeared rather broken.

In Africa, in the 1980s and the early 1990s the West was able to impose ideologically driven policy that led to continued failure and unfulfilled potential. Structural Adjustment Programmes (SAPs) were inflicted on all East African countries and the entire continent, as they would be on post-communist Russia. This shock therapy prescription led to well-documented hardship and suffering.[20] In addition, the USSR's collapse meant global powers withdrew from Africa's security concerns, which unleashed repressed security dynamics and created a wave of violent civil conflict. East Africa remained in perpetual crisis. The 1994 Rwandan genocide was an extreme crescendo to the years of insecurity and marginalization suffered by many groups, the perverted logical conclusion of an ethicized politics that was prevalent in all states who would eventually be EAC II members. The 1994 Rwandan genocide was the perverted logical conclusion of an ethicized politics, insecurity and marginalization suffered across all states who would eventually be EAC II members. Tanzania, the only possible exception, had a stagnated economy and endemic simmering tension between Island and Mainland. The fall-out from Rwanda led to the catastrophic Congo Wars that engulfed the entire continent, killed five million people, and included direct military confrontation and proxy war between Uganda and Rwanda.

China paved a different course. It retreated from Africa, prioritizing its own domestic development and an export-orientated growth strategy which inserted China into the international division of labour. Capital was needed for its investment in infrastructure and communications networks, for which Africa was not needed. This re-structuring was done *carefully and slowly*, and eventually led to spectacular success.[21] Even during China's retreat and regrouping, it retained a special relationship and notable historical link with East Africa. Beijing stayed closer to Tanzania than elsewhere, agreeing to renovate sixty former aid projects. Its non-interference principle was also re-interpreted by Beijing, which now allowed Chinese management of its African

68   *Ugandan Agency within China–Africa Relations*

initiatives (this was queried by Nyerere).[22] Relations with Kenya also improved, and Ugandan instability did not prevent low but steady interactions.

In the mid-1990s, China emerged victorious as a manufacturing powerhouse that now needed minerals and resources to continue fuelling is exponential growth, a market for its products and allies in its resistance to US hegemony. Africa was needed again; and East Africa would remain a crucial and unique component of its larger African agenda. Having restructured and reimagined itself China had become a key part of the global economy. These trends occurred separately in East Africa and China, but at the beginning of the 2000s these ancient partners' fluctuating relationship began to coalesce once again. Complex personal dynamics between leaders in East Africa and Kenya's contested hegemon status created challenges and opportunities for China.

East African Community II – a shared agenda?

Revival and rivalry

Amidst the continued chaos, the arrival in East Africa of Museveni as Ugandan President in 1986 – who would become clearly and consistently the most vocal champion of EAC rejuvenation – led to tangible steps towards a shared regional agenda. From 1991 onwards, a decade of slow but steady progress occurred despite continued regional difficulties. The Treaty for the Establishment of the East African Community was signed in November 1999, and formally launched on 15 January 2001. In a similar way to how China embraced a capitalist market-based approach to development (albeit with unique characteristics and controls), the EAC partners also moved away from EAC I's common ownership and towards a neo-liberal free market doctrine. Executive powers were more evenly spread in the new EAC II, and the agreement included the principle of more civil society and grassroots organization (at least in theory).

National differences between economies and leaders, however, continue to cause rifts. The scars of EAC I, and China's role within them, have had their repercussions. Tanzania's active role in the Front Line States against Apartheid South Africa (whose liberation struggles Beijing had supported), along with the failure of EAC I, encouraged its southward drift into what became the Southern African Development Community (SADC) in 1992.[23] This dual membership causes problems to this day. 'When you tell Tanzanians to withdraw from SADC they don't understand you,' says a Clerk at the EAC, 'because Tanzanians have suffered there, they have lost blood, they have lost resources, to ensure that those countries are liberated.'[24] Tanzania lacks the security and economic incentives for integration that Uganda, Rwanda and Burundi have due to them being landlocked, and it lacks the economic clout and business acumen of Kenya. Tanzania therefore sees itself as justifiably cautious towards EAC integration, especially regarding the espoused end-goal of political federation.[25] In 2011, members were presented with a draft model of what federation could look like but Tanzania 'got cold feet' about it. This led to the creation of the Coalition of the Willing: Uganda, Rwanda and Kenya (the Northern Corridor countries) agreed to proceed with various projects alone without Tanzania and Burundi (the Southern Corridor).[26]

This Coalition of the Willing (CoW) dominated media attention for the next several years. A restructuring of the EAC institution became possible, or even a complete split. This emerging collective of three states pushed forward whilst viewing – and being viewed by – Tanzania with suspicion. 'It's a different leadership and policy and philosophy and values and principles system that drives them in Tanzania,' according to an ex-Director of Uganda's External Security Organisation, due to Tanzania's historical preference for mediation and dialogue rather than the more belligerent policies of other EAC partners.[27]

The risk of a north-south divide in the EAC also highlights the geo-political forces within Africa that both compel and frustrate a collective EAC security arrangement. It is clear that 'South Africa as a Big Brother in the SADC has responsibility in the stability of Great Lakes Region', meaning that EAC members must take account of Pretoria's interests.[28] This is exacerbated by Tanzania's SADC membership. Northwards, the continental (and global) politics around the river Nile is a huge consideration. Egypt is a clear strategic concern, as are all riparian states.[29] A former-Director of the East African Standby Force, explains that the Coalition of the Willing developed at least in part as a means of strengthening a collective fight against the power and influence of Ethiopia and Sudan. This emphasizes how important it became to bring South Sudan into the EAC arrangement:

South Sudan of late since they got independence has been so huge for both Kenya and Uganda that its inclusion in EAC becomes fundamental. So to the Northern Corridor it is a perfect move. Now for the Southern Corridor countries, Burundi and Tanzania, it is secondary. Because for them they would rather have a southward drift than a northward drift.[30]

Within this unstable, fluctuating regional dynamic, the EAC's security function is of crucial significance.

The crucial role of defence and security

Kenya does not possess the regional hegemonic status of powers such as South Africa in Southern Africa or Nigeria in West Africa, despite being the EAC's most important economy. In East Africa, military and economic capacity is more evenly distributed (with the exception of Burundi who remains exceptionally poor), meaning that the role of individual leaders can shift relations and regional dynamics considerably. Museveni's militarism and security mind-set has been in line with EAC II developments, and Uganda has remained central to regional (in)security throughout its existence. A somewhat improved security environment is one of the most tangible developments over the history of EAC II.

Defence and security has been a building block for integration and the EAC as an institution. Cooperation and MoUs around defence and security existed pre-EAC treaty, as 'it was felt that it was important that if those people in Defence can work together, then it will be easier for the others'.[31] The EAC 2012 Protocol on Cooperation on Defence Affairs and 2013 Protocol on Peace and Security are as natural developments, growing organically from the ad hoc arrangements that were taking place into being a stronger, more permanent arrangement.[32] Although the Protocols were the culmination of a longer-term trend and effort in the EAC, the more recent threats facing the region 'facilitated a quick response and rapid intervention toward completing them'.[33]

From a collapse of EAC I and the 1978–9 inter-state war between Idi Amin's Uganda and Nyerere's Tanzania, EAC II's security cooperation is helping to forge better security cooperation between partner states. The Protocol's explicit and obvious impacts are so far limited; however, 'the *spirit* behind them is important, to a larger extent that spirit has cemented security relations, that idea that there will be more coordination and cooperation across the region.'[34] This cooperative environment has made violent inter-state conflict increasingly unlikely.

EAC officials cite a distinct gap in the African Peace and Security Architecture (APSA), whereby East Africa's borders and multiple Regional Economic Communities (RECs) make control of the proposed East African Standby Force (EASF) more complicated than is found in other regions. An East African Legislative Assembly (EALA) representative is passionate in his critique of the current arrangements:

> The unfortunate bit is this: Uganda has boots on the ground in Somalia, Burundi has boots on the ground in Somalia, Kenya has boots on the ground in Somalia, not using an East African framework but using an African framework, it is outrageous! ... the command structure of these three partner states is in East Africa but using an AU framework. Tanzania is in DRC not as party of EAC but as part of AU through SADC, Rwanda is in Central African Republic as part of the AU. So all our countries have presence in the neighbourhood, but it is not neat, it is not properly coordinated, it's not properly organised. It has to be organised from our framework.[35]

The EAC as an institution is trying to carve out its own operational space within uncertain, overlapping regional governance and security agreements, and within the continental security architecture proposed in APSA.[36] There is also agreement to establish a permanent EAC Peace and Security Council to report to the Summit on security issues.[37] In 2014, the Coalition of the Willing partners also signed a Mutual Defence Pact and Mutual Peace and Security Pact 'to guarantee each other in the event that they are attacked from outside'[38] (although implementation of the Pact was stalled as of 2018).

Currently, this EAC security arrangement remains fluctuating and unstable; and individual leaders can affect that instability significantly. Uganda's Museveni is not the only President to exert agency and seek to influence the nature of regional progress in order to suit his personal and domestic agenda: they all done and have done, to varying degrees of success. And although the likelihood of violent confrontation has lessened, it has not approached a stage where conflict is unthinkable. Far from it. The Assistant Commissioner in Charge of Planning in the Ugandan Ministry of Defence explains:

The kind of mechanisms they have put in place, conflict management and things, would not allow any conflicts between EAC members from happening. But for us here fighting in the region we know Tanzania and Uganda it's not so long ago, Uganda and Rwanda although we were doing it in Congo it's not very long ago ... practically I don't see it because of the close relationship. But just because it has not taken a lot of time, people will say ah but you never know![39]

Personal animosity and state rivalry remain important and conflict is possible. The role and interests of individual leaders in all countries can have serious regional consequences. Tanzania consciously watered down the EAC Defence Protocol, due to its membership of SADC and what it perceived as a confusion between what was being marked as police versus military matters.[40] Its 2013 involvement in the United Nations Force Intervention Brigade as part of MONUSCO in Eastern-DRC (which had an unusually aggressive mandate) extended Tanzanian military operations into an area highly sensitive to Rwanda. This caused a serious schism. Tanzanian President Kikwete appealed for Rwanda to negotiate with the FDLR – the remnants of the génocidaires and Kigali's nemesis that operates in DRC. Rwanda's Kagame reacted by publicly threatening to punch Kikwete, and Tanzania then expelled Rwandans from its Kagera region.[41] Museveni's influence in shaping dynamics was evident when he intervened and managed to quell the hostility, by getting Kagame to become less overtly confrontational. But unresolved issues remained.[42] Arguments on the matter took place at the EAC Council of Ministers meeting in August 2013, at the same time as Tanzania and Burundi officially recorded their apprehension at the trilateral discussions taking place amongst CoW states.[43]

Contemporary relations – China's structural role in East Africa

So, what is China's role within East Africa and these developments within EAC II in recent times? Within the institution itself and with partners states? China of course is a major world economy and nuclear power: it has the military and economic power to overrun East Africa in any kind of 'colonial-style' arrangement it so desired, in theory. The power dynamic between China and East African states is clear and obvious. But that possibility is clearly very constrained: the reaction of the other great powers, the UN charter, global norms of behaviour etc, make such behaviours very unlikely. And for China, they are also 'self-constrained' by their own narrative of south-south cooperation and non-interference (in the same way as the West are by their promotion of human rights discourse, even if obvious contradictions of behaviour occur within that). How then, does China assert influence and protect its interests? What impact does it have on the region? It occurs both by the overarching structural context which China helps create and EAC states must operate within; and through direct and indirect Chinese roles in specific security issues that are prevalent on the ground in East Africa.

The shifting environment

The historical narrative of peaceful trade and support for liberation movements set a context in which China–East Africa relations occurs. This is important and cannot be ignored. It is strikingly different to the much maligned colonial-master history that the West carries with it. Meanwhile, EAC integration efforts would be occurring with or without Chinese presence. The institution is actually 'playing catch-up' with local and regional dynamics that compels integration. This includes serious conflicts occurring at its border. The decision to expand to include Rwanda and Burundi in 2007 was taken (at least partly) in order to help stabilize those countries after their intense and brutal civil conflicts, and the significant volume of cross-border trade with South Sudan made their inclusion somewhat inevitable.[44] Somalia has also applied to join and will likely be accepted in future, as may the DRC. Ethiopia is also touted as a possible future member (so is Sudan, even considering the historical animosity there has been between it and member states).[45] So resentment at the continued European presence in the region, and the effort to integrate and expand EAC would be occurring whether China had undergone such rapid economic transformation or not. China's re-emergence as a serious global power with a penchant for mega-construction sees them 'aligning themselves with a maturing EAC, because they are chasing larger projects . . . China is just fitting in the architecture into something that was already working.'[46] But is that Chinese presence shaping what was already underway? And what does that presence and alignment mean for the region?

Chinese incursion into the East African market provides serious competition to partner states' own comparative advantages and industrialization strategies. East African economies already suffer from lack of complementarity – they each produce too many similar goods, rather than sharing different specializations across the region which would foster better, more integrated trade. China now also supplies many of those same goods, as well as ones that could potentially be manufactured in the region and hence spur East Africa's own transformation to a manufacturing hub. Some prophecies have been rather damning. In 2013, Joseph Onjala wrote:

> Continued threat by China is likely to tilt the trade balance against the EAC member states. This turn of events can be of concern, especially when it is considered that that regional imbalance in particular with regard to industrialisation contributed to the collapse of the EAC four decades ago ... the expanding trade between China and the regional market provides a direct threat to the future viability of the economic integration since the process is likely to undermine many of the trading benefits envisaged in the formation of EAC integration.[47]

But the EAC is more than just an economic group that seeks to trade basic goods between members. China's engagement with the institution and its partner states is a multi-layered, multi-level approach that is having even more significant ramifications for the institution and its security role.

The EAC as an institution – increasing interaction

China has appeared in the consciousness of EAC II and East African Legislative Assembly since its creation (notably by Ugandan EALA representatives in particular), but initially China was seen and spoken of as an inspiration rather than strategic partner. In January 2002, the first Secretary General of the Community, Nuwe Amanya Mushega from Uganda, stated to EALA: 'you know what China can do, and nobody attacks it. But what is the secret behind China? ... It is the size of its population and landmass.'[48] James Wapakabulo, Ex-Officio member and Uganda Minister of Foreign Affairs, was even uncompromising and explicitly anti-European in his own statement:

the China that the Europeans used to rejoice in humiliating, the China which was despised by Europeans, is no longer available ... East Africa, we all agree, is despised, and Africans are despised ... For East Africa, we must be very serious on the question of unity, the question of the East African federation.[49]

There has been occasional criticism over sub-standard Chinese goods and pollution levels in Beijing on the floor of EALA, but generally the subsequent years saw repeated comparisons and policies to emulate. These include reference to: having tariffs on foreign trade; China's industrialization strategy and use of Small and Medium Enterprises; utility of government subsidies; agricultural development; promoting its culture globally; China's access to the sea and lack of debt; and use of biogas.[50] At a January 2014 EALA speech, Museveni himself said that East African states should be comparing themselves to high-performing China rather than their struggling African neighbours.[51] China's emergence as a key partner clearly influenced EAC negotiations with the European Union (EU) over Economic Partnership Agreements (EPA), leading to a prolonged and confident battle over the EU's demand of retaining favoured nation privileges.[52]

Meanwhile, China itself gives very little finance directly to the EAC as an institution directly. Relations between China and partner states have been more important, where Chinese companies have acquired large state-to-state deals as well as winning open bidding contracts. But a relationship with EAC emerged around our time of focus (early 2010s). EAC officials insist that their ideas and proposals for large infrastructure projects occurred without Chinese influence, but there is no doubt China's engagement and propensity for such projects has been welcomed. The senior member of the EAC secretariat confirms:

> I am happy that China stepped onto the plate, because we requested all our partners to come and support the projects. So our projects are not development partner driven we developed them, agreed them at the regional-level, got the heads of state to endorse them, and then asked our partners to help us in those. And China has stepped up to the plate especially in rail.[53]

In November 2011, the China–EAC Framework agreement was signed to further institutionalize the relationship, the first of its kind between China and an African REC. It encourages Chinese involvement in a variety of sectors including trade, industry, people-to-people relationships and technology transfer.[54] Infrastructure, however, 'is the main crux of the matter'.[55] Similar in nature to EAC agreements with the US and EU, the framework agreement does not compel partner states to work with China on particular projects, but provides an overarching set of principles under which relations operate. It was initiated and is monitored by diplomats and technocrats from both China and the EAC, and was not discussed at EALA or within EAC committees. It agrees to have annual meetings between the EAC Secretary General and Vice Minister for Commerce of China, have more regular meetings between the EAC Director of Infrastructure and Chinese Ministers, hold regular trade shows, and have certain aspects and agreements taken to the Ministerial and Heads of State level.

The most unique outcome vis-à-vis other agreements is size. According to the EAC Director of infrastructure 'the Chinese of course you know they work big. So they come in big groups with big people. But the arrangement is the same, the format is the same as other agreements.'[56] Importantly, the agreement also retains the principle that arrangements for and implementation of projects occurs bilaterally between China and relevant partner states. Unlike the EU, which can negotiate directly with the EAC, the Chinese agreement ensures that Beijing's preference for state-to-state deals remains intact. This is an important difference: the EAC Summit (meetings between Heads of State) has regular explicit agenda items to discuss agreements such as the EPA, the US African Growth and Opportunity Act (AGOA) and COMESA–EAC–SADC tripartite; but the China Framework Agreement does not.[57] The sovereign loan arrangements for most (if not all) mega-infrastructure projects mean that bilateral relations and state level implementation remain essential.

Private Chinese individuals also have an interest in EAC affairs. In April 2015, a group of Chinese investors asked the EAC to implement a double taxation agreement to ease their investment in the region.[58] A senior member of the secretariat explains that 'the network of individual Chinese business people operating in our different countries form a very strong group that backs us'. With their counterparts in China, they form a network who engage EAC through the East African Business Council.[59] The Chinese business model is perhaps uniquely suited to the East African environment. According to a Chinese businessman whose family has worked in Arusha, Tanzania for the last twenty years: 'Most Chinese use the same principles as back home to get contracts . . . the main problem with the whole relationship is the bribery that goes on.'[60] Non-interference only applies to governance and government relations, not the terms of business deals which are actually far more stringent than most Western partners. Local economists are concerned:

> There is no competition, you know it is very very opaque, very opaque. I mean I have been in this business of reporting contracts and things for many years, but there are things I have not seen before. I mean the subject of tied aid and tied procurement is an old subject, and we used to say oh no it is not fair and all that. But the Chinese have taken it to a different level.[61]

Museveni has also been ever-present in the history of EAC II's revival, and has pushed for political union more forcefully than any other leader. At an early session of EALA, the Ugandan Minister of Foreign Affairs, James Wapakabulo announced: 'Tell us when you want to discuss it. I can speak for Uganda; we are ready any time to begin discussing the question of a federation.'[62] In 2004, Museveni pushed Kenya's Kibaki and Tanzania's Mkapa to 'fast-track' the process; and when that agreements also became delayed Uganda continued to push ten years later at a time when other partners were more resistant.[63] Museveni's role as elder statesmen in the region carries weight: Justice Kanyeihamba, noting his age and longevity, explains 'that matters, in an African context to say he is our senior, it's very important to anybody'.[64]

Material capabilities and the geo-political realities of being landlocked or coastal state have, of course affected regional dynamics, but the individual presence and personality of Museveni has undoubtedly shifted the level of power and influence that Uganda might otherwise enjoy. And because China's implementation of major deals remains overwhelmingly at the nation-state level, opportunity for national leaders to influence relationships and regional progress remains firmly in place in the contemporary 'Chinese era'. So what interactions and impacts are occurring between China and EAC countries? And how is Museveni also asserting influence within partner states?

Notable influence in Kenya

Kenya's economic strength in the region makes it of obvious interest to China, and its leaders particularly powerful: Kenyan Presidents are therefore of interest and concern to Museveni. However, despite relatively high-levels of trade, China's overall impact has been somewhat mixed. In 2005, the University of Nairobi was the site of Africa's first Confucian Institute (CI), with two more set up since (South Africa is the only other African country to have three CIs). But the warning noted above that Chinese goods are a clear threat to East African industrialization applies to Kenya in particular, who could potentially become a manufacturing hub. China supplying the EAC with items such as soap, paper products, footwear exports, clothing and textiles poses a partial and direct threat to Kenya's export market to the EAC and elsewhere.[65] In 2005, Kenyan business leaders were publicly questioning China's impact on Kenyan exports, and Kenya's government were expressing concern privately.[66] This did not stop President Kibaki (in power 2002–13) beginning something of a going-East policy of courting Chinese finance and initiating large-scale projects. China has subsequently become a significant player in Kenya's political economy and been sold to the public as worthy allies in the fight for Kenyan development.

Museveni has also carved a greater role for himself in Kenya's political economy than might be expected considering economic and geographical imbalances clearly favour Nairobi. Museveni was initially hostile towards Moi (President of Kenya 1978–2002) although relations quickly improved with the reinvigoration of the EAC. But Museveni became genuinely influential within Kenyan politics under the Kibaki Presidency. The Kenyan opposition ODM party has supporters who dislike Museveni's apparent meddling in Kenya's internal affairs.[67] According to a Ugandan Ministry of Finance spokesperson, 'it's an unspoken or open secret' that Museveni has influence in Kenyan politics, and that after Kenya's disputed 2007 election Kibaki was ready to concede defeat and quit office but then came to speak with Museveni. He subsequently claimed victory, which sparked Kenya's post-election violence.[68]

Launched by Kibaki in 2008 after that election conflict had dissipated, Kenya's Vision 2030 development programme has infrastructure construction as a key component to its growth strategy. Large Chinese supplied projects are an increasing feature of the political and economic landscape in Kenya, having almost entirely displaced Western contractors. Uhuru Kenyatta's indictment to the International Criminal Court (ICC) in 2011 encouraged a continued and more purposeful turn from the West when he became President in 2013; Museveni also took advantage of this. Museveni became paternalistic to Uhuru and gave outspoken backing to his younger Kenyan counterpart. Whilst Kenya was at loggerheads with the West, Museveni 'was a good support to Uhuru so of course then he has some gratitude to Museveni'.[69] Flexing his own muscles and taking advantage of the presence of new global partners, Uhuru explicitly mocked the West whilst championing China during a 2013 speech to the AU:

> The imperial exploiter crashes into the pits of penury. The arrogant world police is crippled by shambolic domestic dysfunction. These are the spectacles of Western decline we are witnessing today. At the same time, other nations and continents rise and prosper.[70]

The China–Kenya relationship is largely at the elite level having been 'captured by people who are close to the power centre'; according to an anonymous economist working for the Daily Nation newspaper, 'it looks like a very insular thing, they have just captured this place and they are just rolling projects all over the place'.[71] In April 2015, Kenya's Ethics and Anti-Corruption Commission published a report naming and shaming 175 government officials, with some major examples of graft and corruption involved in deals or attempted deals with Chinese companies.[72] China is now being given 60 per cent of the digital TV frequencies being offered by the government, and became Kenya's largest bilateral lender in December 2014.[73] Arms sales are increasing, and a September 2015 MoU for China to build a Nuclear Reactor in Kenya would be a pilot project for nuclear technology transfer to the continent, if undertaken.[74] Notably, however, in 2011 Ireland's Tullow Oil refused to partner with China National Offshore Oil Corporation (CNOOC) for renewed oil exploration, after CNOOC quit the country in 2010. Unlike in Uganda where Tullow and CNOOC are in partnership (discussed in later chapters), this means Kenya's oil industry remains dominated by Western firms.[75]

Shared histories and resistance in Tanzania

Tanzanian support for China at the 1971 UN vote made them a prominent global actor, despite being one of the poorest nations on earth. They also maintained more of an 'all-weather friendship' than elsewhere during China's 1980s from Africa. Museveni also has strong historical ties: Julius Nyerere – a giant of African agency – providing him with ideological tutelage and then material support during Museveni's struggle for power. Tanzania's own Pan-African spirit and East African ideology means that 'Museveni is probably philosophically closer to Tanzania than anywhere else',[76] at least in terms of his publicly articulated goals.

Post-2000 large Chinese projects include the $1.2 billion 532 km natural gas pipeline funded with an EXIM loan,[77] and a $412.5 million Chinese financed logistics hub at Dar es Salaam begun in 2014. A 2013 state visit from President Xi Jinping sealed $3.7 billion worth of business and an $11 billion deal to build a new, mega-port at Bagamoyo (part of the Chinese Belt and Road Initiative, alongside the wider intra-regional transport networks in East Africa).[78] Iron ore and coal mine sites are also receiving substantial attention with grants and soft loans.[79] The Chinese military continue to supply Tanzania's People Defence Force, and a Chinese company built the jointly funded national defence college.[80] A Tanzanian EALA representative believes that the massive funding required for the much-desired infrastructure projects, and hesitancy of the IMF and World Bank to supply such monies, means that 'you have two choices: either you don't develop; or you do it with the Chinese. That's it.'[81]

Tanzania's major Chinese funded projects have not yet thrown up serious corruption allegations that others have experienced. And although the 22,000 plus Chinese residing in Tanzania have caused some local-level friction and reaction (as per elsewhere), the government seems conscious of the need to manage and address that issue in order to maintain steady relations.[82] New 2015 laws restrict the number of foreign workers that can be employed by companies, with tighter government control of work permit issuance. Afrobarometer surveys, despite some continued criticism, observe that locals have a generally positive view of China.[83] Tanzania's more democratic governance system has also affected relations with Museveni. Aside from his longevity and experience naturally affording him some status, Tanzania's relative stability and regular democratic transitions have not provided opportunities for Museveni to gain ground in the political economy. Ugandans are often outspoken in their praise for the historical debt owed to Tanzania by Museveni's National Resistance Movement (NRM), yet Tanzanian hesitancy over EAC integration is at least in part inspired by Museveni's lack of democratic credentials. Tanzanian hesitancy over the fast-tracking agenda from 2005 onwards has partly stemmed from Museveni's personal role in pushing it.[84] In March 2013, the Citizen Newspaper quoted a senior Tanzanian cabinet minister as seeing the Coalition of the Willing (CoW) as being the brain-child of Museveni, who had grown increasingly frustrated by Tanzania hindering his ambition to be President of a federated East Africa.[85]

Rwanda's development state challenges

China's relations with Rwanda floundered in the 1970s and 1980s, although there was $9 million worth of arms provision between 1980 and 1985.[86] Notably, after the 1994 genocide, President Mobutu of Zaire took the fleeing wife of Juvenal Habyarimana on a state visit to China where she purchased military equipment costing $5 million.[87] That did not stop relations during the Kagame era from expanding, however. China is visible in Rwanda at all levels, from local hawkers to larger construction projects. Trade levels are increasing and China has been a notable player in Rwanda's drive to become a regional leader in ICT.[88] When Western donors withdrew aid over Kigali's support for the M23 rebels in DRC, China provided $35m in interest-free loans and grants (despite China's strong support for DRC's Kabila government).[89]

Rwanda's President Kagame (President from 2000 onwards but essentially in power from 1994) has been a strong regional influence and also used an example of African agency in the contemporary era. His personal relationship with Museveni is long and complex. Kagame was part of the guerrilla movement which landed Museveni in power, and Uganda then backed Kagame's Rwandan Patriotic Front (RPF) invasion and conquest of Rwanda.[90] A former Rwandan Ambassador says: 'I think there is a history which link the two people, with support for each other's struggles ... we have a strong relationship by the past, and I think it remains between the two peoples.'[91] The 2000 violent confrontation in eastern DRC between these supposed allies when UPDF and RPF soldiers attacked each other led to a student-beating-master style animosity, but Museveni was then instrumental in Rwanda gaining entrance to the EAC arrangement. Mutual suspicion has remained, and one can imagine some jealousy from Museveni against Kagame, whose Rwanda is often depicted as a potential 'African developmental state model' in a way that Uganda is not. But outwardly, at least, relations during this period greatly improved, and the CoW would not have emerged without rapprochement between these two leaders.[92]

But in the same way that Rwanda has lingering suspicion over Museveni and his personal agenda, Rwanda's emerging developmental state has also seen more wariness of China than elsewhere. Chinese presence is less than in Tanzania, Kenya and Uganda. Rwanda's former Ambassador to the UN explains that 'the business China are doing in Africa needs to be structured, needs to be focused on the progress of Africa ... we refused some Chinese offers because we thought that it is not really what Rwanda wants'.[93] President Kagame said it was 'pathetic' that Africans could not finance the construction of their own headquarters – a lone critical voice amongst leaders during the unveiling of the AU building in Addis Ababa. This was a criticism of Africa more than China, however (China built Rwanda's Ministry of Foreign Affairs in 2008 for $8.5 million).[94] In April 2015, Rwanda cancelled the contract with state-owned Beijing Construction Engineering Group (BCEG) to build its ambitious $300 million Kigali Convention Centre after continued delays. But Kigali then quietly negotiated with China over this controversy in order to avoid possible litigation and not to jeopardize relations or prevent future investment. A May 2015 MoU was signed with Sinohydro to build the 120 MW Nyabarongo II power project.[95]

Instability in Burundi with fluctuating interest

Suspicious and complicated China–Burundi relations still allowed economic and technical agreements, and military support, in the 1970s and beyond. Post-2000 relations have increased, but impoverished Burundi remains very much peripheral to China–East Africa relations. China have not undertaken any high-visibility, large-scale mega-projects as per elsewhere in Africa, or sent the same high-level delegations.[96] A local explains that 'sometimes I heard it is going to construct the State House offices, but we have been waiting – I haven't seen that.[97] Cultural and sports exchange programmes do exist along with modest military and economic assistance, however, and the Burundi Senior Normal College has been expanded.[98]

Museveni has been a more significant figure in Burundi than China historically. His chairmanship of the regional peace initiative that ended the 1993–2005 civil war, and support for Pierre Nkurunziza, who became President in 2005 following that process, means it is natural to some extent that 'they will listen to him, they will have some loyalty to him'.[99] A Burundian working at the EAC stated in early 2015:

> I know that he is somebody who likes unity, he doesn't like people to be in conflict . . . he is a very peaceful man, he likes peace, he likes integration. He is very engaged in it. In Burundi people are thankful of him, he is very much respected, very much.[100]

With chaos once again threatening the country amidst violent protests, deaths, coups and government crackdowns following the 2015 election, it was Museveni whom EAC leaders chose to mediate between government and opposition. This was unsurprisingly welcomed by President Nkurunziza and criticized by the opposition.[101] China did not play any noticeable role in the political economy of Burundi until this election trouble.[102] Burundi's underdeveloped mine reserves and the proposed Southern Corridor Standard Gauge Railway (SGR) linking Tanzania's Bagamoyo mega-port to Burundi and potentially DRC (discussed further below) increase Burundi's potential importance to China, and the violence saw them taking more noticeable interest. In May 2015, Russia and China blocked a UNSC statement calling for an end to violence and an inclusive electoral process (the situation and violence subsequently got much worse).[103]

As the situation deteriorated rapidly during 2015, the international community also backed Museveni's mediation, as did the largely toothless AU who took a default position of deferring to the EAC (until December 2015 when they threatened a peacekeeping operation which did not ultimately occur).[104] China apparently pledged $25 million to help fill holes in the government's aid-starved budget in August 2015, whilst Nkurunziza became distrustful of the EAC – reserving particular enmity for Kagame who he saw as destabilizing his regime.[105] The EAC nonetheless kept Museveni as its figurehead in efforts to prevent Burundi backsliding, and Nkurunziza's gamble that the continued support from China and Russia would block any kind of serious UN intervention force was ultimately correct (he remained President until his death during the COVID pandemic in 2020).

In summary, therefore, China has taken up position in each of the EAC partner states to varying but notable degrees. China has also formed direct links with the EAC institution directly, albeit within a framework that retains bilateral relations as centrally important. Likewise, Museveni has a unique history with each country and has carved out a distinct role for himself in all partners to varying extents but with notable degrees of influence in each. Regional security concerns have caused prolonged and deep problems for all countries and the entire region, but also encouraged collaborative efforts that see security cooperation a central component to wider EAC integration. So, what is the relationship between these key forces in EAC – China, Museveni and security concerns – and how has the presence of each shifted the importance of the others?

Security trends and challenges – China's impact on dynamics

China's new global position and status in the world, continent and region means it has increasing interests that need protecting somehow; this poses challenges to its non-interference and respect for sovereignty principle. This is the same way in which dominant Western norms of democracy and human rights challenge its fundamental concern with stability. The EAC's Conflict Early Warning specialists – working as part of APSA's Continental Early Warning System – appreciate that China is unlikely to remain neutral if its interests are threatened, and that it 'doesn't have a choice' as to whether it becomes involved in complex conflict situations.[106] EAC specialists are somewhat wary of China's principles – Sudan's presence looms large in the region, and China's role there in supporting the brutal Bashir regime is not forgotten. One states:

> As a person who supports democratic governance, you can see the impact is already there … they have this non-interference principle, so if you are

fighting then we will still sell you guns; if you want to move your troops as per of some conflict, that is fine we will still build your roads and assist; if there is almost a genocide taking place then we will still sell to you. Those are situations where the West would not do that, but China is willing to. So that is not a good precedent ... you have children being roasted alive and they still sell guns.[107]

This specialist thinks that East Africa's relative stability affords opportunities for progressive relations with China to be utilized and exploited, but is concerned that if conflict engulfed the region then China's presence could become problematic. But presently – without the same obvious and brutal conflicts that have appeared in Sudan and elsewhere – what security threats are occurring in the EAC in which China plays a role? The discussion below presents terrorism and oil as two serious security threats facing EAC member states. In both cases, China's global-level role helps create a structural context under which events and relations between partner states fluctuate within, as well as contributing directly to local-level security issues.

Terrorism – global implications and China's local-level role

EAC partners are at persistent threat of terrorist attack, due to lingering internal instability serious conflict occurring in its neighbours, and a post-9/11 global jihadi ideology penetrating the region. China's non-interference policy does not prevent it from becoming entwined into this security issue. Whether intended or not, Chinese presence and action feeds into the terrorist menace which has destabilized regional dynamics but also helped compel cooperation between partners.

A unifying fear with illicit Chinese involvement

Terrorism is potentially becoming a unifying force within the East African security agenda, provoking fear and uncertainty, which also lead to greater cooperation. In May 2014, the EAC Presidents issued a joint communique explicitly calling on security agencies to intensify their cooperation and to implement EAC's counter-terrorism strategy as a matter of urgency.[108]

86   *Ugandan Agency within China–Africa Relations*

Somalia's Al-Shabaab currently forms the focus point. A Ugandan EALA representative says:

> In terms of the region . . . at the moment one of the most important things is terrorism, definitely. That is top of the agenda, and this region appears to be a target, Al-Shabaab mainly and whatever goes with it. That's why Uganda is in Somalia. That is definitely a big part of the regional agenda, although that's under the AU arrangement.[109]

Kenya was originally wary of Somali intervention but eventually 'had no option' but to joined AUs AMISOM due to increased security risks. Kenya has received the most deadly and spectacular Al-Shabaab atrocities with the September 2013 Westgate mall and April 2015 Garissa University attacks killing sixty-seven and 147 respectively, and persistent violence in coastal areas of Lamu and Mombasa. The 1998 US Embassy bombings in Tanzania highlighted its vulnerability to Islamic terrorism, further exemplified by more recent grenade attacks on Churches and Western friendly areas in Arusha and Zanzibar (although not thought to be Al-Shabaab). Burundi's role in AMISOM sees credible public threats from Al-Shabaab (US officials banned its personnel from walking outside after dark or using public transport in October 2014 after one such warning).[110] Rwanda, perhaps facing less direct threat, is nonetheless a possible source of operatives and affiliates. The US Special Envoy to the Great Lakes Region also stated there is a very real possibility of Al-Shabaab forming links to rebels in eastern DRC, which would have clear repercussions for Rwanda.[111]

Historically China has not engaged the terrorism issue as willingly and obviously as the West; however, the ivory trade and Small Arms and Light Weapons proliferation creates a link between China and terrorism. China is not the only market for ivory, but it is certainly driving a poaching epidemic underway in East Africa. EAC security experts have no doubt that 'the poaching is increasing massively and yes that is to do with the influx of Chinese, it's one result of the influx for sure'.[112] And although terrorist groups are not the primary cause of the problem, experts are certain that 'there is a high connectivity with Al-Shabaab and ivory, definitely . . . they might not do the poaching themselves, but they do it through their couriers, it's a very big thing', as will be discussed further in later chapters.[113] Whilst not linking itself to terrorism, the Chinese government are aware of their role in the poaching and insist to EAC officials that it is not intentional on the part of government.[114] A November 2014 report by the Environmental Investigation Agency alleged, however, that Chinese officials and high-ranking businessmen have been involved in Tanzania. This included officials who were part of a President Xi Jinping delegation and others from a naval task force returning from Gulf of Aden operation, both in 2013.[115] Whilst this was denied by China, accusations of official collusion are not without precedent elsewhere in the region and Africa.[116]

SALW proliferation is an enabling factor in ivory poaching,[117] as well as in the wider terrorist menace and structural instability in East Africa. SALW has long been the most consistent, prominent, complex and far-reaching security issue faced by the region, an EALA representative noting that 'there is governance issues, there is economic issues, there are neighbouring conflict situations, it's extremely complicated. You can't get into a more varied and multifaceted area than this.'[118] A representative from Uganda's National Focal Point on SALW was clear that, despite the difficulty in getting precise figures, 'Chinese made arms are the main arms in the region, the main ones. If you have been to Tanzania, the AK-47s they have are Chinese versions. All along here. You go to DRC, South Sudan, that is it.'[119]

EAC and Chinese stifled reactions – new dialogues but traditional outcomes

The impact of China's role has been to make anti-poaching endeavours critically important, which helps promote a militarized response to security issues already being furthered by Chinese SALW supply. Rapid Chinese incursions into East Africa and this associated rise in ivory poaching means that at the regional-level, 'it has quickly become a big issue', having previously been largely ignored at the EAC.[120] A senior member of the EAC secretariat admits that 'it is an area we are getting involved with as a region we have not been involved in. It has been a national issue. We now realise it is a bigger problem so we are beginning to get involved.'[121] East Africa has become 'ground-zero' in Africa's ivory poaching industry,[122] with Tanzania becoming the main hub of the trade with its elephant population being devastated.

Concern has become clear and palpable within EAC: species extinction is discussed as a possibility.[123]

The original version of the EAC Peace and Security strategy did not include references to the poaching issue, but the updated version sees it fully included and articulated. It is also explicitly in the Security Protocols.[124] EAC's role as a coordinating body, however, means more bilateral talk takes place than with the EAC itself, and the institution also does not want to be too critical of the Chinese. In August 2013, an EALA motion urging protection against poaching noted that ivory is 'being exchanged for money, weapons and ammunition that support local and regional conflicts'. During discussions the original reference to Chinese demand helping fuel the upsurge in killings was removed, to avoid unnecessarily 'picking quarrels with our new partners in development'.[125]

Regarding SALW, between June 2012 and June 2014 Saferworld helped organize numerous activities under the Africa–China–EU dialogue on conventional arms control, which included the Nairobi-based Regional Centre on Small Arms (RECSA), where the link to the ivory trade has been identified (the Saferworld initiative is discussed more in Chapter Three in relation to Uganda). Whilst outside an EAC framework, representatives from partner states' National Focal Points on SALW and RECSA participated in the dialogues and told China 'that the supplies that are coming from there are causing chaos … China was specifically brought into these discussions, knowing that the weapons have their origins in China.'[126] EAC expert attendees also brought China's role in the SALW-Ivory dynamic to Chinese officials' attention during meetings, although the EAC have never fully articulated it officially within a high-level security forum.[127]

From the Chinese side, FOCAC V's Action Plan regarding Peace and Security cooperation stated explicitly that China 'will continue to support African countries' effort to combat illegal trade and circulation of small arms and light weapons'.[128] Despite the clear link between ivory poaching and SALW, however, the EAC peace and security specialist explains that Beijing sees the issues in somewhat different ways:

> With the ivory they admit there is a market in China and that it is only the Chinese government that can do something about that. On SALW there is no direct response, because officially you can track what China has supplied and it has been supplied to governments only, on official business.[129]

China therefore 'haven't really been helping on this', regarding EAC efforts at combatting SALW proliferation.[130] To be certain: there is no evidence at all that China supplies SALW to particular terrorist groups for their own purposes or with a view to destabilize regional security more generally; or that they engage the ivory trade for any kind of strategic purpose beyond individual businessmen (and some officials) personal profit. But they are entwined within these destructive processes whether they would like to or not, and there can be no doubt that China is aware of malpractices or where some of their arms end up. But Beijing's ideology and non-interference narrative prevents them engaging fully on SALW proliferation: that issue must be seen as primarily the responsibility of the recipient government. It does, however, allow for recognition of their domestic ivory market's role and the need for them to act therefore in that sector. For image-conscious China, Dr Cobus van Staden, Co-founder of the China–Africa Project, notes that there has been severe 'brand failure' regarding the ivory trade, resulting in a wider anti-China narrative being channelled through the ivory debate.[131] Steps have been taken by China following widespread media attention and a global campaign against the trade, including publicly agreeing to phase out the legal domestic market (which eventually occurred at the end of 2017),[132] and taking part in a coordinated international law enforcement operation to arrest individuals and seize illegal ivory stocks.[133]

A former Chinese Ambassador to Zambia, however, argues that during his numerous years working in Africa, no local President ever brought up this issue, but were instead preoccupied with development. One official in an unnamed country even asked him to help sell their seized ivory stocks to help finance their budget deficit. He believes:

> The communication channels are there. If African governments believe this is so important then they need to discuss it with their counterpart . . . If your government does not think it's so important then maybe it is not a topic for discussion, but it's up to your President . . . It's not a Chinese issue, the killing is done by your own people! So pointing fingers at the Chinese people, that's not fair.[134]

An Executive Director and Co-Founder of the Elephant Action League agrees, saying research from Kenya and Tanzania shows unequivocally that 'ivory and rhino horns are pushed out of Africa as much as they are pulled out by foreign consumers', and that 'equal if not more blame should be placed on African traders, businessmen and the political elite'. He believes East African governments use the excuse of China not to act as they should. He explains:

> African governments keep asking the US and the EU for millions of dollars, for drones, automatic weapons, Special Forces, when actually in the majority of cases what is needed would not cost much. We are talking about more accountability, greater will and a genuine fight against corruption.[135]

Utilizing the ivory trade to gain military hardware is mirrored in the wider fight against terrorism. For all countries in the region, 'the expenditure on arms and the military is on the increase by very very large proportions. So there is a quiet arms race going on which people don't want to admit.'[136] All countries in the EAC increased their military budget during this period – for 2014/15, Tanzania by 34.4 per cent, Kenya 20 per cent, Uganda 10.8 per cent, Rwanda 9.3 per cent and Burundi 8.3 per cent – perceived as a response to the increased regional terrorist threat.[137] Compared to the East African Standby Force, which has multidimensional military, police and civilian components, the EAC security apparatus is 'still military heavy' (although regional police chiefs do meet).[138] So despite the EAC's perceived economic aims and espoused people-centred approach, the militarization of its security agenda remains in place.

This militarized agenda is very much in line with Museveni's own ideology and opens space for him to exert agency: he has certainly used the AMISOM mission and Al-Shabaab menace has helped to centralize Uganda's role within this wider terror threat. The EAC see the AMISOM intervention as nothing other than entirely necessary and inevitable, as 'you cannot allow a terrorist state to sprout next door'.[139] Despite Kenya now coming on board in AMISOM and understandably 'some quiet rivalry' between them and Uganda, an expert notes that the AU effort essentially remains a Ugandan mission. Kenya has ongoing disputes at the International Court of Justice between Kenya and Somalia over off-shore claims to oil and gas exploration blocks; historical baggage from the 1960s Shifta War that saw ethnic Somali's in Kenya attempt to secede and join Greater Somalia; plus obvious Kenyan business interests in Somalia, meaning Uganda remains the most credible lead force within AMISOM. Uganda furthermore was the first to commit troops and remains the largest contributor, and the Uganda People's Defence Force (UPDF) expanded outwards from the capital.[140]

The EAC remains generally reactive to the terror threat: its obvious consequences are tackled forcefully, whilst there is limited capacity to proactively rid the region of the underlying causes of SALW proliferation (or to aggressively and publicly question China's and other powers' global roles). Constrained by the EAC's institutional reach and legislative power, the member states' National Focal Points are the primary driver in combatting the issue. The EAC is only able to try and link partner state's SALW agenda, which it has struggled to do.[141] Similarly regarding ivory, the 5th Meeting of the Sectoral Council on Tourism and Wildlife Management in July 2013 noted that anti-poaching measures were uncoordinated and required concerted actions.[142] At their 4th Meeting in September 2011, poaching was not even on the agenda, again indicating that a reactive rather than proactive approach has occurred.[143]

Museveni's militarism and willingness to intervene means that he is of central importance to any EAC agenda aimed at confronting the terrorism issue. China's presence helps to enable his active role in the region. Museveni's agency is not present in direct confrontation against China on this issue, or in directly challenging regional partners; China is not in East Africa as a direct challenger or overt threat to Uganda and Museveni that needs to be countered or resisted head on. Instead, his agency is manifest in his clever ability to take advantage of the impacts of Chinese presence to further his own goals and status. This terrorist and Al-Shabaab threat to EAC would exist whether the Chinese regional presence had increased or not. Nonetheless, China is a key player in setting the global context: it has been crucial to SALW supply, both historically and in the contemporary era. SALW proliferation has contributed significantly to a general instability being pervasive across the region, which creates notable local-level security issues and results in the militarized EAC security agenda. China's role in the ivory trade is unique and centrally important to the poaching epidemic underway in the EAC. Al-Shabaab – whilst not driving the poaching industry – are known to be involved in the trade. So, in similar fashion to SALW, the ivory issue again operates beneath a globalized context of illicit China–Africa networks operating alongside legal enterprises, which feeds into serious local-level security issues.

Oil – threat of the curse and the integration drive

Conflicts over oil in Africa have occurred through a toxic mix of nefarious foreign interests taking advantage of poor domestic governance structures, combined with and exacerbated by the high expectations local populations invariably have over what they perceive as bountiful new oil wealth.[144] The possibility of this dangerous mix, and the potential insecurity occurring amidst increased resource wealth, is undoubtedly present throughout East Africa. Chinese oil companies are directly involved in East Africa's burgeoning oil sector and China is an obvious market for its eventual output. Again, China is deeply engrained into this high security risk, regardless of its intentions or desires.

Troubling finds but an opportunity presented

Throughout the EAC, oil and gas finds are occurring 'in the marginal areas, at the border point, at the pastoral lands, communities that have not been integrated'.[145] Existing tensions within nations between neglected regions and centres of national power become amplified by the presence of oil. Kenyan EALA representative explains 'in fact people from those areas think that is God's answer to neglect by previous administrations'.[146] Emerging security issues – partly mimicking the terror threats discussed above – may be exacerbated due to oil prices plummeting in 2014, which increases the likelihood of the expected benefits not occurring. Bunyoro, the main oil region in Uganda to be discussed in subsequent chapters, has a maligned history of marginalization from central Ugandan authority that is mirrored in the Turkana and west Pokot regions of northern Kenya, where oil deposits are found. EAC Early Warning specialists working on reducing Turkana-west Pokot tensions admit 'that situation has become a lot more complicated ... their conflicts used to be about cattle rustling, or about water issues, but now with oil the potential is there for it to become a curse'.[147] In November 2014, the Kenya Defence Forces performed a 'massive military operation' to hunt down armed bandits in Turkana who had killed twenty-one police officers (and community tensions and consistent low-level violence have continued ever since).[148] Elsewhere, Tanzanian oil exploration is contentious due the politically sensitive border demarcation between the mainland and Zanzibar island.[149]

There have also been small-scale attacks by Somali-based pirates off the east coast where exploration is underway.[150] Rwandan FDLR rebels have kidnapped oil workers in DRC.[151]

Uganda's proposed oil refinery and crude export pipeline to the Indian Ocean clearly make their sector regional in nature, and oil companies are often involved in side-meetings at regional heads-of-state summits.[152] The pipeline project has become a key development issue for the whole of the EAC, and its construction will interconnect and rely on other priority projects such as the Standard Gauge Railway.[153] The regional implications and value of Uganda's refinery are therefore substantial. EAC members agreed to its construction in 2007 as part of the EAC Strategy for the Development of Regional Refineries (although at that time Uganda predicted oil production was possibly five years away).[154]

Despite China National Offshore Oil Corporation's 33 per cent stake in Uganda's oil find, it is UK-, Norway- and French-based companies seemingly taking a strong position in the East African oil sector regarding concessions. Clearly China is also seen as a major market for the sector, however. A Tanzanian EALA representative noted 'most of it will be going outside anyway, it's not going to cause any issues. If the volume is sufficient there could be three refineries, and the Chinese will drink all of it.'[155] The balance of power and economic clout within the region also shifts as oil and gas sectors are developed. Infrastructure like refineries become geo-strategic and logistical hubs, making those involved in their construction critically important. Wider infrastructure also connects to the oil sector, by its direct involvement in related industries or from its construction being financed through future revenues. The Ugandan EALA representative remarks:

> Oil is just part of the bigger agenda, because the bigger agenda is to build an integrated economy of East Africa looking at a wide range of economic initiatives. Top on the agenda is infrastructure development. Actually even oil comes under this, because a great deal of it will need a certain level of infrastructural capacity. You are talking about the rail transporting this and that, we are talking about road transport, we are talking about energy. So there is a big big commitment on infrastructure.[156]

The level of interest and involvement in the infrastructure agenda from the heads of state has increased dramatically in recent years, and is linked directly to the combination of China's appearance and new oil finds (as well as new mineral and gas deposits).[157] Against the backdrop of the Kenya 2007/8 election violence which greatly disrupted Northern Corridor trade routes, in 2008 EAC Ministers visited China on an infrastructure fact-finding mission.[158] A subsequent EAC Heads of State retreat in June 2008 noted the multi-billion dollar costs required for the agreed regional projects, and recommended that states spend at least 25 per cent of their national budgets on infrastructure projects.[159] Infrastructure then became much more prominent at EAC discussions – and the 2008 projected costs were dwarfed by the subsequent massive plans and contracts – with dedicated agenda items and regular meetings set up.

The development trajectory and current emphasis on infrastructure is publicized by EAC officials as an entirely East African-led and initiated agenda. These plans have existed for some time; but it is only now that China is apparently willing and able to fund such projects. A Tanzania EALA representative notes:

> With those master plans you have got billions of dollars to spend to get them to life. And there is only one country that can do that, it's the Chinese ... China see this region as being critical to the supplies of critical resources, extractive predominantly, for China in exchange for building the infrastructure.[160]

The massive finance required, along with the symbolic and practical importance of the Standard Gauge Railway project, make it a defining feature of modern EAC integration efforts and China–East Africa relations. It is clearly one of the flagship projects stemming out of the 2011 EAC–China framework agreement, and played a crucial role in the emergence of the Coalition of the Willing. The SGR connecting Mombasa–Kampala–Kigali (as well as Juba) is estimated to have an eventual cost of $11 billion, with the Ugandan section placed at $6 billion in 2013: China was always hoped and assumed to be its main financial backer.[161] Even if it is circumstantial, 'there is a project putting three countries together, and there is a country that is willing to support it. So basically that defines that relationship.'[162]

The Director of Infrastructure at the EAC explained that the long-standing development strategy master plan originally advocated rehabilitating the old colonial railway line with a gradual development of SGR. CoW's emergence then saw heads of state intervene to prioritize SGR construction rather than the long-term gradual approach which they argued risked prices increasing.[163] The Chairperson for Uganda's Parliamentary Committee on the EAC says China has been key to the CoW developments:

> The emergence of China offering opportunity of funding such huge projects could be one of the reasons why the three states have said I think we should exploit this opportunity. Let's move and grab it. Because you would do nothing if there was no available opportunity for having such a huge project, having a funding source or investor interested in investing. So it directly involves China.[164]

The CoW effort was inspired by Tanzanian reluctance to forge ahead with integration. According to a leading EAC expert and advisor to regional governments, 'the CoW really came as a wild card for Tanzania ... Tanzania top brass were taken aback by it and didn't really know what to do. They had been warned, but were surprised by it.' The SGR project in particular was intended to show Tanzania how quickly progress could be made and the benefits therein, as a method of encouraging them to embrace the regional agenda more willingly.[165] After three years of controversy and perceived splits occurring around the CoW, in March 2015 Tanzania announced it would spend $14 billion on its railway network, financed through commercial loans with a twenty-year repayment period from an undisclosed consortium of banks.[166] Somewhat inevitably, in June of that year it was announced that Chinese companies would build this new SGR route linking Dar es Salaam with DRC, Rwanda and Burundi, as well as rail lines to mining sites and towards offshore gas deposits.[167]

China taking advantage of EAC capacity issues?

Chinese impact occurs by encouraging and enabling particular development projects to be pushed forward, despite the region being vulnerable to problematic schisms occurring when such projects are implemented. There are serious concerns that the EAC's institutional apparatus is not sufficient to deal with a mega-industry like oil and the resultant regional security implications. The creation of a permanent desk to coordinate regional petroleum exploration activities, recommended in October 1996, never happened. And the Ugandan EALA representative admits within the regional parliament itself 'I think there is yet to get serious debate on that', with the EAC instead relying on the annual oil and gas conferences which member states attend.'[168] A leading expert on EAC integration is worried that oil exploration 'is just being done and exploration concessions are being awarded to the Chinese and others without a regional framework'. This absence of a coordinated proactive regional approach to the oil sector risks security issues appearing which will inevitably necessitate a reaction, but that reaction will only occur after the issue has become overly complex (coordinating thoughtful action before issues become manifest would likely be easier). The EAC expert laments the lack of this detailed regional oil and gas framework from which member states can draw their own plans. He dismisses the regional conferences as largely meaningless:

> The consequences of this loose management of the oil sector are that you can't integrate the economies properly, certainly not effectively. You will have distinctly separate energy sectors in each country, with different contracts and companies. And the energy sector is absolutely fundamental to regional integration; it is crucial ... everything you do depends on energy.[169]

The various sectors and committees of EAC link to oil, security and infrastructure, but do not discuss the sector coherently and in a coordinated fashion. So although the Regional Affairs and Conflict Resolution committee is not mandated to discuss natural resources, its clerk nonetheless sees the development of the Peace and Security Protocol as of central importance to the region's new oil-producing status:

> The committee had been discussing issues like if we don't have a common army, for example, and one commanding force to intervene in case of when conflict occurs, the region would end up in smoke in the future ... if these natural resources are not managed well they are going to cause problems. And how are we going to manage well? We need institutions to take care of these resources. So such kind of mechanisms are being looked at in order to try to guard these precious resources for the region.[170]

The EALA committee on Agriculture, Tourism and Natural Resources recommended new legislation, more equitable distribution of resources and greater transparency after touring Tanzanian mining sites and Uganda's oil region in 2008 and 2009.[171] It was also working with the National Democratic Institute to create regional transparency and distribution laws around oil and gas, but the effort fizzled out.[172] EALA politicians are working on a freedom of information bill due to government's preventing parliamentary oversight of the industry. Whilst recognizing the justified sensitivity of such agreements, the Kenyan representative remarks:

> If you have justification that can be understood within democratic practice, then you establish a legal framework that allows for either limited access or distance or time. But you can't say we will not submit. The executives must submit to parliamentary scrutiny.[173]

This Kenyan EALA representative also feels that EAC partners need to negotiate better terms with China and any other investors, not only to receive favourable financial terms but also 'to open up the question of local participation particularly by local business'.[174] The EAC Director of Infrastructure admits that at present the EAC's ability to negotiate skilfully 'is not good, I must tell you it is not good. But it is improving.'[175] Lack of coordination around the energy sector and security issues, and capacity issues about getting the best deals from China and international partners, are also reflected within the wider infrastructure agenda.

The viability of the entire SGR project is questionable. Despite often being cited in the China–Africa narrative as a beacon of China's prolonged friendship with Africa, the TAZARA railway has in fact helped inspire unusually stringent conditions to be imposed in Kenya's SGR. The Chinese originally pushed for 100 per cent of cargo coming from Mombasa to be used on the rail. This was resisted, but significantly high percentages will still have to be transported and EXIM Bank insisted on a railway tax being imposed on Kenyans. This stringency leads an expert to remark 'when we start looking at those contracts we say hey, Chinese are no different from any other lender!'.[176] A well-known Kenyan economist is scathing in his critique of SGR's economic viability vis-à-vis an upgrade of the old colonial line. He states:

> It is the biggest white elephant project I have seen or had experience of in my 25 years in this business . . . I have never been able to figure out this, it is one of the dumbest things I have ever seen! It is so dumb that I can't possibly say why, or who would do such a thing in their right mind.[177]

The EAC Director of Infrastructure is also concerned as to whether SGR on its own is viable, stating that 'the idea that I am hearing is that it will reduce the trucks, it will reduce the time and delays; but I am asking myself and saying is that enough?'[178] It is also unclear whether Tanzania's SGR construction is an integration measure with Kenya and the EAC, or in fact a rival project. Kenya's push on SGR and the aggressive promotion of infrastructure projects was partly in order to counter the threat from Tanzania's Bagamoyo mega-port, in order to remain the preferred trade route for Uganda, Rwanda, Burundi and eastern DRC.[179] And Tanzanian Transport Minister, Samuel Sitta, stated of their alternative SGR effort that 'we are in competition at all times with the Mombasa port ... it's a competitive business, so we need to be efficient'.[180]

This kind of regional geo-politics is also played out within extra-regional infrastructure drives. Outside the EAC, Kenya's LAPSSET project (the Lamu Port Southern Sudan–Ethiopia Transport corridor) is a wildly ambitious infrastructure development plan. It involves constructing a huge thirty-two-port berth at Lamu; an SGR line, highways, crude oil and product pipelines connecting Kenya, South Sudan and Ethiopia; and three international airports, three resort cities and a merchant oil refinery in Kenya. Although in existence for many years, the project received impetus by being a key part of Kenya's Vision 2030. The total cost is thought to be $24.5 billion, with Lamu Port's thirty-two berths alone costing $3.1 billion.[181] When Juba had problems negotiating oil pipeline exports with Khartoum, they looked to Kenya and Lamu port as an alternative transport route. Uhuru Kenyatta's pledge to work closer with China during his 2013 election campaign saw China inevitably moving into the LAPSSET project. China Communications Construction Company will build an initial three berths at Lamu Port, which an expert notes 'basically are going to be in my opinion oil, oil, oil, they are making them for this oil'. And when agreement was reached for China to finance the Juba–Lamu pipeline, 'it looked like the first major thing Lamu Port was going to do was that project'.[182]

Uganda was originally locked out of this arrangement and Museveni's plan for a Ugandan oil refinery was undermined. The East African security specialist notes that serious cooperation on that scale between Kenya, South Sudan and Ethiopia 'can shift the regional geo-politics, so definitely it is something of very serious concern to Uganda'.[183] Museveni pushed into the project using Uganda's oil and officially became part of the plan in June 2013 at an infrastructure summit in Kampala, utilizing the CoW whose quickening agenda was very much mindful of China's willingness to invest.[184] 'They started a regional infrastructure thing at the EAC level, and the scope changed,' according to a leading economist. 'It was no longer about a pipeline from Juba coming this way, there were railways, the connections and all that.'[185] Museveni regionalized Uganda's refinery by offering EAC states a 10 per cent stake in the Ugandan government's 40 per cent share, an important move that has gone down well amongst EAC officials.[186] In January 2015, Kenya agreed to a 2.5 per cent stake in the refinery at an estimated \$67.2 million, Rwanda has clearly expressed interest, and it is hoped that Tanzania and Burundi will also invest.[187] Kenya coming on-board with Uganda's refinery showed its intention not to fight an important asset of that kind being in Uganda whilst it develops its own through the LAPSSETT project, and was seen as 'really good diplomacy, good relations, its economics, its good politics'.[188]

Future oil revenues and China's willingness to fund the mega-infrastructure agenda have helped Museveni position himself as central in the whole regional project. In 2010, Ms Kate Kamba from Tanzania praised Museveni at EALA for saying his army would build the railway in Uganda (discussed further in Chapter Three), and the speed at which he and Kenya approached China to build such projects, stating:

> (I) urge the leaders of East Africa not to wait for World Bank Missions to come and write proposals, but to ask the Chinese to build the railways . . . We need such practical actions for our projects; not these feasibility studies and consultancies.[189]

When addressing EALA, the EAC Secretary-General Dr Richard Sezibera also gave plaudits to the Ugandan President amidst applause from representatives, following Museveni's efforts at the 2013 BRICS Summit in Durban in agreeing large deals with regional implications for EAC:

> I want to say that I was privileged to be with President Museveni at a Summit in Durban early this year. I want to say that I was proud to see this leader in moving the EAC Project forward in a practical manner. (Applause) He has personally taken it up to look for funds for the railway network. (Applause) He passed on these projects to the presidents of Russia and China. He has

also taken it up to look for funds for the energy sector, ports and harbours and for all the projects that the Summit adopted in November last year. I wish to pay tribute to him and the leadership of our Community in general for taking us forward.[190]

So whilst not dominating oil concessions at present, China's availability and willingness to fund necessary and associated mega-infrastructure (notably the SGR), make it of central importance to EAC's regional security dynamic. This has allowed Museveni to become something of a figurehead for the large regional projects, even though SGR and other initiatives were begun initially by Kenya.

Security fears around African oil sectors are well documented and justified, with the locations of finds within EAC occurring in particularly unstable territories. Chinese interest in oil resources, as well as mineral and gas deposits, is palpable. Along with the CNOOC's stake in Uganda's crucial oil find, China's unique willingness to construct or finance much-needed multibillion-dollar infrastructure sees EAC partners progress their development agenda with the knowledge that increasing resource revenues will soon be available. Alongside inevitable local-level tensions in oil areas, the wider infrastructure agenda – whilst seemingly a progressive integration measure – also risks instability as regional geo-political rivalry plays out and the EAC's structural environment shifts. This context has allowed Museveni to exercise agency by, again, claiming space for himself and Uganda as centrally important to the regional oil and energy sector, as well as within EAC's wider development ambitions.

Conclusion: spaces being opened

This chapter first outlined that China's engagement with East Africa is of central importance to the historical narrative of the entire China–Africa relationship. From ancient times to the modern era, regular and varied interactions occurred amidst changing global dynamics of different eras and epochs. Some of the issues leading to the collapse of the EAC at least in part can be linked to Beijing, such as the ideological divide between member states and the southward drift of Tanzania. The personality of leaders, however,

China and the East African Community 101

played a far greater role in the security dynamics and threat perceptions within the region.

As China's concerted post-2000 push into Africa allowed modern relations to truly flourish, the global, continental, regional and domestic levels in the relationship all remain unstable. The consequences of friendship towards China at the expense of an increasingly resented West at the global-level remain uncertain, and EAC's continental role within APSA is malleable and unclear. Regional security dynamics are shifting and shiftable, as national rivalry exists alongside cooperation. The power of individual leaders and their personalities is ever-present. Sub-national threats to domestic and regional structures remain evident throughout.

The EAC is attempting to forge its own institutional security arrangement, with bilateral security inter-dependence between members increasingly strong, with a historic and continued effort to expand membership to neighbouring countries that have clear security implications for partners. China impacts these developments structurally through its global role as a Great Power partner within the EAC's development agenda, and also at the local sub-national level within specific security threats.

Uganda is key to regional progress. A more reluctant Tanzania highlights the central importance of Uganda to any Chinese regional ambitions, with the historical Tanzania–China links unlikely to have such a regional integrationary impact. Kenya's wealth makes it naturally attractive, but to China and all players, meaning that interests would likely continue whether EAC integration proceeded or not. Rwanda is the most capable nationalist state with a clear domestic developmental agenda whether regionalized or not. And Burundi is the poor man of East Africa, never integral to any regional agenda. Engaging Uganda, however, finds the nation without which there is no link, no EAC region as such beyond the sea-bordering Kenyan and Tanzanian rivals. Uganda is the nation capable of networking the regional arrangement from Kenya deeper into Rwanda then Burundi, as well as to both DRC and South Sudan; it also has extra-regional reach as far as Somalia and CAR.

This thereby offers opportunities and risks for both China and Museveni to exercise their agency and influence outcomes in the EAC. Museveni's agency in shaping this emerging regional security arrangement is evident in the way he successfully uses Chinese presence to promote himself as central to the

EAC's increasingly interlinked security dynamics. The East African Community, with a prominent role for Uganda's Museveni in its integration efforts and as a notable force in member states' political economy, has seen its shared security issues compel military and security cooperation to a greater extent than is sometimes acknowledged. As the institutionalization of the China–EAC relationship is cemented through the Framework Agreement, bilateral relations nonetheless remain a key component to understanding China's relationship with the region. Museveni has rather successfully exploited China's presence in the region to further his own agenda, by shifting Uganda's role within two key security issues facing the region.

China, therefore, whether intentionally or not contributes to destabilizing impacts in EAC which provide operating space to Uganda. The two terrorism and oil security issues show varying levels of Chinese involvement and impact, which Museveni has exploited to a greater or lesser extent. The ivory trade is a serious direct and obvious problem, which China is rightly noted and spoken of as exacerbating. That retains something of a link to Al-Shabaab, as does Chinese role in SALW proliferation, which is underemphasized by EAC officials. China accepts its role in the ivory trade to some degree: this acceptance allows EAC partner states to deflect their own responsibilities, and remains in line with China's respect for sovereignty norms. The SALW issue is largely ignored by both sides: Museveni and the EAC do not have the same interest in apportioning blame to China in this instance, instead pursuing a militarized security agenda and even a regional arms race. Uganda's crucial role in countering terrorism increases Museveni's standing and importance in the region dramatically.

China is not dominating the East African oil sector in regard to concessions. China being a likely destination for the extracted crude, however, and the key partner in the construction of mega-projects that will be paid for with revenues means that China is fully inserted into the industry nonetheless. Such mega-projects have at times threatened Museveni's agenda. LAPSSETT potentially locked out Uganda's oil find until Museveni was able to insert himself successfully into the project and shift focus on to the CoW of which China is such a key part. Museveni has also retained importance in the flagship SGR project which will define China–East Africa relations in the modern era.

Other leaders have also exerted agency against China and within the EAC. Uhuru Kenyatta utilized Chinese presence to push back against the West during his ICC indictment, and Kenya's material wealth and regional position clearly gives its President some influence over Uganda's development trajectory. Tanzania's Kikwete has resisted some Chinese presence through the enactment of certain employment laws whilst generally continuing their history of friendship as a development partner, and has clearly influenced EAC regional dynamics in preventing what are perceived as unwise rushed moves towards federation (as noted throughout this book). President Kagame has not allowed the same degree of Chinese presence in Rwanda as has become common throughout Africa, and has a long, complex history of pushing against and actively meddling in Museveni's regional ambitions. And Burundi's Nkurunziza openly resisted Museveni and EAC influence in his election trouble and domestic political economy, whilst engaging China to subtly assist during that difficult period.

So, the argument here is not that Museveni is an omnipotent force against regional rivals, or the only major actor that China needs to be cognizant of. But Museveni's hegemonic aspirations do see him push Ugandan influence beyond what natural endowment may have allowed for. And China's regional engagement with EAC seemingly creates a context whereby such ambitions are potentially enhanced amidst fluctuating, emerging security dynamics.

3

China's role in regional security and the nature of Museveni's methods

'Without security you cannot develop.'

Shem Bageine, Uganda Minister of State for the
East African Community[1]

We have seen so far that Museveni has quite skilfully incorporated Chinese engagement into Uganda's political economy in a way that ultimately benefits his Presidency, and that China's role in East Africa more broadly also affords Museveni opportunities to assert his influence and maintain his importance in the region. We now focus in more detail on two prominent security issues in Uganda, and China's role within each one. The entry point for the discussion is to focus on pressing Ugandan security concerns with regional implications, and then uncover the Chinese role within them, rather than taking Chinese action as a starting point and looking for the security implications of those. The Africa-centric starting point ultimately uncovers more intriguing and nuanced impacts and roles for China than might be otherwise discussed, and centralizes the importance of African agency in the conversation.

The nature of 'terrorism' and 'oil' security issues show that Museveni is the key agent in producing a militarized response against these threats; and that domestic considerations in Uganda (rather than Chinese interests) are the most important factor in deciding how he behaves. Although the international political economy and China's role within it are of course a crucial factor in shaping Museveni's behaviour and the outcomes produced, he has asserted his agency successfully within both these issues and used them to maintain his importance. China impacts these security issues in distinct ways, but in both instances Museveni's agency has enabled him to utilize their engagement to shape regional security dynamics so as to benefit his regime.

Chinese-supplied Small Arms and Light Weapons (SALW) have been used by various terror groups in Uganda who also benefit from China's domestic ivory market, and these groups linkages to Sudan have created serious instability. Museveni has used these issues, however, to maintain his militarized government and response to threats in a way which elevates his regional status as a key security actor. With the oil threat, China plays a key role directly within the oil sector and within Uganda's wider development agenda. Chinese involvement has aided Museveni's domestic power plays and utilization of the Uganda People's Defence Force (UPDF), and made China an important partner in his successful manipulation of EAC states. Thus, as per China's engagement in Uganda and East Africa more generally, Museveni has exploited the Chinese presence in these specific security issues to centralize his role in the East African Community (EAC).

This chapter is broken into four main sections. The first '"Ugandan" terrorism', provides a brief history of the Terrorist security issue in Uganda, showing how Museveni merged three disparate groups into a narrative appropriate to the US Global War on Terror (GWOT) discourse, which has encouraged collective security arrangements in the EAC. The second section, 'Chinese Small Arms and Light Weapons (SALW) – impacting all levels', outlines China's role in this terrorist issue, through its supply of SALW globally, regionally and domestically. It also notes the role of the ivory trade in Uganda. The third section, 'Museveni's oil', moves to the oil security issue. It explains that Museveni's tight control of the sector is coupled with his effort to position the UPDF into the wider infrastructure agenda deemed essential to Uganda's development. The fourth section, 'CNOOC and Uganda's development dream', shows Chinese investment in both the oil sector and these associated infrastructure projects has provided distinct opportunities for Museveni to impact regional dynamics. The chapter ends with a brief conclusion, summarizing how Museveni has used the Chinese presence to shape regional security dynamics in a way beneficial to himself.

'Ugandan' terrorism

During the period of focus, 'terrorism' was unquestionably promoted and accepted as the most critical security concern facing Uganda. Al-Shabaab grew into the most prominent group within the 'terror' discourse, but Uganda had experienced its own brand of home-grown terrorism in the preceding years. Museveni successfully combined a series of distinct threats into a coherent strategy which positions him and the UPDF as the fulcrum in a shared regional battle against terrorism.

Securitizing home-grown and global terror – LRA and ADF to Somalia and Al-Shabaab

Joseph Kony's Lord's Resistance Army (LRA) had been the most prominent Ugandan security issue since 1986, but never a genuine threat to Museveni and the country as a whole. The insecurity LRA caused until the mid-2000s was contained entirely to the thoroughly neglected Acholi region in Northern Uganda. Having fled Uganda circa 2008, LRA inflicted a degree of carnage in neighbouring eastern DRC and the Central African Republic (CAR), but the number of LRA fighters and their capability have substantially decreased. ADF-NALU is the amalgamation of a disgruntled Rwenzururu movement in Western Uganda (NALU), combined with an Islamist Allied Democratic Forces (ADF) grouping who fled to the Uganda–DRC borderland region between 1989 and 1993, after Museveni's new regime cracked down heavily on the group. ADF-NALU has since become part of local conflict dynamics within DRC,[2] but there have been consistent cross-border attacks into Uganda that, in June 1998, included burning alive eighty school students and bomb blasts occurring in Kampala. Sporadic attacks on civilians, the UPDF and police continue until the present day (although their leader Jamil Mukulu was captured in Tanzania in April 2015).[3]

Although we should not ignore the serious security threat that these groups did indeed pose, especially to local populations within their vicinity of operations, Museveni promoted their significance to a higher degree than they were perhaps worthy. He cleverly created a narrative that these were part of a wider global trend of extremist groups threatening the very fabric of a civilized world order. Following 9/11, Museveni shifted from describing LRA as 'bandits' to being 'terrorists' linked to the 'Arab Fundamentalist' regime in Khartoum (which they certainly were).[4] The ADF's Islamic roots and sponsorship from Khartoum also made them fit easily into a post-9/11 global 'terrorist' threat. On 12 September 2001, Museveni publicly grouped them with Al-Qaeda:

> We in Uganda know very well the grievous harm that can be caused to society by terrorists, having suffered for many years at the hands of Kony and the Allied Democratic Forces, terrorists supported by Sudan ... Indiscriminate violence in the pursuit of any cause must be condemned and terrorism in all forms needs to be eradicated.[5]

The emergence of Al-Shabaab in Somalia then fully inserted Uganda unequivocally into the US Global War on Terror. Following 9/11, US crackdowns resulted in the decentralization and localization of Al-Qaeda in East Africa, which then saw Al-Shabaab emerge mid-2000s from the chaos of Somalia's collapsed state. By 2007, Al-Shabaab began using terror and suicide bombings to save resources and men, whilst other factions engaged in the heavy fighting of the ongoing Somali civil war. Al-Shabaab also gained popularity due to Ethiopian troop's invasion and occupation of the country.[6]

With the LRA and ADF already successfully inserted into the global narrative around 'terrorism', the inclusion of Al-Shabaab in Uganda's noble fight against terrorism took place during the launch of the AMISOM mission in March 2007. This AMISOM mission became the main foreign force in Somalia after the 2009 Ethiopian withdrawal. Deployment was backed unanimously by the African Union (AU) but this was, in effect, a Ugandan mission. A UPDF Lieutenant Colonel admitted: 'I think there was a certain degree of unilateralism in our deployment in Somalia, because I mean it doesn't happen very often, just one country deciding to deploy.'[7] In Parliament, the Defence Minister justified the action due to Uganda's moral duty in assisting regional security, the threat of light arms proliferation in Northern Uganda, and the links between Uganda–Somali populations, amongst other domestically focused justifications. But Al-Shabaab were easily presented as 'terrorists' within the GWOT. Museveni stated in a 2009 meeting with Washington's UN envoy that it was 'important to send a strong message to terrorists that they can't go on terrorizing populations in Africa'.[8] By volunteering to become involved in the intensely complex Somali civil war, Uganda created a direct danger to itself that had not objectively existed prior to deployment. The 2010 Al-Shabaab bomb attack in Kampala, killing seventy-four people, was open revenge for the UPDF presence in Somalia.

Successful grouping of threats

This successful articulation of these groups into the GWOT's 'terrorist' discourse helped ensure a heavy militarized response that became fundamentally important to Museveni's relationship with the US and West. Following 9/11, the LRA and ADF were almost immediately included on the US Terrorist Exclusion List, in 2008 the US State Department named Kony a 'specially designated global terrorist' and in 2011 the AU officially designated LRA a terrorist organization.[9] During the 1990s and 2000s, UPDF suppression of LRA certainly contributed to the suffering of the Acholi population in the form of Internally Displaced People (IDP) camps and general maltreatment. Actions against the ADF include, indirectly, the launch of the Congo Wars and persistent manoeuvres against the group thereafter. AMISOM is an obvious militarized response against Al-Shabaab. In Uganda, although criticism against the UPDF's harsh measures in the north has occurred, no serious resistance to the campaigns against the LRA, ADF or Al-Shabaab has ever emerged. In speaking with a range of security specialists and local actors in Uganda, 'terrorism' was persistently named as the most pressing security threat facing Uganda, with Al-Shabaab, the ADF and the remnants of LRA all well-identified.[10]

Throughout the conflicts, Museveni and Uganda have successfully painted solutions in purely militaristic terms and courted the US to accept Uganda's lead, offer support to the UPDF, and even help pursue the LRA into CAR with US Special Forces.[11] A year after the July 2010 Al-Shabaab attacks, then Chief of Military Intelligence, Brigadier Mugira, reported that ADF was regrouping and seeking to form links to Al-Qaeda in the Maghreb region, Al-Shabaab and Al-Qaeda in the Horn of Africa along with its affiliates in East Africa.[12] In January 2013, Museveni described eastern DRC as a 'terrorist conservation project', and UN peacekeepers there as 'tourists'.[13] Eastern DRC has a series of interlinked, well-documented security issues and 'MONUSCO itself has now taken it (ADF) as their mandate ... it's one of the commitments to rid that region of negative forces including ADF'.[14]

Whilst LRA and ADF remain important components of Uganda's narrative on the terrorist threat, Al-Shabaab took centre stage, especially around regional security within the EAC. Currying favour with the US as an ally in the GWOT was a significant contributing factor to AMISOM deployment: Museveni's personal decision to interne in Somalia occurred at a time when Western donor support was lagging due to Uganda's heavy crackdowns on new opposition parties and their foolhardy second invasion of the DRC. AMISOM thus reasserted Museveni's role in protecting Western security interests and helping deflect attention from governance issues. There have been allegations of sexual abuse by Ugandan and Burundian soldiers against locals, and a scandal involving Ugandan troops selling fuel and food to local networks, but Uganda's involvement has been largely successful.[15] Somalia, deeply insecure by any reasonable standard, began showing clear signs of improvement and resilience to catastrophe during this 2010s period which continued into the 2020s. A Ugandan expert on the Somalia effort says:

> When I first went there in March 2007, it was complete chaos; just utter chaos there ... that has improved somewhat since then, partly because Ugandan forces had just arrived and are now there and first secured the airport at least. So there is some improvement, there is a semblance of government now. In 2007, there was none to speak of.[16]

Al-Shabaab at this time continued to be seen as 'the principal threat to peace and security in Somalia and throughout the Horn of Africa', however, and its inner core having become 'more operationally audacious' by emphasizing actions outside Somalia.[17] AMISOM means Al-Shabaab remains a pressing security concern for Uganda and various credible warnings have been made of further terrorist attacks on its territory. Essentially, however, Al-Shabaab (like the LRA and ADF) will not affect the Ugandan state-building project writ large. A UPDF Brigadier notes that 'the terrorist threat might cause panic, might affect business for some time ... It's a nuisance, it's costly, but it's not a countrywide threat to Uganda as such. It's costly because the man power you use.'[18] Ultimately, the terror threat has highlighted Museveni's ability, willingness and capacity to act regionally in a way that others cannot. A well-known Ugandan academic notes that 'Al-Shabaab is a bigger threat to Kenya but Kenyan forces are not in Mogadishu, it is Ugandan forces in Mogadishu! And making progress there as well!'[19]

Furthermore, terrorism has played a role in enabling the pacification of key domestic constituents. 'Ghost-soldier' scandals in the North saw UPDF leaders claim funds for non-existent soldiers, and Congo War booty helped fund the increasingly important patronage networks.[20] AMISOM proved lucrative due to donors' financial and political support, especially after 2011 when pay was upped to UN levels.[21] According to a prominent Ugandan journalist whose brother is a Commander in the UPDF, troops are rotated every nine months, thereby increasing the numbers who receive an approximately seven-fold pay increase, and the US (through the UN) replaces each piece of military hardware used.[22] In addition, by 'timing the Western mood to perfection' after 9/11, Museveni passed the thoroughly restrictive Anti-Terrorism Act in 2003 without any US criticism. This law was then used against opposition supporters.[23] An updated anti-terrorism law was passed in June 2015 that provided even stronger laws that the government could manipulate to crack down on opposition activity.[24]

Regional cooperation and the shared danger

Museveni resisted regional cooperation against the LRA, despite a May 2003 East African Legislative Assembly (EALA) resolution that sought to establish a committee whose purpose would have been to seek ways to negotiate an end to the crisis.[25] A Kenyan and Tanzanian offer in 2005 to send military assistance against the LRA was also rejected.[26] Museveni's clear preference was for a Uganda-only solution: regional cooperation was only sought and gained after the LRA fled Uganda. Museveni invokes regionalism when it suits his agenda, not when it does not, and AMISOM partners have copied Uganda' template of securitizing 'terrorism' to suit domestic political purposes by linking it to the more global narrative. Having suffered the most brutal attacks, Kenya's large Somali community has received severe police crackdowns and reprisals in Nairobi. Addressing the UN General Assembly in 2014, President Uhuru stated that 'in Kenya, we stand at a critical moment. As we deepen our democracy, we find our nation thrust into the front lines of a regional and global war against terror.'[27] Burundi's low global status make it a less likely target than its AMISOM partners, but danger remains. In 2010, President Nkurunziza called on the international community to increase its assistance in their fight, 'because it is going to ignite world terrorism from the Horn of Africa'.[28] During the 2015 election trouble, discussed in Chapter Two, the government justified the heavy government crackdown by saying that 'these demonstrations provide cover for a terrorist enterprise'.[29] And in Nkurunziza's first public appearance since the failed coup attempt in May 2015, he stated he was concentrating his attention solely on the regional fight against Al-Shabaab.[30]

Regarding the other EAC partners who are not active in the AMISOM mission, Tanzania helped foil planned attacks in Kenya during the 2013 election and Uhuru's subsequent inauguration.[31] In March 2015, the Home Affairs Minister stated that Mohammed Emwazi – the infamous 'Jihadi John' – had been stopped from entering the country in 2009. At the same time, President Kikwete hinted that an attack killing one solider in Tanga may have had international links.[32] And in the build-up to the October 2015 elections – one of the tightest fought by the dominant ruling party – Chama Cha Mapinduzi (CCM) Secretary-General Abdulrahman Kinana wrote that if his party lost then 'the country stands to become a new front for terrorists', due to Islamist threats to Zanzibar. He also made unsubstantiated claims that opposition party Uamsho is a Boko Haram affiliate.[33] In Rwanda, despite Western reluctance to class them as such, EALA representative Abdul Karim Harelimana stressed in an interview that the FDLR génocidaires operating in DRC are 'another terrorist group'.[34] In October 2015, at the EALA organized 'Nanyuki Series' meeting focused on security threats to EAC, Rwandan delegates insisted on other members formally acknowledging FLDR as a 'terrorist' entity.[35] Kigali has also accused Human Rights Watch of spreading the equivalent of 'political propaganda for terrorist groups', by criticizing government extra-judicial killings.[36]

Hence the East African Community has terrorism embedded into its regional security dynamic, which is tied to global interests in the issue. And within the EAC, Al-Shabaab is seen as linked to Uganda's other regional security issues. According to an EAC expert, Al-Shabaab and LRA did seek to establish links, but these failed due to a lack of shared Islamist ideology. He states, however:

China's Role in Regional Security and the Nature of Museveni's Methods 113

There is a connection with ADF and Al-Shabaab in that network. ADF have been in the DRC for years, looting timber, tusks, other ivory for a long time, and they are connected to Al-Shabaab . . . all the recent intelligence says they are in contact and connected and use those kinds of networks.[37]

This EAC analysis came at a time when a UN Group of Experts Monitoring Group found no evidence that the ADF had links to other Islamist terrorist groups.[38] Certain EAC experts are wary of Museveni's militarism and its regional impact, however. 'When I look at the way Uganda is arming itself, I don't see that many enemies for whom to spend so much on Defence,' says an anonymous EAC security expert. With the severely decimated capacity of the LRA and lack of serious threat from the ADF, 'any strategic thinker would say this is something that is worrisome to the region.'[39] But that view is not reflected institutionally within the EAC. A UPDF Colonel says that 'we face the common threat of terrorism and that has brought us together like never before,'[40] and the Tanzanian EALA representative remarks, 'I don't think there is any entity in the community that is more integrated than our militaries, it is incredible.'[41]

Uganda's role in combatting terrorism, therefore, positions Museveni at the forefront of the wider regional security agenda. 'Terrorism' has been made more prominent by Museveni through his interlocking three disparate groups into a collective discourse that incorporates domestic, regional and international actors. The LRA was the product of a complex domestic context in northern Uganda, albeit with a regional base and support from Sudan, which took many years to expel fully into Central Africa. LRA received increasingly significant international attention and direct support from the US to fight against. The ADF, born in Uganda but quickly becoming Congolese and again with Sudanese assistance, now faces collaborative efforts against it from the Congolese army and MONESCO. The ADF has received far less international media or government interest. Al-Shabaab was an extra-regional force garnering strong US attention, then becoming a specific domestic threat whilst remaining a wider regional menace. Against these distinct but conceptually collectivized 'terrorists', Museveni provides a UPDF force which promotes a narrative logic that helps justify its deployments to domestic, EAC, AU and international constituents. Museveni's UPDF also supplies tangible and significant successes in the field. No other leader in the EAC can lay claim to have fought terrorism for so long, in so wide an area, and with such success.

114   *Ugandan Agency within China–Africa Relations*

Situating China's role in this key security issue is, therefore, crucial to understanding their impact on Museveni's position within regional security dynamics.

Chinese Small Arms and Light Weapons (SALW) – impacting all levels

China is not active militarily in the region in the same way the West is. China does not offer anti-terrorist support to Uganda, for example, unlike the US and UK.[42] FOCAC VI did pledge $60 million over three years towards APSAs Standby Force – the five rapid reaction regional forces referred to in Chapter One – but until that time China had only given minimal amounts of support to AMISOM, (including $2.3 million to Uganda in 2012), and $0.5 million to the Somali Transitional Federal Government in September 2009 (and the FOCAC VI package still means that Chinese overall financial support for African security issues has been paltry compared to the West).[43] China has vocally condemned LRA action in CAR at the UN and publicly applauded the regional efforts against the group, but when doing so always emphases China's allegiance to the UN and AU mechanisms: championing regional or continental efforts are the only way China can voice its support for security operations whilst maintaining is 'non-interference' policy.[44] There is no evidence of the Chinese peacekeepers within the UN MONUSCO operation in eastern DRC ever having encountered ADF.

It was noted previously, however, that SALW proliferation and the global ivory trade links China to security issues around terrorism. This is particularly notable within Uganda's 'terrorist' security issue, where China's regional role in Sudan has been particularly significant. Chinese arms appearing in Uganda and the region have impacted on each of the terrorist groups that Museveni has merged into an all-encompassing terrorist discourse, as well as contributing to other domestic dangers. In Uganda, the SALW proliferation issue occurs through arms leaking from domestic facilities, regional smuggling across porous borders with conflict-prone neighbours and international problems with the global supply chain: China is involved to some extent in all three of these factors.

International trade

A significant portion of the SALW circulating have been in the region for many years. It is thought that Idi Amin's fleeing soldiers left up to 60,000 AK-47s in the Karamoja region at various bases,[45] and caches left from LRA and long-defunct rebel groups are found fairly often by authorities and criminal networks. Another portion comes more from recent government purchases that are then handed out by nefarious officials or soldiers/policemen who flee with them.[46] The spread of ammunition receives less attention than arms, but 'clearly it is a vital part of the problem ... controlling the spread of ammunition has huge implications also for tackling SALW proliferation.'[47] Within the murky world of SALW procurement, it is not easy to apportion 'impact' on a particular level or nation: violence and criminal networks operating in eastern DRC, South Sudan and Somalia make it very difficult for Ugandan authorities to identify individual suppliers.[48]

The Chinese link, however, certainly exists and is tangible. The argument here is not that Chinese arms are the primary causes of these security issues, or that Beijing is deliberately or covertly aiding certain groups for their own purposes. It is that Chinese made arms clearly play a substantial role in the destructive capability of such groups, and that Beijing officials must be aware of this. Other countries and actors certainly embark on similar practices – that is not in question. And precise quantities and details of supplied SALW are difficult to state unequivocally. But there is no doubt that Chinese made weapons have played a role in each of the threats that have been discussed here and are therefore significant. China's historic engagement with Africa during the liberation struggles and info the modern era has made Chinese arms a key feature since colonial times. 'The Chinese made weapons have been in this region for years,' says the Ugandan Minister of State for Foreign Affairs. 'The AK-47 that is awash in Africa today came from China, came from North Korea, and came from USSR, initially as a means to help us with the armed struggle.' He continues:

> Our radar in Uganda here captures on average per week, up to 400 small aircraft that come from North Africa and land on the thousands of runways in Eastern-DRC. Intelligence tells us they bring weapons, and then they get the gold, diamonds, and then they fly out of there. Now the kind of weapons they bring here are not Western weapons, we never find Western kind of weapons, they are mainly Chinese.[49]

116   *Ugandan Agency within China–Africa Relations*

In 2010, Uganda was the third largest export destination for China's SALW.[50] Their supply to other regional powers like Sudan (discussed below and in previous chapters) and porous borders between states mean that the LRA and ADF certainly used Chinese-manufactured AK-47s during their campaigns.[51] As well as using Chinese-made arms, significant quantities of Al-Shabaab's ammunition are also made in China. A Small Arms Survey reports that Chinese-made ammunition is the most available in Mogadishu markets and from arms dealers, and has been recovered during various raids on Al-Shabaab hideouts.[52] Chinese-made Type-54 pistols are also becoming the 'weapon of choice' for criminals in Somaliland.[53]

Sudan's regional presence

China's links to Khartoum are well-documented and have been briefly noted in previous chapters. Bashir's regime created clear and consistent geo-political, regional and local security issues in Uganda and Greater East Africa. The historical links to the LRA were not severed after the group fled Uganda. In September 2014, a UPDF Lieutenant Colonel explained that Kony was located in the Kafia Kingi enclave near the border with Sudan, 'so we suspect that he could be dealing with some Sudanese Generals, this is something we are still investigating'.[54] As well as support for subversive groups, Khartoum sparked a regional arms race enabled through its China links:

> Sudan was looked at as a pariah state and in anticipation of that they armed themselves a lot, they have a lot of money. And what did this do, it changed the balance of power within the region. As a result, different countries had to try and match that imbalance, and so also armed themselves. Sudan had airpower and we had to match that air power. Sudan used to bomb us and we didn't have the deterrent capability, they used to bomb Northern Uganda with impunity and so we had to get that capability, the deterrent. When we acquired it, that stopped. Sudan was supporting the rebellion; we had to prepare ourselves for that. In that way the Chinese involvement in Sudan indirectly led to this regional arms build-up.[55]

Despite years of open hostility against Khartoum and Bashir, neither Museveni nor the NRM have ever publicly linked Chinese support with

Sudanese actions. As noted previously, Museveni has never publicly disparaged the Chinese in the way he has regularly done with the West (even when in receipt of their donor funding), and has certainly not tied the Sudan menace to the presence of China there. But as noted by the Ugandan security specialist, 'strengthening Khartoum's military capabilities and defence industries is something that is definitely of strategic concern . . . it tilts the balance of power militarily in the region. So you can't just ignore it.'[56]

China has maintained a somewhat impressive ability to remain neutral amidst fierce conflict even when whilst its arms supply has remained crucial to particular sides. During South Sudan's war with Khartoum, 'China which was losing money did not flex its muscle.'[57] After 2011 independence, rebel groups in South Sudan continued to receive Chinese arms through north Sudanese sources, whilst China was also supplying the now independent Sudan People's Liberation Army (SPLA) with weapons to help fight against those same rebels.[58] In July 2014 (whilst the Machar-Kiir conflict put South Sudan on the brink of famine), $38 million worth of missiles, grenade launchers, machine guns and ammunition arrived courtesy of China North Industries Group Corp (NORINCO) for the SPLA government. China claimed the contract had been agreed many months earlier, hence not violating an international agreement to stop sales to the increasingly war-torn young country.[59] But a UN Panel of Experts report in 2015 alleged that a further $20 million worth of arms were sold by NORINCO to Juba in 2014, even after that previous controversy and Chinese promises to cease trading in arms there.[60]

China's official neutrality became increasingly difficult to maintain during the period of focus here. The Chinese government was unusually public in its condemnation of the 2013–14 civil instability. China began an experimental 'mediator-like' role acting as something of a broker between sides, with limited affect. China realized the immense complexity in resolving the conflict when it convened a special meeting of the Intergovernmental Authority on Development (IGAD) in January 2015 that failed to end hostilities. This resulted in China pulling back from discussions and focusing instead on supporting IGAD's own efforts. It also supported sanctions on belligerents, which was a markedly different policy from preceding years when China resisted the sanctions being imposed against Khartoum whilst it was an international pariah.[61]

The Kiir-Machar conflict gave Museveni the opportunity to position Uganda as being centrally important to China's regional interests (including those in Ethiopia, who was very much involved in South Sudanese issues). Beijing's priority is a functional oil sector in South Sudan and they would back any party who could enforce that. Generally, however, it is thought they preferred President Kiir to remain and that they were privately supportive of UPDF's late-2013 intervention in South Sudan.[62] In September 2014, the rebel Machar withdrew his complaint of the UPDF presence in the country just days before he was summoned to Beijing to discuss the crisis.[63] The IGAD's efforts to replace UPDF in South Sudan with troops from Kenya, Rwanda and Ethiopia amounted to nothing. Eventually, China committed 700 combat troops as part of the UNIMISS force there in late 2014, although they were not guarding oil fields (as had been initially reported).[64]

Museveni's regional manoeuvring continued in early 2015, when Uganda and Sudan set up a joint security committee, and in September 2015 he visited Bashir in Khartoum for the first time in ten years. One month later, the UPDF withdrew from South Sudan after a UNSC Resolution warned of appropriate measures against those preventing the initiation of an August peace agreement, and was replaced by UNMISS forces (Uganda had ignored a forty-five-day withdrawal timetable from that August agreement). A role for China in the Museveni–Bashir reconciliation would be speculative (Bashir had visited Beijing earlier in the month and signed several economic agreements), but this certainly signified a serious geo-political shift, which undoubtedly impacts on China. A Kampala-Khartoum alliance will ensure maintenance of Uganda's influential clout in South Sudan's affairs even without UPDF presence. Analysts suggest Museveni was willing to then ditch support for Kiir and was preparing himself for an alternative regime in Juba (possibly even led by the rebel Machar), although Kiir has survived any potential manoeuvring and remained President into the 2020s.[65]

Ugandan and Chinese reactions – National Focal Points with regional efforts

Domestically, as of January 2014, Uganda's National Focal Point on SALW claims that the government has destroyed '1,500 tonnes of unexploded ordnances and 120,000 pieces of small arms and weapons since 2008'.[66] But the country (especially the north) remains awash with weapons. The Karamojong – from the impoverished, intensely unstable Karamoja region – get most of their arms and ammunition from across their border with South Sudan, through trading or capturing from other groups in Uganda and by purchasing from Ugandan state security forces. By far the most common ammunition used in the region – the 7.62 × 39 mm Warsaw Pact standard cartridge – comes from China and is found across the Great Lakes Region (GLR) and Horn.[67]

Of further interest is Luwero Industries, a domestic parastatal arms factory in Nakasongola, which manufactures and refurbishes small armaments and bullets. It was built between 1987 and 1992 with aid from China's Wanbao Engineering Corporation. A 2014 Parliamentary Report said the plant has been dilapidated and unproductive since 2010.[68] Ostensibly it operated to supply the UPDF but its ammunition is found throughout Karamoja and elsewhere, and in the 1990s it was accused of producing and selling landmines in Central Africa and across the Great Lakes Region.[69] Jacqueline Mbabazi, wife of sacked Presidential rival Amama Mbabazi, ran the Luwero Industries plant during the 2000s. She began that role around the same time that her husband was appointed Defence Minister in 2001, which created some controversy due to accusations of there being conflicting interests and incorrect reporting lines.[70] Wafulu Oguttu and Kizza Besigye claim that China continued operating the facility alongside the Ministry of Defence. Besigye further alleges that Mbabazi's wife 'is the one who developed the intimate relations with the Chinese companies from that vantage point', which eventually led to Mbabazi becoming viewed with suspicion and as a rival to Museveni years later.[71]

China believes the SALW issue is best dealt with by increasing local capacity to handle the matter or by initiating conversations through its own FOCAC setting. But as its own security interests and responsibilities as a global power increase, China is becoming more willing to accept at least some responsibility around the SALW issue and agreed to partake in the Africa–China–EU dialogues referred to previously, after many years of effort from Saferworld.[72] Stockpile management and the recognition that 'China's African partners fail to comply with end-user clauses, which are key elements of China's export control practices and supply contracts' were key outcomes of the Saferworld Working Group.[73] Uganda was particularly keen to build and improve its own storage facilities, but whether this was ever undertaken is unclear.[74] China is willing and available to fund certain projects that are presented to them precisely, succinctly and coherently, especially when they are focused on domestic supply-side issues. According to a participant in the dialogues and China expert, 'if it is about paying a few million to build a facility or improve record keeping, China would be very willing to do that'.[75]

Ugandan and African governments, however, habitually produce long lists of requests, rather than being explicit and precise. Uganda has also not been entirely forthcoming regarding Chinese and others efforts at combatting SALW proliferation. Those undertaking field work in 2013 by the Saferworld Working Group were not allowed access to any military facilities – including Luwero Industries in Nakasongola – and Ugandan officials were generally uncooperative.[76] China itself also remains constrained by its own narrative and international position. Its statements during such dialogues always reiterate its adherence to increasing local capacity and non-interference.[77] Likewise, at the UN, Beijing emphasizes its adherence to arms embargoes and claims 'strict compliance with the principles of never impairing regional peace and security and of non-interference in the internal affairs of recipient countries'.[78] Delegates at the Saferworld dialogue commended the passing of the UN Arms Trade Treaty (ATT) in April 2013, which 'establishes clear international standards for the international transfer of conventional arms, including SALW and ammunition'.[79] China was slow but did eventually join the ATT in July 2020 (it entered into force on 24 December 2014). Burundi, Rwanda and Tanzania have signed but not ratified the ATT; Uganda and Kenya – as well as the Sudan, DRC and Somalia – have done neither.[80]

Ivory trade – suppression of issues and military responses

China's role in the international ivory trade is another indirect link to Uganda's terrorist security issue and the SALW issue. Ivory has long been a source of income for rebel groups. Charles Kisembo says that 'in the 1990s LRA was poaching and was selling these tusks into Southern Sudan at that time. And Sudan in exchange would give them arms, food, medicine.'[81] This practice has continued. Although Kony is not any kind of kingpin figure in the ivory trade, the LRA currently garners substantial income from illegal elephant poaching as part of a wider regional network that includes Al-Shabaab and other militia groups. It has been estimated as much as 40 per cent of Al-Shabaab funds come from ivory, increasingly seen as akin to the blood diamond trade in profitability.[82] Because the current record-level monetary value for ivory products is being fuelled largely by growing demand in China, it can therefore be assumed that LRA- and Al-Shabaab-supplied ivory is appearing there.

Uganda is a source, consolidation hub and major transport route in the global trade. The Executive Director of the Elephant Action League explains that:

> Uganda don't have a serious poaching problem anymore in the way others do, but they do have a serious problem with trafficking . . . Fighting trafficking is a different job than fighting poaching in the bush, and on this issue Uganda did not show enough capability and commitment yet.[83]

At the 2014 International Union for Conservation of Nature, Uganda narrowly escaped sanctions for not doing enough to fight the illegal ivory trade and serious problems persist.[84] The militarization of the anti-poaching effort can spur something of an arms race between poachers and anti-poaching units across the region. Ugandan security forces have been implicated in profiting from the trade, and in 2012, whilst supposedly searching for the LRA in DRC, they allegedly killed twenty-two elephants from a Mi-17MD military helicopter. In 2013, Tanzania's shoot-to-kill anti-poaching operation resulted in serious human rights abuses, and Kenyan wildlife rangers were accused of killing eighteen poachers to cover up official collusion in elephant poaching in 2014.[85]

In 2014, Museveni intervened to prevent Uganda's head of tourism from questioning the UPDF Colonel coordinating security and law enforcement for the Ugandan Wildlife Authority (UWA), after over one tonne of seized illegal ivory was stolen from the UWA vault. This was despite members of the UPDF being involved in the theft.[86] Museveni instead let the Inspector General of the government handle matters, again showing his dislike of investigations into the UPDF that he cannot control (as per Saferworld's SALW efforts). The director of the Lusaka Agreement Task Force, a Nairobi-based inter-government agency fighting ivory trafficking, feels that Uganda's role in the issue is growing. Museveni wants UPDF presence at the UWA in order to monitor rebel movements, and does not pre-occupy himself with concern over their possible collusion in ivory poaching and smuggling.[87] In July 2015, forty-eight boxes of ivory were seized on a flight leaving Entebbe Airport by Aviation police, the fourth such seizure of the year, indicating the persistence of Uganda's role in the trade.[88]

Unlike SALW, however, Ugandan government, officials and security personnel are more willing to highlight China's role in the ivory trade and try to engage them on the matter. 'We discuss with them yes,' says a source within UPDF Military Intelligence, whilst highlighting that Uganda is simultaneously strengthening its own domestic laws.[89] Equating the ivory trade to prostitution, whereby 'you have to stop the buyers of prostitutes,' Henry Okello says he has talked to Chinese ambassadors and diplomats in international fora about the matter. Okello believes that 'they have accepted it and tried to work to reduce and eliminate the trading in ivory products in their country. There is evidence that they are trying.'[90] Although not publicly linking itself with the LRA and Al-Shabaab, China – along with the measures discussed in Chapter Two – has also burned ivory seized inside the country, has prosecuted increasing numbers of smugglers, and in 2013 sent text messages to foreign travellers reminding them not to purchase ivory products.[91]

China's domestic interventions in its ivory trade are in line with its own narrative logic. Its global position as arms supplier historically and currently, however, and its regional interests in Sudan have superseded any efforts to halt its supply-side role in SALW proliferation. Likewise, Museveni's priority in maintaining his domestic position has prevented his full engagement in tackling the issues. He has avoided investigations into possible UPDF collusion, resisted regional assistance in tacking Ugandan security threats, failed to utilize Chinese potential assistance and consistently adopted a militarized response to issues that ultimately require a more holistic approach. Regarding terrorism, therefore, China affects Museveni's role in regional security dynamics indirectly: China has provided noteworthy contributions to terror groups through supply of SALW, its support to sympathetic governments, and as a market for illicit goods. But these terror organizations ultimately depend on a multifaceted array of factors for their appearance and continuation. Museveni's agency is evident in his actions against the overt military manifestations of these issues (i.e. violent terrorist groups), rather than through serious engagement with tackling the complex underlying factors leading to their creation (such as poverty, marginalization, and so forth). The security threats that these groups produce has helped cement Museveni's key role in tackling regional security issues, with the West and EAC partners generally accepting of his militarization of regional security dynamics.

Museveni's oil

Uganda's oil sector will define the country's next decades. Museveni's long-term legacy ultimately depends on how successfully or not he plays the various forces influencing its progress. He has therefore centralized his personal role in the oil sector and anyone who challenges his authority is presented as a security threat to the nation. Domestic elites, Kingdoms and locals, and regional and international partners are all vying for spoils. Museveni has needed to deploy a combination of accommodation, subjugation, balance and coercion in order to maintain his tight control of the sector. As the oil industry grows and determines the ambitions of Uganda's wider development agenda, the UPDF is being enlisted to play an increasingly important role in constructing Uganda's future under Museveni.

Oil as a national security asset

Oil and Ugandan security are intricately linked. Following the NRM's 1986 victory, Museveni began sending geologists, geo-chemists and others to be trained abroad (Uganda's oil potential was known due to colonial-era speculation).[92] The Lake Albert–Albertine Rift region – crossing borders with Congo – was divided into blocks and survey-exploration activity increased in the 1990s, whilst ADF and other rebel disruptions occurred. Oil was not a driving force for Uganda's Congo Wars effort, but that dimension must at least have been considered. As the Second Congo War officially ended in July 2003, Ugandan exploration efforts intensified. The NRM Director of the External Security Organisation at that time said in an interview, 'even when we withdrew the troops from the rest of Congo we left them in Ituri to protect this oil ... you can shell that oil field from Ituri'. He also believes that Khartoum's support for rebel groups like the LRA and ADF was, in part, due to Bashir not wanting Uganda to exploit its oil sector and potentially become a rival to Sudan's.[93]

With relative calm in the region, commercial viability was confirmed in 2006. In 2012, Ireland's Tullow Oil, the longest serving of the international oil companies (IOCs) who had bought out Heritage in 2010, completed a three-way split 'farm-down' to the China National Offshore Oil Corporation (CNOOC) and France's Total.[94] Uganda's oil – estimated as 1.4 billion recoverable barrels – will provide funds for the following thirty years or so. A 2012 Oxcarre study estimated that initially low profits will rise after ten years to between 3 per cent and 9 per cent of Uganda's GDP.[95] Although up until 2014 Museveni was publicly saying First Oil would be in 2017, but it is now planned for 2022 at the earliest, following periodic delays. Uganda plotted and planned in the post-2000 commodity boom phase, but the drop in global oil prices provoked renegotiation of awarded contracts in 2015 and a delay in issuing production licences, and Tullow in particular struggled. The lower half of the Oxcarre estimate is now more likely.

Oil money is crucial to Uganda's future development strategy. The ambitious Vision 2040 document outlines plans for transforming Uganda from a low- to middle-income country within thirty years, described as 'the wet dreams of the government and the political class around oil resources'.[96] Vision 2040 discusses investment in infrastructure, technology, urbanization and industrialization; however, Ministers and officials emphasize that infrastructure is where oil revenues will primarily be spent. Surveys show that Ugandan locals also hope and expect that oil revenues will be invested in infrastructure.[97] There are concerns, however, that continued borrowing for infrastructure projects such as the oil refinery, Standard Gauge Railway (SGR) and other projects could mean that debt sustainability levels are breached. Yet there is a clear belief that infrastructure is key to development: the NRM Deputy Chief Whip stated that 'infrastructure is seen as stage one, which will then lead to jobs in future by encouraging more businesses to come here'.[98] Museveni promotes infrastructure as countering the stability risks of underdevelopment, saying in November 2014 that 'if you do not solve the problem of electricity, the railways, no jobs will be created and very soon you will have the Arab Spring'.[99]

The oil sector is presented as a national security issue: a threat to the oil sector functioning is seen as a threat to Uganda's development objectives, and this crucial national asset is under threat of sabotage or mishandling. Linking oil to the terror security issue discussed above, the UPDF is explicitly vocalizing and reacting to the DRC/ADF menace to justify the militarization of the oil area. The UPDF Chief Political Commissar has stated that 'certainly they might attack. ADF is getting stronger than they were before', and that 'we know their plans and movements, we are on our guard, and we are in charge ... we have put in place measures to ensure that the oil wells are secure'.[100]

But threats to the oil sector also move beyond the terrorism issue, with the suggestion that anyone opposing Museveni and the NRM's managing of oil money threatens Ugandan progress and stability. During the 2011 election campaign, Museveni proclaimed that 'I can't leave the seat when we have just discovered those resources like oil', saying that the opposition could not be trusted to handle the find appropriately. He suggested that the FDC's Besigye wanted the Presidency only for his personal enrichment through oil wealth.[101] And in 2015, Museveni stated to supporters that 'you hear people say "Museveni should go." But go and leave oil money? They want me to go so they can come and spoil the oil money. These people want me to go back to the bush.'[102] Foreign meddling is likewise seen as a risk. The Minister of Security in an interview explicitly labelled the NGO movement in the oil region as a security challenge for Uganda:

> I don't think there are serious problems with oil. The challenge probably we have felt and found is from the number of foreign NGOs, fuelled either by their opposition to the exploitation of oil or something. You know they have become so numerous and go into the oil region ostensibly saying they are just sensitising people about the oil and so on, but they end up actually inciting people to stop the exploitation or to make the exploitation of oil very very difficult. Lots of them, foreign NGOs.[103]

These risks require Museveni's direct involvement to prevent the development opportunity being wasted. Whilst updated oil legislation was passing through parliament in December 2012, Museveni wanted all negotiating powers to be handled by the Minister of Energy and Mineral Development, effectively meaning the President, rather than under Parliamentary scrutiny. There was even a threat of military intervention if Parliament did not cede, which they eventually did. An MP states that '[Museveni] didn't come himself and say that, but he has his mechanism and the message was on'.[104] Although denied publicly as being an explicit coup threat, messages from Museveni and the Ministry of Defence that the so-called 'bad politics' of Parliament would not be allowed to continue were backed up by the Chief of Defence Forces. General Aronda stated:

> The message was well taken for those to who it was intended. Stand warned. Stand advised. Should you not change course, other things will be brought into play. Let no one return to the past. We have seen enough, almost 25 years of turmoil ... the message was deliberately sent out and we leave it at that.[105]

The importance that Museveni places on the oil sector has encouraged exemplary professionalism from the Petroleum Exploration and Production Department (PEPD). Whilst bribery allegations have been thrown at the IOCs and NRM's inner circle, the technocratic PEPD has fought cleanly and dogmatically to protect Uganda's interests. A prominent journalist exclaims that the lack of corruption thus far in the oil sector 'is because the core actors in it are very, very strong and honest people. They have been extremely, extremely honest and tough-minded, it is unbelievable!'[106]

Submission to Museveni's tight control

The oil sector has been tightly controlled by Museveni and the oil region physically secured. The UPDF is also playing a role in Uganda's infrastructure agenda which is linked to the oil sector and revenues. A 2010 directive written by Museveni to senior colleagues stated that no oil agreement 'should ever be signed without my express written approval'.[107] The four NRM rebel MPs discussed in Chapter One were particularly vocal in criticizing the oil bills and expelled from the party and Parliament. The Production Sharing Agreements (PSAs) between the government and IOCs have been kept secret from the public and are only available to MPs through unusually stringent conditions, even though Uganda got an extremely good deal.[108]

Despite significant protestations, ultimately Parliament has succumbed to Museveni's control by passing the oil bills. In physical terms, the External Security Organisation (ESO), Internal Security Officers (ISOs) and the Chief of Military Intelligence (CMI) are operating in the oil area along with a newly created covert Oil and Gas Operations Unit.[109] The state's physical control has of the resources has been tied directly to Museveni's personal control: the UPDF built a large military base nearby; overall security operations in the region are controlled by Museveni's son, Brigadier Muhoozi, under the Special Forces Group; and Saracen Uganda Ltd has private security contracts to guard all oil installations and Museveni's semi-notorious brother, Salim Saleh, as a major shareholder.[110] Such tight state and personal control of the oil region highlights to foreign companies the importance of maintaining good relations with Museveni.

Most oil-related activity to date takes place within the Bunyoro Kingdom, a historically marginalized area with deep seated resentment against central government neglect. The oil-rich Albertine Graben stretches north into Acholi, and deposits are thought to be elsewhere including Karamoja, meaning that finds are located in the most volatile areas of Uganda. Bunyoro (and other Kingdoms) will receive 1 per cent of oil royalties despite their formal request for 12.5 per cent.[111] Lack of credible institutional resistance from Bunyoro and other Kingdoms to this announcement is largely matched by a passive local populace seduced by the expectations around oil wealth. Clashes and deaths have occurred amongst themselves, however, in the Ruwenzori, Bunyoro and Acholi regions, as existing land tensions are exacerbated by potential value increasing dramatically.[112] According to a Physical Planner in Buliisa District within the oil-rich Hoima region, the inequality likely to emerge once production starts means that 'I anticipate a major conflict . . . you will see fire'.[113] In countering such latent security concerns, a UPDF officer says:

> There is a grand plan, it's both a development plan and a security plan . . . I think the challenge is not really these local sentiments, these local sentiments can be taken care of if you have a strong security machinery. Because Uganda is not like Nigeria, ours is different. Our security forces are very competent and capable of dealing with some of these concerns before they escalate into violence.[114]

The state also employs militarized responses against the internationalized NGO movement. Museveni again resists Western influence, which occurs through their funding of civil society organizations, in this key domestic sector. Security forces have prevented 'disruptive' organizations from attending community debates, where vocal troublemakers have also been beaten.[115] Parliament also passed an extremely restrictive NGO Act in November 2015.[116] So despite a lack of institutional capacity, government special measures in the local area mean a well-known journalist sees that the Kingdoms 'have now become front and centre of political calculations'.[117] Engaging locals and Kingdoms therefore become a key concern for any oil sector actors.

Furthermore, under the wider development agenda 'the military is going into infrastructure, like what America did after World War II'.[118] With oil revenues to focus primarily on infrastructure, UPDF will be involved in the construction of key projects as Museveni views them as more efficient and less corruptible, stating that 'the army was disciplined right from the bush days ... if the political class were half as disciplined as the UPDF, Uganda would go very far and fast'.[119] The journalist recognizes that this means the 'UPDF are not only the last line of defence, but really that they are the only option left for those things'.[120] Museveni has now begun engaging UPDF Generals around planning national development, with the army pitching itself to the public as the most dependable institution. A UPDF officer who was interviewed saw public perception and the role of the army as fundamental to Ugandan progress:

> Our relationship with the public is very important because there is a lot of trust in the forces today, a lot more than what it was in the past. You see if you look at what happens in other countries where there has been conflict, as long as the population does not trust the security forces you can't be sure that it won't become ugly. So if we can maintain the discipline, if we can maintain the cohesion, if we can continue with training, our country will continue to develop.[121]

This further cements the oil sector as a key national security issue by centralizing the UPDF's role in the economic development of the country, through constructing key oil-revenue-funded infrastructure projects. Museveni's personal relationship with the UPDF remains critically important and makes other development partners' engagement with the army of increasing significance.

Regional necessity – interactions and possible conflicts

The oil sector provokes security issues that can necessitate regional cooperation as well as induce conflict within EAC and outside. The Minister for Justice and an ex-Director General of the External Security Organisation, and ex-Minister of State for Regional Cooperation, emphasizes the clear risks that any intra-regional rivalry could create:

> There is going to be resource competition in the region. Oil, gas, minerals and so forth. And business people are not exactly charitable people, so I am afraid business interests can generate business competition, which if not properly handled degenerates into destabilisation ... if we the indigenous do not handle our assets and exposition properly, it could degenerate into friction. That's my concern.[122]

The ever-looming eastern DRC remains the most immediate external security threat around Uganda's oil, made even more complicated by shifting river beds beneath the oil potentially moving borders and demarcations.[123] Cooperative military strikes against the ADF and LRA have occurred, and government relations are more cordial now than in previous decades. Yet DRC is still seeking $23.5 billion in reparations from Uganda over its Congo Wars looting through the International Court of Justice, and military build-up on both sides has continued.[124]

Within the EAC, Uganda's infrastructure agenda – both that supporting the oil industry and that being funded by future revenues – remains key to regional integration and security dynamics. The company Total claims the fact that Uganda's crude oil pipeline will be underground will prevent any Nigeria-style bunkering and associated issues,[125] but clearly the security issues around its construction will be enormous (Total was especially concerned about which particular routes would be chosen, discussed further below). Regarding the wider agenda, an expert on EAC integration and advisor to the Ugandan government has no doubts that the regional infrastructure drive, discussed in Chapter Two, is the correct one. 'We need the infrastructure. It is correct to make that the number one priority,' he says. 'We can't move, physically and developmentally without it. We need to just build it! ... we need the infrastructure and we should build it immediately.'[126]

As with terrorism, oil has now become centrally important to the EAC's regional security dynamics and the increased linkages between member states. The Defence Pact and the Peace and Security Pact signed between the Coalition of the Willing (CoW) is part of this wider infrastructure agenda. 'You cannot talk about integration and development without infrastructure, without industry ... you need the energy, you need the roads, you need the railways', according to the UPDF Brigadier. And importantly, in order for those necessary projects to be initiated and functional, 'they are saying let us put this in place, but you need to provide security for that'.[127] The need to provide a more stable security environment to satisfy the demand for large-scale infrastructure projects intricately links Ugandan oil to EAC security dynamics. Article 2 of the Mutual Peace and Security Pact agrees to joint cooperation in safeguarding against instability that might be caused by the new development initiatives.[128]

Uganda's oil sector will be a vital feature of the emerging East African security cooperation for the coming decades. Museveni's agency appears through his presentation of the oil sector as an important security issue and successfully positioning himself as *the* key decision maker within that sector. This also, therefore, centralizes his own role in those regional dynamics. The interplay between Museveni's 'terrorism' and 'oil' security issues in Uganda is readily apparent. Terrorism is a risk to the oil sector whose funds are intended to drive NRM's infrastructure agenda. The infrastructure required for wider development is crucial to a successful oil sector and a likely security challenge. This has clear, wide-reaching and openly acknowledged regional effects that have helped spur on what is hoped to be a more structured security framework amongst EAC member states. Uganda's pending oil-producing status has helped to spur a development agenda that views infrastructure as crucially important. Oil sector infrastructure such as the refinery and pipeline is coupled with a Standard Gauge Railway project expected to handle a major portion of associated traffic. Its future revenues also encourage other expensive high-profile dam and road construction projects. All have regional implications or components, further solidifying Museveni's importance. It is therefore essential to assess China's impact on the Ugandan oil sector in order to uncover why Museveni's agency within regional security dynamics is affected by their presence.

The CNOOC and Uganda's development dream

Uganda's oil sector exemplifies the Global Mix policy pursued by Museveni: he has micro-managed the sector in order to avoid over-reliance on any one actor.

Western companies were chosen for the exploration phase, but Uganda then deliberately turned East when costlier infrastructure was required for production.[129] China's increased presence within the oil industry has become a key feature of their wider Ugandan incursions. The China National Offshore Oil Corporation is a key partner, and it is impacting upon the multifarious influences within Uganda's political economy that Museveni must balance in order to maintain control of the industry.

Chinese incursions more generally in Uganda have also shaped the oil sector and oil's role in Museveni's domestic and regional agendas. China's presence in Uganda has helped Museveni to avoid US interference within the latent oil industry and encouraged costly infrastructure projects to be implemented. Chinese companies have also made it easier for Museveni to use the UPDF within his domestic development agenda and they have become crucial players in his regional geo-politicking.

Resisting interference

China's entry into the Ugandan oil sector is an intended consequence of their wider relationship with Museveni. In 2009, whilst America's Exxon Mobil was hoping to buy into the sector, WikiLeaks cables show that the US embassy believed claims that rival Italian firm ENI was bribing Mbabazi and other Ministers in order to secure an oil deal done with Heritage. This would have reduced the value of Exxon's proposed deal with Tullow. The US and UK were considering 'tougher action' of travel restrictions for Mbabazi and others involved in corruption scandals, and writing complaint letters to Museveni over the issue.[130] Firstly, Museveni allowed Tullow to buy out Heritage rather than ENI in 2010; then he ignored a 2011 parliamentary resolution that halted any further oil agreements when he sanctioned the farm-down deal between Tullow–Total–CNOOC.[131] Museveni publicly admitted that he had instructed the Ministry of Energy personally 'that you work with especially the Chinese', instead of the others vying for oil rights.[132] He also explained to MPs that China's National Defence and State Councillor, General Liang Gaunglie, had urged him privately not to delay deals and negotiations further.[133]

In typically cunning fashion, these manoeuvres by Museveni initially gave the impression that he had heeded donor warnings by cutting out ENI, which

US and UK donors were accusing of corrupt practices, but then Museveni actively prevented the US (and their inevitable nagging) from getting involved. A Chinese oil expert working in Uganda says that international oil industry standards mean that in terms of expertise and capability, 'I can't say that when CNOOC comes to Uganda that it can do much better than BP or Shell etc ... CNOOC has its advantages, but specifically for this programme I can't say that there is anything very special.'[134] According to the East African security specialist, therefore, this planned strategic decision to balance between a Chinese and European company 'speaks volumes ... it is purely on a geo-political basis.'[135] Other organizations that try to perform oversight roles in Uganda believe that China and the CNOOC's presence indirectly encourage Museveni's aggressive protection of the oil sector and incentivize him to hinder their oversight activities. A member of the Democratic Governance Facility says when discussing the fall-out from the oil bill controversy:

> China's presence makes life more difficult for us to do what we do ... Museveni made a speech immediately after the bill, which had been extremely contentious. He talks about civil society and the MPs we worked with being traitors and quislings, and talked about 'nefarious foreign interests' behind them all, which is more or less us. There was a level of hysteria there.[136]

The rebel MPs expelled from Parliament following their demands and outspoken criticism of the secrecy surrounding the oil bills and government negotiations around oil contracts also see China playing into their predicament. 'Partly I was a victim because of the Chinese engagement with government, stemming from the oil,' says one rebel MP, as he and other rebels were particularly concerned around the farm-down deal to Total and the CNOOC. He believes:

> We are seeing that once we come out as MPs the government is quick to come in and say no leave, the Chinese are our friends ... I think that is why the President said no we are making much noise, and it was time that we were dismissed.[137]

The CNOOC is not party to the Extractive Industries Transparency Initiative (EITI) and has been accused of lack of transparency, lack of appreciation for human rights issues and poor working conditions. During interviews, donors and NGOs claimed that the CNOOC showed lack of awareness around corporate social responsibility.[138] However, the corporation has actually managed its image in the Bunyoro oil region extremely well. Following early consultation meetings with locals, the CNOOC provided annual cash prizes for the ninety best-achieving students at primary and secondary school in Hoima district, and sponsors an annual football tournament for local teams where cultural leaders attend. A Municipal Planner for Hoima Municipality explains that the CNOOC 'is more popular than other companies. It has brought up this issue of stakeholder engagement, it has worked closely with the people, unlike other companies.'[139] Bunyoro Ministers and elders are impressed:

> For us CNOOC in particular is doing well in the Kingdom. Because it has come forward to give assistance in reviving the youth of Bunyoro Kingdom, through sports ... CNOOC also is well liked by the indigenous people, so they really like China now ... when it comes to educating their children, physically, that is skill development. If it means sport, CNOOC is coming in again to give aid. And if it means employment, again CNOOC is coming in, the environment is open.[140]

The nature of the farm-down deal, therefore, shows that China has influence in the oil sector and has seemingly benefitted from the secretive control by Museveni. It has also avoided serious hostile criticism of its activities from locals in the oil areas, despite donor criticism. But Chinese involvement in the sector extends beyond oil concessions. As the exploration phase moves to production, the well-respected geological experts within the technocratic PEPD lose importance.[141] A prominent journalist notes that as more Ministries become involved in the procurement projects related to the oil, 'they have to involve other players and those other players are rotten to the core, they are not the core team in the Ministry of Energy'.[142] China's relationship with those other actors and their projects is therefore of vital importance.

Contentious infrastructure: the refinery and beyond

Within the oil sector specifically, the oil refinery was the most contentious issue between government and IOCs. Negotiations were clearly long, complex and challenging. The MoU eventually signed requires oil companies to support government efforts at building the 30,000 bpd refinery expanding to 60,000 bpd according to market demand, and the government to assist the companies in surveying for and building the pipeline through neighbouring countries.[143] Oil companies had never seen a President so directly involved in such discussions for so long as the way in which Museveni was involved through all stages of negotiations.[144]

Museveni has used the refinery to reward and punish companies. A Chief Executive Officer for the Africa Institute for Energy Governance believes Museveni has never forgiven Tullow for thwarting his original intention to build a 5,000 bpd refinery as part of its Early Production Scheme, saying that 'the President got annoyed, and most of the problems Tullow have been facing are also associated with their refusal'.[145] Museveni was apparently 'dazzled' by China's promise and belief in his refinery project whilst others wavered in supporting such a costly endeavour.[146] The issuing of production licences stalled over the government's insistence on building the refinery, but CNOOC had been the most outspoken advocate of its construction.[147] Following the 2014 MoU's signing, the President of CNOOC Uganda, Mr Zongwei Xiao, briefed the media that his company could fund the entire refinery project independently if required.[148] So it was of symbolic significance that the CNOOC was awarded the first licence in September 2013 despite its later entry into sector (it was more than eighteen months later that any of the other partners were).[149] According to the Chief Executive, 'so the government is telling Total and Tullow if you don't go with the way we want, we are going to ignore you'.[150]

The CNOOC has not seemed as frustrated as Total and Tullow around the delays to Uganda's oil sector, having itself seen progress in its own role. According to a representative from International Alert, who had regular contact with all three companies during the 2010s when these difficult negotiations were occurring, 'CNOOC out of the three has been the one that has pushed the government less on things ... CNOOC seems to be laid back, even when we interact with staff we don't talk much about government.'[151] And within Uganda's wider infrastructure agenda, China has clearly become a major player. Only the Chinese have put serious money on the ground towards the costly procurement projects required – if all planned infrastructure projects involving Chinese are completed, the cost will be $10+ billion (not including oil pipeline and refinery). In 2013, the then Prime Minister and openly pro-China Mbabazi officially confirmed that China would be granted all priority infrastructure projects in Uganda, due to their acceptance of future oil revenues as payment.[152]

This followed the handshake agreement between Museveni and Xi Jinping on the sidelines of the 2013 BRICS Summit, referred to in Chapter Two, agreeing that China would build Uganda's major infrastructure through state-to-state deals. This model of agreement aids Uganda's new preference for UPDF involvement in projects. According to the EAC Director of Infrastructure, projects done by the military are problematic to audit so multilateral lenders are reluctant to fund them. Therefore, 'the beginning point for the military to take part in a project is that the larger part of the funding is government ... the basis of the funding is what will bring in the military'.[153] Beijing are also specifically involved in assisting UPDF's involvement. The UPDF Brigadier explains that 'we are having them train our engineers, our military engineers, a lot of that'.[154]

Domestic manoeuvres: China and the UPDF

The oil sector and associated infrastructure agenda sees Museveni politicking with domestic, regional and international forces. Domestically, the complex Ugandan fronts and power centres (discussed in Chapter Two) pose difficult questions for Museveni and the NRM elite. Museveni needs to deliver vital and flagship regional integration projects that are required for oil production and wider development, whilst appeasing the domestic power structures by somehow incorporating them. China's willingness to take future oil revenues as payments is coupled with its ability and willingness to engage those local networks, as discussed in Chapter Two. A well-known local journalist and oil expert believes:

> Oil in a sense, and the Chinese involvement in all these multiple high capital intensive projects, just sets the stage for an era of Chinese investment. But it also sets the tone for what that investment is going to be like, because the Chinese have taken like fish to water as far as the course of doing business in Uganda.[155]

A member of the Uganda Overseas China Association, with more than ten years' experience investing in Uganda, says the public fights which can occur in media and court between this complex network of local fronts sometimes impel government bigwigs to get involved:

> Chinese private and state-owned businesses are corrupt, they don't mind paying bribes or whatever they have to do. In fact, I think the Chinese state-owned companies are the most corrupt ... When there are delays and issues, eventually the Chinese government gets involved and has to try and sort it out. It's like a cartel really, remember these are all state-owned companies, but they behave separately. But when it gets complex the government can get involved. They have a meeting and it gets fixed, they ask what's going on and decide what to do ... The Chinese government know about the local dealers and corruption, they know. It all runs very deep.[156]

To deliver a functional oil sector and the espoused wider infrastructure agenda, bids for contracts ideally need to be assessed on merit. As noted by Uganda's Ministry of Finance spokesperson, 'if you allow the politics of the project to get to you then you are completely finished'.[157] But these internal power plays are a crucial component of Museveni's machinations, and he protects those interests ahead of China's. At a time when CNOOC's progress within the oil sector combined with a shared narrative arch and generally flourishing China–Uganda relations, China seemed somewhat poised to take command of the industry. However, the Chinese consortium which bid for construction rights to the refinery (along with ones from Russia, the UAE, South Korea, Switzerland and Japan), then dropped out of the process in late 2014. It was fairly well accepted that Mbabazi was behind the Chinese bid for the refinery,[158] so having signalled his displeasure towards Tullow by awarding of CNOOC's production licence, this move over the refinery was part of Museveni's distinct message to China regarding who runs the country (discussed in detail in Chapter Two).

The Russian consortium was awarded the contract in February 2015, defeating the remaining South Korean option.[159] A leading expert on the oil sector explains that Museveni apparently preferred South Korea due to their stronger potential to scale petro-chemicals out of the refinery, whereas important UPDF players preferred Russia as they offer better military equipment procurement opportunities.[160] Already, in 2011, Museveni purchased six Russian fighter jets for $740 million without permission from Parliament, later admitting the government coffers used would be topped up with future oil revenues.[161] Speaking before the announcement that Russia won the refinery bid, the oil expert says:

> The choice of the lead investor, the politics of it, will show one of two things. One is just how much influence the High Command in the army has in getting a partner that can bring in more things; the second will be how much interest Museveni has in growing a domestic oil industry that is part of his legacy. So within there you have got the real two tensions Museveni is grappling with, one would be the power and one would be the legacy.[162]

Maintenance of power was clearly prioritized. The Russian Consortium winning the refinery is part of Museveni's manoeuvring of the UPDF into Uganda's development plans. The UPDF is a key constituency he needs to keep on-board. The complexity and intrigue over the refinery then continued in subsequent years, however: negotiations with the preferred Russian bidder eventually collapsed; the South Korean consortium was again engaged; and there was then a back and forth between Chinese-led and US-led offers, before eventually, in April 2018, the Albertine Graben Refinery Consortium seemed to sign a definitive agreement and is now building the refinery (mainly a combination of companies from Mauritius and Italy, and the Uganda National Oil Company).[163] This refinery story is an important example for, firstly, emphasizing how Museveni was keen to prioritize the UPDF's preferred choice initially, at the expense of the more development-minded long term legacy enhancing South Korean offer, and secondly, showing the real-life complexity of how major oil contracts are awarded that cannot simply be done on the whim or intention of an individual leader or powerful group within the state – these can only be one amongst many other considerations.

This complex balancing of Museveni's wishes, powerful Ugandan local networks, and the need for development projects has also occurred in other Chinese contracts. Within the wider development agenda, a dual process has emerged where high-level agreements are reached and publicized even as the intensely complex domestic networks clash with local legal procedures, so that the actual logistics of the deal have not been finalized. China Harbour and Engineering Corporation (CHEC) signed an MoU with the Ministry of

Defence to construct a key section of Standard Gauge Railway in 2013. This meant a 2012 MoU between China Civil Engineering Construction Corporation (CCECC) and Ministry of Works for the same section was terminated, despite a July 2014 High Court ruling that this termination was illegal. Museveni negotiated with interested parties whilst MPs tried to block the new CHEC contract and wrote to EXIM Bank requesting they did not release funds, and CCECC tried to recoup costs in court. In October 2014, Museveni officially launched the initiative anyway saying that the contract would be signed and paid for later with oil funds. CHEC was allegedly fronted by Museveni's son-in-law, businessman Odrek Rwabwogo, and backed by 'some powerful people'.[164] They also offered to train UPDF engineers and technicians and remodel Tororo Barracks into a polytechnic, meaning that Museveni preferred that option despite it being $500 million more expensive. A UPDF officer explains:

> Now we have a very special understanding with the China Harbour and Engineering Corporation ... They have agreed to establish a polytechnic, from which we are going to channel quite a number of engineers, trained fully to construct railways. So we are really moving very well in terms of training ... the idea is they work together during the construction with Chinese workers. Then after that we should be able to build a critical mass that can do that kind of work on our own later in future, which is a very good thing.[165]

This domestic infighting put Uganda's SGR project one year behind schedule. The 600 MW Karuma Dam project (requiring UPDF protection of the construction sites outer rim[166]) has faced similar problems, with public arguments and bribery accusations against Chinese companies. Museveni and the Chinese Ambassador got involved to stop embarrassing public spats and to decide which Chinese company got the tender, eventually resulting in the East African Court of Justice case, discussed in Chapter Two. The confusion meant that work began on Karuma without EXIM Bank having fully agreed terms for releasing funds.[167] A government advisor on hydro-power issues explains that EXIM was 'being careful, taking their time, checking every nitty gritty to make sure they will get their money back'[168] (Karuma is set to be commissioned in June 2022).

Museveni has established himself as the solution to Chinese concerns over the implementation of projects. He has proved to the Chinese that he is the player who retains the most leverage over the competing domestic forces. A Chinese embassy official stated after the Karuma incident that 'from now on we deal only with the President'.[169] Museveni's shrinking inner core of loyalists makes his development agenda increasingly difficult to achieve; but thus far he has been able to exert his authority to the extent that China rightly view him as being the essential deciding factor in how projects will be undertaken.

Regional manoeuvres: unravelling the CoW

The lack of centralized planning at the EAC within the oil sector has also allowed Museveni to play politics regionally with the associated infrastructure. Chapter Two explained how Uganda pushed into Kenya's LAPSSET project using Uganda's oil find. As Uhuru Kenyatta became preoccupied with the CoW Northern Corridor initiatives, in 2013 he and Museveni successfully pushed South Sudan into a new export pipeline project involving Uganda, even though a pipeline to Djibouti makes more economic sense to Juba.[170] The security specialist believes that part of Uganda's incentive for intervening in the December 2013 South Sudan crisis was because it 'was an opportunity for Uganda to reposition themselves as a country, to say hey guys, you see, we are the guys who can stand by you', in order to cement South Sudan's links with Uganda and East Africa ahead of their partners in the Horn.[171]

A game of brinkmanship then ensued between regional leaders and the oil companies, as the failure of Uhuru's International Criminal Court (ICC) indictment unleashed a greater possibility of schisms between him and Museveni. In August 2015, Museveni and Uhuru announced that the 'Northern Route' oil pipeline to Lamu would be built. Uhuru addressed the Ugandan Parliament – a rare honour for a foreign Head of State – stressing the regional impact of Uganda's refinery and importance of the CoW Northern Corridor initiative. This was something of a victory for Kenya. The Ugandan pipeline would potentially kick-start Kenya's long dreamed for LAPSSET project and reduce costs of exporting Kenya's own oil finds (thus far somewhat disappointing). Museveni and Uganda's oil therefore carry weight, however. Seeking better terms, Museveni then signed an MoU with Tanzania to build the pipeline to Tanga on the north-eastern Tanzanian coast, reneging on the pronounced Kenya agreement. Nairobi apparently never believed Museveni would shift the route so unexpectedly south: Kenyan officials assumed he was bluffing until the MoU with Tanzania was signed.[172]

Museveni clearly used China's regional presence to suit his own agenda, by linking his interests to different EAC partners in a way that shifted the shared security dynamics between them. Lamu port is preferred by Uhuru, even though the area has serious security challenges. But despite China building berths in Lamu, the CNOOC is the most relaxed Ugandan IOC regarding the pipeline route: the debate between whether to build to Lamu or Tanga was essentially between Tullow and Total interests.[173] Whilst Chinese finance remains essential to the regions development ambitions, Museveni has learnt that Chinese companies are economically focused: there does not seem to be an apparent overarching geo-political strategy for their various interests (logic around national interests would assume that the CNOOC would push harder for the Lamu port due to Chinese presence there).[174] Museveni has thus sought the best terms possible for Uganda. He first muscled in on Kenya's LAPSSET dream, and then risked the dream's failure by pandering to Tanzania.

Likewise, Museveni has used Chinese money and oil revenues to manoeuvre expertly within the regional SGR project. The SGR plan initially began bilaterally in 2008 with talk of developing Kenya–Uganda railways in order to construct a Mombasa-Kampala line. But then in 2011, 'the Chinese and their smart guys, their local players' approached the former Kenya Minister of Transport and offered to do only the Mombasa–Nairobi section, which created tension with Uganda.[175] Museveni then managed to push back in with an agreement that the second phase would link Nairobi to Western Kenya and then through to Kampala, thus creating the flagship project of the China–EAC Framework agreement and entire CoW agenda.

After several years of seemingly steady progress within CoW, at the Northern Corridor Summit in June 2015, Museveni announced reluctance to link SGR to Kigali as was originally agreed and would instead prioritize building to Juba (this was then confirmed in December). Kenya's huge business interests in Rwanda and DRC were undermined by this move, with Tanzania's expressed intention to build a Southern SGR route from the improved Chinese-built Bagamoyo port already threatening Mombasa's dominance. Uganda is extremely mindful that once oil production is ramped up, SGR will capture much of the associated traffic and the Juba route is seen as more economically viable considering Uganda's trade with South Sudan. In a rebuke that had become rare during the CoW era, in August 2015 Kagame had criticized Museveni over prioritizing Juba (especially considering its non-EAC status),[176] and in December was said to be 'deeply disappointed' due to Kigali needing the Kampala route in order to link with Mombasa port.[177]

Museveni's regional politicking around SGR is again draped in Chinese presence. Rwanda failed to get an EXIM Bank loan for their SGR section, as China Civil Engineering Construction Corporation wanted confirmation over the Kampala section before agreeing to build into Rwanda. But an MoU between EXIM and South Sudan did occur to build SGR from Juba to Nimule on Uganda's border. This will also mean there is little economic case to build an additional route from Juba to Kenya, which Nairobi had also hoped for. Uganda explained the Kigali route would only occur once oil revenue flowed (then thought to be around 2020 but subsequently delayed to at least 2022 at the time of writing). Uganda's minister of Works and Transport, John Byabagambi, stated that 'we have interests in oil and we cannot ignore prioritising it. If we get more funds, especially from oil, we will embark on developing all infrastructural projects.'[178]

China is a long way from setting the oil agenda in Uganda and EAC at present, and Museveni's agency has been crucial in utilizing Chinese finance without becoming overawed by their presence. Uganda's refinery will not be built by the Chinese, and the CNOOC's role in constructing and deciding the pipeline route is balanced with two Western IOCs. However, interests and influence in Juba, and capacity for constructing necessary infrastructure, does ultimately make China a key component in calculations of regional actors positioning themselves within EAC. Museveni has utilized this engagement to a far greater extent than any regional leader as a means of playing geo-politics amongst EAC partner states, at a time when mega-project construction dramatically impacts upon important linkages within the EAC. Museveni centralized Ugandan oil into the seemingly progressive CoW grouping whose multi-billion dollar flagship projects relied almost exclusively on the presence of China. He then concentrated on Uganda's interests by shifting SGR to Juba and oil pipeline to Tanga, to the detriment of Rwandan and Kenyan partners. Chinese projects also provide significant opportunity to keep on-board key domestic constituents, notably the UPDF. In regards to oil, therefore, China affects Museveni's role in regional security dynamics directly. The geo-strategic restructuring of EAC through crucial infrastructural development, with associated schisms and jockeying amongst partner states, would not be possible without the emergence of China. Museveni has used that emergence to improve Uganda's regional status and his personal importance in implementing regional projects. Oil's security threat would remain, and the pipeline still likely to be proceeding without China; but the wider agenda – including refinery, SGR, dams and roads – in which Museveni has centralized his importance within regional security dynamics would not have occurred without China's might and muscle.

Conclusion: necessary reactions enabling regional security impacts

Analysing how and why China–Uganda engagement affects Museveni's role in regional security dynamic uncovers how he successfully utilized the 'terrorism' and 'oil' security issues to suit his domestic interests and regional agenda. Museveni's presence – as both spiritual and institutional head of state and commander-in-chief of the army – promotes local insurgent threats domestically and regionally with regard terrorism. Oil is presented in national security terms with considered moves to promote Museveni's survival as being crucial to oil revenues developing Uganda, specifically regarding infrastructure development. Museveni's leadership ensures domestic concerns are the most influential in determining Uganda's regional behaviour. This sees him positioned as a crucially important actor in the increasingly interlinked security dynamics between EAC partner states.

Rather than taking China and Chinese action as a starting point, this chapter (and book) discusses prominent security and development issues within Uganda and East Africa and uncovers China's role within them. This enables a more Africa-centric analysis that uncovers both a strong African agency and more consequential role for the new and increasing Chinese actors. China's impacts upon African security issues do not occur primarily through their UN peacekeeping, anti-piracy efforts or protection of their own citizens, for example. Greater impacts it occurs through China's role in intra-regional geopolitics, complex local security issues, and through the manipulation and behaviour of particular leaders.

China – intentionally or not – contributes to these regional security concerns through various means. China has not entered Uganda as a direct opponent to Museveni's regime, far from it; but as the rising global power of the age with material resources vastly outstripping his own, Chinese presence needs to be understood, engaged with and managed for Museveni to maintain his position. The role of such powers in Uganda and Africa historically is, of course, very well known. Museveni is therefore mindful of China's role and incorporates them into his strategizing moves in order to further his domestic and regional standing. Terrorism and oil have been promoted as security threats in Uganda, and their appearance – along with China's role in each – has aided Museveni's regional agenda. 'Terrorism' has been prevalent in Uganda since 9/11, with a clear shift in usage of the term to describe groups that had been active beforehand. Al-Shabaab has now grown to encompass the most prominent exporter of the concept following the deployment of AMISOM. China's supply of SALW forms a vital component in the role of terrorism, regardless of other supplier's involvement in the industry or the undoubtedly local factors that tie into the proliferation issue. China's historical relationship with Sudan has had far-reaching ramifications in this area, and its domestic ivory market provides income for terror groups. Somewhat ironically, this source of weaponry and income for destabilizing forces may ultimately encourage a more institutionalized security apparatus amongst EAC members as they move to tackle the issue. The challenges that Uganda faces through SALW proliferation have meant that they have engaged regional mechanisms and China on the matter to some extent, but always on Museveni's terms whereby full investigations into domestic roles are prevented and overt reference to China's role not presented. Conversations and pressure around ivory have resulted in some Chinese responses.

Oil, supposedly a major factor in China's African incursions, will shape the development and security trajectory of Uganda and the region over the next thirty years. Museveni has successfully pushed for his tight control and military oversight of the industry. Thus far, the sector exemplifies Uganda's own Global Mix policy and ability to balance different international partners and actors, without over burdensome domination from any. Whilst China's later insertion and seemingly well-structured relationship with government and locals means CNOOC has enjoyed early success in the sector, the Mbabazi fall-out and refinery bidding process reminds China of Museveni's agency. He is well capable of preventing China from obtaining an obviously preeminent position. The oil sector does, however, create both a direct necessity for related procurement contracts, such as the Standard Gauge Railway, as well as significant funds for wider development infrastructure, which China seems uniquely positioned to take advantage of and impact upon. The refinery, pipeline and SGR have obvious regional geo-strategic implications. Museveni's actions mean he is (rightly) considered the most influential domestic force in initiating such projects, and thereby capable of creating China's often preached 'win-win' scenarios. In Uganda, Museveni assumes that the maintenance of his position above all other things is the driver of development. However, his domestic constituency remains complex and problematic, and requires pandering to, which creates problems in projects being delivered.

The continued impossibility of separating Uganda's domestic security concerns from both regional developments within the EAC, and extra-regionally with the Sudan's as well as DRC and Somalia, makes it inevitable that China's bilateral relations effectively become multi-lateral regional engagements. The local, domestic and regional drivers of the future East African security dynamics may remain most important. But China's global position and appearance in each of those lower areas, whether wilful or otherwise, clearly influence the direction that the EAC's security arrangement takes. Indirect involvement in terrorism, through SALW supply feeding into threats, and direct involvement in oil, through concessions and infrastructure funding, both provoke obvious regional benefits to Museveni. Tackling the two most pressing security threats facing East Africa cannot conceivably occur without Museveni taking a prominent position and tangible action. This central role in directing and manipulating regional security dynamics has always been one of Museveni's leading ambitions and would not have been achieved in the way it has been without China's considerable rise.

Conclusion

Museveni as agent of Africa?

'Some people think that being in government for a long time is a bad thing. But the more you stay, the more you learn. I am now an expert in governance.'

President Museveni, April 2012[1]

This book told a story of African agency, specifically within the modern ongoing China–Africa relationship. Uganda was identified as a key regional protagonist worthy of serious investigation, with its President, Yoweri Museveni, shown to be uniquely successful in manipulating China's presence to suit his regional and domestic aspirations. This book contributes to the literature on African agency by showing how President Museveni – having successfully manipulated the West to support his regime historically – now incorporates China into his pursuit and maintenance of power. Museveni's continuation is made more likely through the increasing Chinese investment, hence adding weight to the argument that China's presence aids incumbent African leaders. It also provides a valuable addition to the literature on China–Africa relations regarding the role of China's non-interference principle in its global relations and the regional nature of Chinese engagement, as well as to knowledge around African regional integration generally and East African integration specifically, by highlighting China's role within the security elements of that process to a far greater extent than has been undertaken previously.

The rapid and unprecedented expansion of China–Africa relations since 2000 means that understanding the nature of interactions and their impact on Africa is very much in its infancy, especially regarding peace and security issues. African regional integration, and East African integration in particular, is likewise an ongoing evolving process with uncertain security implications for the region and continent. The role and nature of African Agency within the relationship has also been under researched. In Uganda, President Museveni's prolonged rule amidst a shifting global environment and unstable region provokes uncertainty within a historically volatile country, despite his continuation presenting an illusion of stability. Assessing how these fluctuating areas of interest – China–Africa relations, East African Community (EAC) integration, Uganda's political economy – interlock to provoke security reverberations is an inherently complex task considering the dynamic nature of all three strands. The book's research attempted something of a 'case within a case study' approach to untangling this complexity: it spoke to African agency within China–African relations as a whole by looking at specific security issues within a specific case study country within a specific region. This concluding chapter summarizes key arguments related to Museveni's role in East Africa, and the lessons therein for African agency more broadly and in relation to China's increasing role on the continent. It ends with final reflections and some brief ideas for further research.

Museveni in the region

The case study of Museveni highlights how an African leader has displayed geo-political agency against China and regional neighbours by utilizing the Chinese presence. China has appeared as a potential friend and partner to Uganda, but one unquestionably more powerful and undoubtedly pursuing its own goals and material interests. Museveni's skill and foresight has ensured that China's investment in Uganda has helped maintain his rule domestically, and China–EAC engagement has been utilized by Museveni to push his regional agenda. China's attempted exploitation of East Africa's various opportunities has ultimately seen it become an unwitting accomplice in aiding President Museveni's machinations. China's finance has helped quell emerging resistance to Museveni's rule domestically by offering a valuable partnership as an alternative to nagging Western influence, and against domestic rivals by providing procurement opportunities which keep his patronage networks in order. Museveni has also been able to avoid and deflect unwanted domineering influence from China itself, by actively preventing its involvement in particularly sensitive areas at particular times, such as: the construction of Uganda's oil refinery when their bid was seen to have been backed by a current political rival; servicing of MPs' debt which would have challenged the NRMs own patronage networks; or within inter-elite rivalries by ensuring Uganda's new Chinese partners were left in no doubt that Museveni remained at the helm indefinitely.

Other leaders in East Africa and beyond have also engaged China successful for their own purposes, such as Kenya's Uhuru Kenyatta during his ICC indictment. East Africa is not simply Museveni's playground where he manipulates rivals and global partners at will: African agency is more complex, nuanced and intriguing. Within Uganda and East Africa, China has encountered in Museveni a leader especially capable of shaping his domestic and regional environment to a greater extent than might have been anticipated by material and normative conditions alone. The rise of China shapes a global context in which the Great Power thirsts for resources, markets and allies, and is able to lend billions of dollars to Africa for much-needed projects. China has not penetrated East Africa by aligning itself with Uganda's security interests against other actors. But Museveni as leader has used China in this context to actively and deliberately forge a more coherent regional security and integration agenda, primarily designed to help maintain his domestic position.

The Uganda case study showed that Chinese 'non-interference' engages the forces and institutions collectively shaping and comprising the state-building process under Museveni, by interacting with Parliament, the judiciary, the elite inner circle, etc. These are not sub-state or non-state actors that are often discussed elsewhere, but are the various features collectively discernible as the state itself whose institutional structure is yet to be determined. MPs' interest in Chinese bank loans and the Prime Minister Mbabazi fall-out are highly visible examples of engagement, occurring alongside subtler avenues of influence such as local traders travelling to China or Buganda Kingdom, sourcing their investment. And whereas Ghana's democratic culture was shown to necessitate Chinese deliberations with civil society over hydropower dam construction, in the Ugandan context Chinese investment interacts with the local network of 'fronts' or 'fixers' that have become engrained in the political economy, thereby further cementing their role. Procurement opportunities resulting from Chinese mega-projects provide financial opportunities for these shadow networks and the patronage system on which Museveni's rule increasingly depends.

Structurally, China provides financial and ideological tools that allow astute, discerning leaders the capacity to impact their domestic and regional environment to a very great extent. On the ground, SALW proliferation and oil interests have intense security implications; however, these negative repercussions of China's engagement can increase operating space for leaders who gain from the exacerbation or prevention of particular threats. A global power has emerged well-suited to aiding African leader's ambitions, with regional patterns occurring across the continent.

China–EAC engagement has been utilized by Museveni to centralize his role in an East African region whose future (in)stability will be determined by its ability to tackle the terrorist menace and produce a viable oil sector. Chinese made Small Arms and Light Weapons (SALW) have been used by various terrorist groups across East Africa, who have also benefitted somewhat from selling poached ivory to the large Chinese market. China's role in East Africa and Uganda, therefore, feeds instability which Museveni can then fight against, and prevents over-reliance on Western donors so that their governance concerns remain of peripheral importance. Hence, China's contribution to these security concerns help Museveni to be seen as a key protector of Western government's regional security interests; and shows that there is no automatic contradiction in actively supporting the Global War on Terror whilst maintaining progressive relations with China. At the same time, China's interest in Uganda and East Africa's oil sector has helped fuel an EAC push for infrastructure mega-projects, creating an integration agenda which Museveni has consistently shifted and influenced as a means of centralizing his importance in EAC development plans. So, whilst China has certainly benefitted from its East African incursions and impacted on security dynamics through its action as well as its inaction, it is Museveni who has risen to paramount importance by incorporating that Chinese presence into his agenda.

China's engagement in the EAC provides security challenges and development opportunities that President Museveni has utilized in order to shape regional security dynamics in a way beneficial to his regime's continuation. Similarly, China's support for Sudan's Bashir in the Horn of Africa created serious regional security challenges, at the same time as Ethiopian leaders have utilized Chinese presence to create commendable economic progress amidst such instability. China has not created the security threats related to terrorism and the East African oil sector. But it has exacerbated these issues to some extent, thereby providing Museveni with a means of imprinting his militarized agenda on the region. An East African region searching for development partners has found a China willing and able to engage, which has aided Museveni's manipulations and machinations aimed at centralizing his importance within the EAC institution. Again, comparable efforts occur elsewhere, although Museveni's successes remain slightly unique. In Southern Africa, for example, President dos Santos forged a Chinese partnership substantial enough to make Angola at least potentially challenge South African hegemony.

Lessons for Africa agency

This book uncovered an Africa leader using the global rise of a Great Power for the advancement of his personal and country's strategic importance. Greater East Africa matters to global affairs, and Museveni's presence is felt throughout it and by the global actors whose vested interests he can help deliver or disrupt. Others searching for African agency often note local actors asserting their demands in foreign business deals, or actively seeking opportunities for their betterment (rather than passively accepted what is offered). But this is far more serious and consequential: oil matters, terrorist activity matters, regional stability matters, long-term development agenda's matter, the arms trade matters and China's new role in the world matters, for the major global power interests of the modern world and for the local citizens across East Africa. Museveni plays an active role in each of these areas, to a far greater degree than material expectations would assume.

This book began by arguing that the rise of China is the preeminent geopolitical issue facing contemporary Africa. Its (re)appearance was presented as, simultaneously, a great opportunity for the continents advancement and betterment; but also as a potential destabilizing presence due to its vastly superior material wealth and considering the long history of great power emergence and rivalry having a detrimental impact in Africa. The book has shown how the continent's own efforts at restructuring its security institutions and dynamics are being affected therein. Museveni has utilized China's Great Power interest to shape his environment successfully so as to increase his own regional stature and Uganda's regional capacity. Museveni's machinations have shaped the regional agenda significantly whilst increasing the security linkages between each of the other partner states. He has incorporated China into those regional manoeuvres and increased linkages, thus making Uganda–China relations central to East African security dynamics.

Museveni expanded EAC to include his neighbours Rwanda, Burundi and now South Sudan. The recent appearance of Juba – with its massive Chinese role in the country – means that this intense thorn in the side of Uganda will now also increasingly link to security concerns of other EAC member states. Museveni's significant political role in Kenya – the stronger, richer, sea-facing neighbour and alleged regional hegemon – has seen power-politics being played using Tanzania. Dodoma has been clawed back from a southward drift by being inspired to build their own Standard Gauge Railway project to Rwanda, as Museveni's reluctance to build his SGR from Kampala to Kigali helped to heal Tanzania–Rwanda relations. His shifting of Uganda's oil pipeline route to Tanga on Tanzania's coast reinforced these moves, by again creating further cross-linkages between member states potentially moving apart. Museveni shows, therefore, that Africa is not a passive space where Great Power interests are inevitably fought out and imprinted, or where supposed regional power-houses hold sway over geographically hindered poorer rivals. Museveni has made Uganda – what would still usually be labelled a 'Weak State' by most Western security scholars – integral to the clear, and dynamic, inter-state rivalry and cooperation increasingly prevalent within the EAC.

The role of China

The historical trajectory of global influence in a region is particularly important in shaping current dynamics and the agency found and exerted therein. Chinese non-interference has not always existed in the way now espoused. Support for liberation groups against colonial government can be justified within the current narrative. The active support for insurgent groups against sitting independent African governments in Cameroon, Chad and elsewhere during the 1960s cannot be. This is both a forgotten era within the historical narrative currently promoted by Chinese and African officials, and is not explicitly emphasized in academic literature as the crude violations of non-interference which these interventions clearly are.

Nonetheless, in the contemporary era China's non-interference does remain a hallmark of its engagement with Uganda, East Africa and the continent, and has been a vital component of it gaining traction amongst leaders. Notable low-level contestation against Chinese workers across Africa is not matched by state-elites who have been largely unquestioning about engaging China. The African Union (AU) is institutionally committed to accelerating its political and socio-economic integration of Africa, and is dependent on regional mechanisms to enact its African Peace and Security Architecture (APSA). China offers consistent rhetorical and minor material support for Africa's regional organizations, as well as engaging the more functional ones directly.

But China helps to cement a paradox within the African Union: that despite its continental reach and reliance on regional mechanisms, the AU remains a forum where national sovereignty is heralded as a means of protecting domestic (elite) interests. China engages the AU as a means of gaining bloc continental support for its efforts within and outside Africa. But Beijing's emphasis on pro-sovereignty nation-state engagement (which aids China's global rise) aligns with this practical reality that power currently remains at the national state level in the African context. The championing of APSA and UN frameworks by China has not stopped African unilateral efforts, as indicated by UPDF intervention in South Sudan, for example.

Africa's naturally regional character has, nonetheless, sucked China into a regional pattern of engagement across the continent: each African region has distinct attributes and associated Chinese impacts that are each worthy of further research. Oil *is* centrally important to relations, along with wider natural resource extraction, but China's methodology of engagement is distinct from the West by the scope of its incursions. Yet despite its material power, China is surprisingly limited in what it can achieve within its own logistical and normative non-interference framework. Financial power remains incredibly influential and seductive nonetheless and retains considerably more day-to-day influence and impact than China's military capability. Non-interference has not shifted towards a Western-style engagement pressuring for particular reforms and actions. Instead, subtle but wide-ranging engagement occurs with a variety of actors and forces within African state and nation building processes. This has successfully led China to become somewhat reified by African governments. China is seen as both an assumed *model* of infrastructure-led development transformation and a *supplier* of that desired mega-infrastructure so centrally important to the AU's Agenda 2063. Africa collectively has not engaged China with the careful and considered steps required to create a genuinely African-led, African-form of (sustainable) structural transformation. This will require more than multi-million and multi-billion dollar roads, rail and dams.

Africa lacks a considered, united voice and collective response to China, yet this book has shown that at the individual state level, Museveni has successfully carved out an operational space for himself and Uganda with significant room for manoeuvre. China's engagement in the malleable East African region occurs whilst the EAC institution sees Museveni acting in hegemonic-like ways despite material and geo-political disadvantages. In Africa, the mechanisms by which governments operate and implement agendas remain problematic and undefined; African leaders, therefore, have a great opportunity to stamp their personality onto the state and regional formation processes currently underway. A leader's operating space in well-defined nations and regions with a structured institutional environment is actually more limited.

China's impact on African regional security dynamics and integration does not occur primarily through their direct interactions with the regional organizations themselves. Instead, it occurs by them providing a structural context and low-level security issues in which bilateral relationships unfold between African states. The EAC case study suggests the possibility of polarity shifts or tensions occurring if particular leaders exploit that context, as might also occur in Southern Africa, the Horn and elsewhere over time. Museveni has utilized China as a means of gaining increased influence over East African states jockeying for position. He has incorporated, adjusted and rejected Chinese efforts as a means of furthering his own goals.

Final reflections and further research

There are three key aspects to reflect on regarding Museveni's agency in relation to this work which is relevant to African agency more broadly (along with an acknowledgement that the books findings can, of course, be challenged or improved). First, it is **strong and powerful**. Regardless of your thoughts and assessment as to the nature of his regime, Museveni provides an example to Africa of how China can be managed and resisted even as they attempt to gain a dominant position, as per his previous success in courting and defying Western donors. Museveni also shows how the appearance of China can lessen Africa's reliance on those traditional Western partners without requiring any distinct break from them (unlike how Zimbabwe's Mugabe acted when he turned East whilst relations with the West were entirely severed, for example).

Developments in EAC have been unequivocally influenced by Museveni's manipulation of China's engagement to improve his own domestic and regional position. Combatting terrorism has increased regional security cooperation in a way which suits Museveni, by centralizing his importance in efforts whilst never risking his domestic position. He has also utilized the geo-political shifts related to oil finds and associated infrastructure more successfully than any other leader in the region. East African states are undertaking the most ambitious of all regional projects by aspiring towards political federation. He is not the only leader to have shaped dynamics, of course, but the influence that Museveni has successfully carved for himself is exceptional. China found him to be a master tactician capable of utilizing China as a ready means of influencing a regional environment yet to be fully negotiated and stabilized. This highlights how lack of collective agency from Africa against China is due to lack of political strategy, rather than lack of capacity.

Secondly, despite that impressive strength, this agency is **limited**. Museveni is not able to bend regional security dynamics and relations with China to his will; and he is not the only leader exercising agency within this regional and geopolitical context. Museveni's continued importance was evident when EAC partners chose him to speak to Burundi's Nkurunziza over the 2015 election crisis, for example, but that intervention proved largely meaningless: Nkurunziza ignored whatever message Museveni relayed (if he had one) and did not change course of action. President Magufuli (now deceased following the COVID-19 pandemic) replaced Kikwete in Tanzania in 2015 and became a more forceful regional actor who revisited and re-imagined several large regional projects that China was involved in. And Kenya remains a regional economic powerhouse whose President will always hold a degree of regional influence. None of these actors, and others, can be ignored or assumed to be Museveni's underlings.

Museveni has also been limited in his achievements. His longevity has been made possible by him being tactically brilliant in his politicking domestically, regionally and in international relations. But strategically he appears less successful. Uganda is most certainly not discussed as a possible African developmental state model in the way that Rwanda and Ethiopia are, for example – he has been unable to structurally alter its economy towards transformative economic development. The Ugandan oil sector and associated infrastructure continues to be extremely problematic, and there is a very real chance its overall impacts will be disappointing at best and chaos-inducing at worst. And Museveni's ambition to federate and lead a united East Africa remains a far-off proposition. This book focused on a distinct period of history where regional progress seemed to be suddenly pushing forward at rapid speed with Museveni at the forefront, a snapshot in time where Uganda's regional status increased and Museveni's regional ambitions were potentially in grasp. The excitement and intrigue around the Coalition of the Willing during the period of interest for this work, however, has quickly unravelled. Just a few years after their supposed rapprochement, for example, there was talk of Rwanda and Uganda going to war after accusations of internal meddling and border closures,[2] and the SGR project is already being labelled another 'lunatic express' within academia.[3] Museveni's overriding interest in maintaining power in Uganda has often had to prioritize short-term gains over long-term ambitions. There must surely be a strong case for arguing if he left office then a united East Africa might become more realizable, for example. But Museveni (and other regional leaders) are far more influential in shaping regional dynamics than is often assumed. In Uganda (and elsewhere), Museveni's eventual departure will have profound implications for regional and global relations in East Africa.

This China–Ugandan relationship is an ongoing negotiation and conversation the outcome of which is uncertain. Museveni has thus far employed his Global Mix successfully since taking power, and resisting Chinese undue influence mirrors his efforts to deflect Western pressure. Museveni's originally espoused Pan-Africanism has been exposed as being secondary to his maintenance of domestic power – only to be supplanted by a federated East Africa that would maintain his substantial influence. Other actors in Uganda's political economy clearly remain influential and will potentially become the pockets of power that unseat Museveni by some means. Chinese state-to-state deals are well-suited to the UPDF becoming involved in construction projects, due to (lack of) auditing requirements and UPDF capacity building add-ons within bids. A role for the UPDF in constructing and planning the development of Uganda is a growing part of Museveni's agenda, and maintaining UPDF support will remain a necessary component of his rule, as it would be for any challenger. The next leader of Uganda must have the support of the army; therefore, China's engagement with that constituency may increasingly define their relationship with the country.

Thirdly, Museveni's agency is **timebound**. China–Africa relations are occurring in real time, in a rapidly changing environment. The genuine impact of China in Africa, which this book helps to expose, will not be known for many years and decades. The book took the reader up to a particular point in the story – the end of 2015 and FOCAC VI – by which time a fifteen-year exponential rate of expansion seemed to be normalizing somewhat. A new structural environment has been created within which events now unfurl. The first instalments of the multi-billion dollar loans are now being demanded, for example, which is changing dynamics dramatically. As will sometime in or after 2022 in Uganda, when the consequences of oil finally flowing creates visible consequences, and the genius or futility of the SGR project begins to be known.

The findings of this book are therefore also time-dependent, as is the nature of Museveni's agency. This work provided a detailed snapshot example of the nature of Museveni's power and influence against China and regional partners within a moment of history regarding particular issues and projects. This does not mean that Museveni has enjoyed and continues to enjoy the same degree of agency across all time, space and issues worthy of study. In addition to the above points about the changing nature of China–Africa engagement and Uganda becoming an oil producer, already the 2020 COVID-19 pandemic has disrupted global geo-politics, China–Africa relations and the Ugandan political economy tremendously.[4] As the climate change and anti-fossil fuels agenda becomes increasingly urgent and prominent, protests against the Uganda–East African oil pipeline are also becoming more vocal and active.[5] And the local hip-hop star turned MP Bobi Wine – who was not any person of note *at all* during the time focus of this book's research – has become the main political threat to Museveni and already has a more prominent international profile than any previous opposition figure in Uganda.[6]

Yet Museveni's longevity remains a defining feature of his NRM regime. He appears in relatively good health and is seventy-seven at the time of writing (Paul Biya of Cameroon is eighty-nine after thirty-nine years of his continuing rule; a frail Mugabe was ninety-three when he was overthrown). Despite many of Museveni's strategic goals being unfulfilled, as noted above, he has adapted himself and shifted tactical plays across various historical eras. Key players within the oil pipeline construction remain on board; Uganda's stringent COVID lockdowns will have further strengthened the control of Museveni's nation state over people's lives, and Bobi Wine's first election challenge in 2021 was very easily swept aside. Thus far, the shifting domestic, regional and international political situations have been exploited by Museveni for his own benefit and do not significantly challenge any of the main conclusions offered here, although precise long-term consequences are not presently determinable. China, however, will remain important to future events. Even before COVID-19 and the emergence of 'Vaccine Diplomacy' that will shape subsequent years, it was clear that China has become an engrained player. FOCAC VI, hosted in Johannesburg, had surprised many observers who had predicted there would be a levelling off or diminishing amount of Chinese money available due to the countries 2015 economic downturn: a record $60 billion was pledged from Xi Jinping to help Africa's industrialization drive. It was also proposed to increase trade levels from $220 billion in 2014 to $400 billion in 2020.[7]

A limitation of the work is that this research was focused primarily on agency occurring at the elite-level within China–Africa relations and the security dynamics between nation-states within the EAC. This therefore focused interest on political leaders such as Museveni. Research still focusing on China's impact on East Africa and Uganda but more interested in human security issues, however, could easily investigate lower-level micro relations taking place and the insecurities felt therein by individuals. Focusing on Bunyoro Kingdom's relationship with the CNOOC and position within Uganda, a worker in Kampala's position within a Chinese company, or the Ugandan house-wife living with her Chinese husband, etc., would identify agency very different from that discussed here.

There is also a risk that this book's findings are biased towards its Ugandan focal point. A similar analysis of Tanzania–China relations within the EAC (or any other partner state), would, perhaps, challenge some of the conclusions drawn here. However, the Ugandan case study was chosen for carefully considered reasons. The findings follow rigorous interrogation of the data derived, and it is highly likely this alternative analysis would, in fact, uncover a central role for Museveni within dynamics and thus corroborate these conclusions. Equally welcome would be a similar-style analysis of any and all African regions, to map continental patterns and contradictions to a greater extent than the time-limits to this work allowed.

In East Africa, having towered over domestic and regional security for so long, Museveni's eventual departure will have a serious impact (for good or bad) on the unfurling dynamic and China's role within it. Whether China identified Uganda as a key regional partner initially is unclear; but Museveni has now positioned himself as crucial to any regional objectives that China may have. It will, therefore, be another serious African challenge for Beijing to react to when any power-transition in Uganda takes place – as it will be for any and all Ugandans and East Africans.

Notes

Introduction

1 Ugandan president tells Chinese construction boss: 'If you are not willing to co-operate, leave', Global Construction Review, 15 October 2014, available at https://www.globalconstructionreview.com/news/ugandan-pre3side8nt-tel0ls-chine6se-constr5uct2ion (accessed 20 April 2020).

2 FACTBOX-Quotes from Uganda's Museveni, Reuters, available at https://www.reuters.com/article/uganda-museveni-quotes-idUKL2207523720080722 (accessed 21 June 2020).

3 Mohan, Giles and Lampert, Ben (2012) Negotiating China: Reinserting African Agency into China–Africa Relations, African Affairs, 112: 446, pp.92–110; Corkin, Lucy (2013) Uncovering African Agency: Angola's Management of China's Credit Lines (Surrey: Ashgate).

4 Ayangafac, Chrysantus and Cilliers, Jakkie (2011) African Solutions to African Problems, in Crocker, Chester A., Hamson, Fen Osler and Aall, Pamela (eds.) (2011) Rewiring Regional Security in a Fragmented World (Washington DC: US Institute of Peace), p.127.

5 Taylor, Ian (2011) The Forum on China-Africa Cooperation (FOCAC) (London: Routledge), p.91.

6 Cáceres, Sigfrido Burgos and Ear, Sophal (2013) The Hungry Dragon: How China's Quest for Resources is Reshaping the World (Oxon: Routledge), p.60.

7 Taylor, Ian (2006) China and Africa: Engagement and compromise (Oxford: Routledge), p.205.

8 de Oliveira, Ricardo Soares (2008) Making Sense of Chinese Oil Investment in Africa, in Alden, Christopher, Large, Daniel and Soares de Oliveira, Ricardo (eds.) (2008) China Returns to Africa: A Rising Power and a Continent Embrace (New York: Columbia University Press), p.109, referring to Gary, Ian and Karl, Terry Lynn (2003) Bottom of the Barrel: Africa's Oil Boom and the Poor (Baltimore: Catholic Relief Services).

9 Carmody, Pádraig and Taylor, Ian (2010) Flexigemony and Force in China's Resource Diplomacy in Africa: Sudan and Zambia Compared, Geopolitics, 15:3, pp.496–515, p.499; Zaremba, By Haley (2020) China Is Rapidly Expanding Its Oil

Resources In Africa, oilprice.com, available at https://oilprice.com/Energy/ Crude-Oil/China-Is-Rapidly-Expanding-Its-Oil-Resources-In-Africa.html (accessed 10 January 2021).

10 Press Release – New Measures on Way for China-Africa Cooperation, Press & Public Affairs Section Embassy of the People's Republic of China in the Republic of South Africa, 26 November 2015.

11 Falling oil prices: Who are the winners and losers?, BBC News, 19 January 2015; Djoumessi, Didier T. (2009) The Political Impacts of the Sino-US Oil Competition in Africa (London: Adonis & Abbey), p.18.

12 Brautigam, Deborah and Xiaoyang, Tang (2011) African Shenzhen: China's Special Economic Zones in Africa, Journal of Modern African Studies, 49/1, p.49.

13 Wade, Abdoulaye (2009), quoted in Brautigam, Deborah (2009) The Dragon's Gift: The Real Story of China in Africa, (Oxford University Press), p.135.

14 Discussed in detail by various panellists at FOCAC VI side-event on China– Africa's maturing relationship, December 2015.

15 The African Standby Force is comprised the East African Standby Force (EASF); ECOWAS Standby Force (ESF); North African Regional Capability (NARC); SADC Standby Force (SSF); and Economic Community of Central African States Standby Force (FOMAC).

16 APSA 2010 Assessment Study, p.19, para. 48; Constitutive Act of the African Union, Article 3.l.

17 Ayangafac and Cilliers (2011), p.142.

18 Lemarchand, Rene (2000) The Crisis in the Great Lakes, in Harbeson, John and Rothchild, Donald (eds.) Africa in World Politics, (Boulder: West View Press), pp.327–31.

19 UNECA (2012).

20 Cohen, Herman J. (2012) Rwanda: Fifty Years of Ethnic Conflict on Steroids, American Foreign Policy Interests: The Journal of the National Committee on American Foreign Policy, 34:2, p.86.

21 Chau, Donovan C (2012) Historical island in a political volcano, African Security Review, 21:1, p.4.

22 Walsh, Barney (2015) Human Security in East Africa: The EAC's illusive quest for inclusive citizenship, Strategic Review for Southern Africa, 37: 1), pp.88–9.

23 Walsh (2015) p.87.

24 'America plots to counter China in EAC with new pact', Business Daily (Nairobi), 20 May 2012; 'China, EAC in new $500m trade, investment deal', East African, 27 November 2011.

25 Uganda Trade Summary Data, World Integrated Trade System, https://wits. worldbank.org/CountryProfile/en/Country/UGA/Year/2018/Summary ;

Gatehouse, Gabriel (2012) Uganda feels China's African involvement, BBC News, 7 August 2012.

26 India and People's Republic of China, 29 April 1954, No. 4307 of UN Treaty Series, Vol. 299.

27 Cable from the Chinese Foreign Ministry, 'Draft Proposal to Strengthen and Develop Friendly Relations with Asian-African Countries after the Asian-African Conference', 12 July 1955, History and Public Policy Program Digital Archive, PRC FMA 107-00065-01, 1-7.

28 Shinn, David and Eisenman, Joshua (2012) China and Africa (University of Pennsylvania Press), pp.34-9; 'Memorandum of the First Conversation between Premier Zhou Enlai and Vice Premier Ri Ju-yeon', 10 November 1965, History and Public Policy Program Digital Archive, PRC FMA 106-01476-05, 41-69.

29 Shinn and Eisenman (2012), pp.39-43.

30 Power, Marcus and Mohan, Giles (2010) Towards a Critical Geopolitics of China's Engagement with African Development, Geopolitics, 15:3, p.475.

31 Odgaard, Liselotte (2013) Peaceful Coexistence Strategy and China's Diplomatic Power, The Chinese Journal of International Politics, 6, p.235; Xiaoyu (2012), pp.364-5; Buzan, Barry (2010) China in International Society: Is 'Peaceful Rise' Possible?, The Chinese Journal of International Politics, 3, p14.

32 China–Africa trade surpassed $200 billion in 2013, East African, 20 February 2014.

33 Cáceres, Sigfrido Burgos and Ear, Sophal (2012) The Geopolitics of China's Global Resources Quest, Geopolitics, 17:1, p.62; see also Tralac (2013b) Africa-China trading relationship, China-Africa Trade Data, 14 April 2013; Africa and China: More than minerals, The Economist, 23 March 2013.

34 Professor Giles Mohan, China–Africa expert, speaking at FOCAC VI side-event on China–Africa's maturing relationship, December 2015.

35 Ezeanya, Chika (2012) Tragedy of the new AU headquarters, Pambazuka News, Issue 567; Mariam, Alemayehu G. (2012) Ethiopia: African Beggars Union Hall? Nazret.com, 2 June 2012.

36 Murithi, Tim (2009b) The African Union's Transition from Non-intervention to Non-Indifference: An Ad-hoc Approach to The Responsibility to Protect?; Constitutive Act of the African Union, Article 4.

37 Alden, Christopher (2007) China in Africa, (London: Zed Books).

38 Walsh, Barney (2019) China's pervasive yet forgotten regional security role in Africa, Journal of Contemporary China, 28: 120, pp.965-83.

39 Lee, Henry and Shalmon, Dan (2008) Searching for Oil: China's Oil Strategies in Africa, in Rotberg, Robert (Ed.) (2008) China into Africa: Trade, Aid, and Influence (Washington, D.C.: Brookings Institution Press), p.109.

40 Seyoum, Mebratu and Lin, Jihong (2014) Private Chinese Investment in Ethiopia: Determinants and Location Decisions, Journal of International Development, July 2014.

41 China's oil fears over South Sudan fighting, BBC News, 8 January 2014.

42 Williamson, Rachel (2014) Briefing: Somaliland, Oil and Security, IRIN News, 7 August 2014; Lanteigne, Marc (2013) Fire over water: China's strategic engagement of Somalia and the Gulf of Aden crisis, The Pacific Review, 26:3, pp.289–312.

43 China negotiating Horn of Africa military base: Djibouti president, Times Live (Johannesburg), 9 May 2015.

44 Shinn and Eisenman (2012), pp.290–306.

45 IMF Trade Data; Economist Intelligence Unit, 'Congo (Democratic Republic)', 11 June 2013, both referred to in Arieff, Alexis (2014) Democratic Republic of Congo: Background and U.S. Policy, Congressional Research Service, 24 February, p.13.

46 Wikileaks cable 07KINSHASA1344, PRESIDENT KABILA DELIVERS UPBEAT 'STATE OF THE NATION' ADDRESS, Democratic Republic of the Congo Kinshasa, 7 December 2007, https://wikileaks.org/cable/2007 December 2007KINSHASA1344.html.

47 Chakrabarty, Malancha (2015) Growth of Chinese trade and investment flows in DR Congo – blessing or curse?, Review of African Political Economy, DOI:10.1080 /03056244.2015.1048794, pp.8–9.

48 New twists in DR Congo's Inga 3 Dam saga, Pambazuka News, 13 March 2014.

49 Former Chinese Ambassador, Interview with author, Pretoria South Africa, December 2015; Former South African Ambassador, interview with author, Pretoria South Africa, December 2015.

50 Taylor (2014), pp.350–1.

51 Adebajo (2012), p.7.

52 Shinn and Eisenman (2012), pp.331–3; Fraser (2013) Zimbabwe is booming – but its future lies in Chinese hands, The Daily Telegraph, 1 August 2013; Carmody (2010), p.27.

53 Power, Mohan, and Tan-Mullins (2012), pp.269–70; Carmody and Taylor (2010), pp.505–7.

54 Vines et al. (2009), referenced in Power, Mohan, and Tan-Mullins (2012), pp.168–9.

55 Shinn and Eisenman (2012), pp.301–5.

56 Sanusi, Lamido (2013) Africa must get real about Chinese ties, The Financial Times, 11 March 2013.

57 Gbemisola Animasawun, Special Assistant in Ogun State 2007–11, Lagos local market expert, interview with author, Arusha Tanzania, January 2015.

58 Brennan, Hugo (2013) North Africa: Are the Chinese Next On Al-Qaeda in the Islamic Maghreb's Hit List?, AllAfrica, 17 December 2013; Peter, Melkunaite, Laura (2013) Research Note on the Energy Infrastructure Attack Database (EIAD), Perspectives on Terrorism, 7: 6.

59 Shinn and Eisenman (2012), pp.238–40.

60 Founder of Chinese NGO, interview with author (online), December 2015.

61 Alden, Christopher (2014) Seeking security in Africa: China's evolving approach to the African Peace and Security Architecture, NOREF, March.

62 Address by H.E. Xi Jinping at opening of FOCAC VI, 4 December 2015.

63 Alden (2014); Saferworld (2011), pp.57–9; Van Hoeymissen, Sara (2010) China's Support to Africa's Regional Security Architecture: Helping Africa to Settle Conflicts and Keep the Peace, The China Monitor Issue 49, March 2010, pp.10–15.

64 Exclusive: U.S. to spend up to $550 million on African rapid response forces, Reuters, 6 August 2014; Fabricius, Peter (2014) The elephant in the room, African Security Review, 23:4, p.415.

65 China signs deal with AU to connect Africa's big cities, Africa Report, 28 January 2015; Agenda 2063, p.5.

66 Taylor (2015), p.26.

67 Grobler, John (2014) Chinese infrastructure lubricates outflow of Angolan and DRC resources, Pambazuka News, Issue 673, 10 April 2014; see also Reopening of Benguela Railway Brings Economic Hope to Angola, The National Law Review, 29 January 2015.

68 Grobler (2014). The CIF and its front Sam Pa broker most of the larger deals in Angola. Despite denials from Beijing and Sam Pa's arrest on corruption charges in October 2015, Pa has been well connected to certain Chinese government elites. See: Sam Pa: The fall of China's trailblazer in Africa, The Independent (London), 24/10/15; Maily, J. R. (2015) The Anatomy of the Resource Curse: Predatory Investment in Africa's Extractive Industries, Africa Center for Strategic Studies Special Report No. 3, May 2015).

69 Litovsky, Alejandro (2014) Renegotiating the colonial-era treaty that gave Egypt a veto over any upstream Nile project is critical, Independent, 28 July 2014.

70 A dam nuisance, The Economist, 20 April 2011.

71 Sally Keeble, UK MP, International Development Minister, 2002–3 (4 June 2007), quoted in Gallagher (2011), p.2303; see also Collier, Paul (2007) The Bottom Billion (Oxford University Press), pp.86–7.

72 Centre for Chinese Studies, Stellenbosch University (2007) China's Engagement of Africa: Preliminary Scoping of African case studies: Angola, Ethiopia, Gabon, Uganda, South Africa, Zambia; Alden, Christopher (2007) China in Africa, (London: Zed Books); Taylor (2006).

73 Chan, Stephen (2013b) Afterword: The Future of China and Africa, in Chan, Stephen (ed.) (2013) The Morality of China in Africa: The Middle Kingdom and the Dark Continent (London: Zed Books), p.141.

74 See Deborah Brautigam's blog, who lists various research ideas, all of which are distinctly micro-level focused: http://www.chinaafricarealstory.com/p/research-topics.html; see Mohan, Giles and Lampert, Ben (2012) Negotiating China: Reinserting African Agency into China–Africa Relations, African Affairs, 112: 446, pp.3–4 for an appeal for micro-, non-state elite studies.

75 A'Zami, Darius (2015) 'China in Africa': From Under-researched to Under-theorised?, Millennium – Journal of International Studies, 43:2, pp.724–34.

76 Bodomo, Adams (2015) Africans in China: Guangzhou and Beyond – Issues and Reviews, The Journal of Pan African Studies, 7: 10, pp.1–9. This is the introduction of a Special Edition of articles dedicated to the African diaspora in China.

77 Mohan, Giles (2012) China in Africa: Impacts and prospects for accountable development, ESID Working Paper No. 12, p.4; see also Mohan and Lampert (2012), pp.92–110.

78 Tisdell, Clem (2008) Thirty Years of Economic Reform and Openness in China: Retrospect and Prospect, Economic Theory, Applications and Issues, Working Paper No. 51, University of Queensland.

1 China–Uganda relations and the regional imperative

1 Ugandan Opposition MP, interview with author, Kampala Uganda, August 2014.

2 Kannyo, Edward (2013) Sino-Ugandan Relations: Themes and Issues, in Adem, Seifudein (ed) (2013) China's Diplomacy in Eastern and Southern Africa (Farnham: Ashgate), pp.107–26, p.110.

3 Shinn, David and Eisenman, Joshua (2012) China and Africa (University of Pennsylvania Press), pp.263–4.

4 Tatum, Dale C. (2002) Who Influenced Whom? Lessons from the Cold War (Maryland: University Press of America).

5 Madina et al. (2010) Impact of China-Africa Aid Relations: A Case Study of Uganda, Economic Policy Research Centre (EPRC), Final Report submitted to the African Economic Research Consortium (AERC) May, 2010; 20 years of explosive growth in China's trade ties with Kampala, East African, 30 January 2014.

6 Kizza Besigye, former leader of FDC, FDC Presidential candidate, interview with author, Kampala Uganda, July 2014.

7 Kalinaki, Daniel (2015) Kizza Besigye and Uganda's Unfinished Revolution (Kampala: DominanetSeven), p.81.

8 Kizza Besigye, interview.

9 Schlichte, Klaus (2008) Uganda, Or: The Internationalisation of Rule, Civil Wars, 10: 4, pp.369–83.

10 Mutengesa, Sabiiti and Hendrickson, Dylan (2008) State Responsiveness to Public Security Needs: The Politics of Security Decision, Making Uganda Country Study and CSDG Papers, Number 16, p.70.

11 Keating, Michael F. (2011) Can democratization undermine democracy? Economic and political reform in Uganda, Democratization, 18:2, p.430.

12 Mwenda, Andrew and Tangri, Roger (2008) Elite Corruption and Politics in Uganda, Commonwealth & Comparative Politics, 4:2, pp.177–94.

13 Kayunga, Sallie Simba (2005) Deepening Political Integration of the EAC Countries: The Uganda Case, in Mohiddin, Ahmed (ed.) (2005) Deepening Regional Integration of the East African Community (Addis Ababa: DPMF), p.203.

14 Kagoro, Jude (2013) The Military Ethos in the Politics of Post-1986 Uganda, Social Sciences Directory, 2: 2, pp.31–46.

15 Museveni (2007), quoted in Brautigam (2009), p.25.

16 Conroy-Krutz, J., and Logan, C. (2012) Museveni and the 2011 Ugandan election: Did the money matter? The Journal of Modern African Studies, 50:4, pp.625–55. doi:10.1017/S0022278X12000377; Chaotic 'walk-to-work' protests put Kampala in spotlight, IRIN News, 29 April 2011.

17 Museveni quoted in Drama at State House, Observer, 28 November 2014.

18 Rukandema, Mwita (2012) Uganda: Reflections of a Passing Generation (Fountain: Kampala), p.134; Tripp, Aili Mari (2010) Museveni's Uganda: Paradoxes of Power in a Hybrid Regime, (Boulder: Lynne Reinner).

19 Izama, Angelo and Wilkerson, Michael (2011) Uganda: Museveni's Triumph and Weakness, Journal of Democracy, 22: 3, p.64.

20 Conroy-Krutz and Logan (2012), p.626; see also de Kock and Sturman (2012), p.15.

21 Private Secretary in State House Uganda, interview with author, Kampala Uganda, September 2014.

22 How the US Can Help Kenya, Heritage Foundation Report, 25 March 2088, p.8.

23 Economist Intelligence Unit (1998) Country Report: Uganda, Rwanda, Burundi, 1st quarter 1998, p.8.

24 I will leave power after East Africa is united – Museveni, Daily Monitor, 10 February 2016.

25 FDC MP, Leader of Opposition in Parliament, interview with author, Kampala Uganda, August 2014.

26 Ugandan journalist and EAC expert, interview with author, Kampala Uganda, September 2014; NRM 'rebel' MP, interview with author, Kampala Uganda, August 2014.

27 Obwona et al. (2007), p.1; for general history also see Sino-Ugandan Relations, Chinese Embassy in Uganda, available at http://ug.china-embassy.org/eng/zwgx/t168251.htm, accessed 28 February 2014.

28 Allen, Kenneth W. and Baguma, Eva (2013) China-Uganda Relations: Closer is Not Necessarily Better, China Brief, Volume XIII, Issue 1, 4 January, 2013.

29 Ugandan journalist, consultant and oil expert, interview with author, Kampala Uganda, September 2014.

30 Western Defence attaché working in Uganda, interview with author, Kampala Uganda, July 2014.

31 Ugandan journalist/consultant/oil expert, interview.

32 Ugandan security expert, NRM MP, interview with author, Kampala Uganda August 2014.

33 Ibid.

34 Fisher, Jonathan (2013) Structure, agency and Africa in the international system: donor diplomacy and regional security policy in East Africa since the 1990s, Conflict, Security & Development, 13: 5, pp.537–67.

35 Source within a Western donor organization, interview with author, August 2014.

36 From the China Aid Data project, see http://china.aiddata.org/projects?utf8=%E2%9C%93&search=&country_name%5B%5D=Uganda; see also Onyango-Obbo (2013a); Sserunjogi (2013).

37 Henry Oryem Okello, Uganda Minister of State for Foreign Affairs, interview with author, Kampala Uganda, September 2014.

38 Zhang Ho, Managing Director of Zhang's Group and Chairman of the Uganda Overseas China Association, interview with author, Kampala Uganda, August 2014.

39 Uganda faces tough choices as donors cut aid, East African, 8 March 2014; see also World Bank postpones Uganda loan over anti-gay law, The Guardian, 28 February 2014.

40 Managing Director China Jiangxi International Ltd Uganda (CJIC), Interview with author, August 2014; Zhang Ho, interview.

41 Western Defence attaché, interview.

42 Western Defence attaché, interview.

43 Ugandan security expert/NRM MP, interview.

44 Museveni (2013), quoted in Museveni says China better trade partner, Daily Monitor, 22 November 2013.

45 Note at the time of writing the author could not discern who attended FOCAC V, but it was not Museveni.

46 Ugandan journalist/EAC expert, interview.

47 Fang Min, owner for the Fang Fang Group, interview with author, July 2014; see http://www.fangfang.co.ug/newsite.

48 Museveni comments overshadow London summit, East African, 1 November 2014.

49 From the China Aid Data project, see http://china.aiddata.org/projects?utf8=%E2%9C%93&search=&country_name%5B%5D=Uganda; Sserunjogi (2013).

50 Bank of Uganda – Statistics, at https://www.bou.or.ug/bou/rates_statistics/statistics.html ; see also Tralac (2013b) for information on top 20 exports-imports; China-Uganda bilateral trade posts 35 per cent growth, Daily Monitor, 20 April 2013.

51 20 years of explosive growth in China's trade ties with Kampala, East African, 30 January 2014.

52 Zhang Ho, interview; see http://www.hisense.ug.

53 Parliament okays $1.435 billion loan for Karuma, Daily Monitor, 25 March 2015; Biryabarema, Elias, Uganda says Chinese firm applies to build $1.4 bln power plant on the Nile, Reuters.com. 11 February 2020.

54 Chinese consortium to revive Uganda's once-vital copper mines, China-Africa Reporting Project, 9 May 2014.

55 Flavia Kabahandra, NRM MP, Chairperson of Parliamentary Committee on Tourism, Trade, and Industry, interview with author, August 2014.

56 Chinese entrepreneur, interview with author (online), December 2015.

57 Chinese Researcher in the Natural Resources Group at International Institute for Environment and Development (IIED), Interview with author, December 2015.

58 Consultant arranging tenders for private Chinese businesses and monitoring contracts, interview with author, September 2014.

59 Chinese business person and ex-Secretary General of Uganda Overseas China Association, interview with author, Kampala Uganda, August 2014.

60 Uganda Ministry of Finance spokesperson, interview with author, Kampala Uganda, July 2014.

61 Chinese business person/ex-Secretary General of Ugandan Overseas China Association, interview.

62 Anonymous Chinese businessman, interview with author, Arusha Tanzania, December 2015.

63 Chinese Researcher, interview.

64 Hydro-power Engineer and Ugandan government advisor, Interview with author, Kampala Uganda, August 2014.

65 Major General (Retired) Mugisha Muntu, President of FDC, ex-Commander of the UPDF, interview with author, September 2014.

66 Mugisha Muntu, interview.

67 Walsh, Barney (2020) Revisiting Regional Security Complex Theory in Africa: Museveni's Uganda and Regional Security in East Africa, African Security, pp.300–24, pp.306–7.

68 Daily Monitor reporter on Oil and Gas, interview with author, August 2014.

69 Mbabazi, Amama (2013) How China can propel Uganda's economic development, Daily Monitor, OpEd, 20 September 2013.

70 Chair of the Parliamentary Committee on Foreign Affairs, interview with author, Kampala Uganda, August 2014.

71 Mbabazi versus Museveni, Daily Monitor, 20 December 2013.

72 Prominent Ugandan journalist and editor, interview with author, Kampala Uganda, July 2014.

73 Ibid.

74 FDC shadow Minister for Water and Environment, interview with author, Kampala Uganda, September 2014.

75 Obore, Chris (2014) NRM delegates fooled as both Mbabazi and Museveni win, Daily Monitor, 21 December 2014.

76 Museveni distrusts Beijing and woos Seoul, Africa Intelligence, Uganda: Politics and Power Brokers, N°1413, 23 October 2015.

77 UPDF Lieutenant Colonel 1, interview with author, Kampala Uganda, July 2014.

78 UPDF Brigadier, interview with author, Kampala Uganda, August 2014.

79 Parliamentary Chair on Foreign Affairs, interview.

80 Henry Oryem Okello, interview.

81 Fred Opolot, spokesperson Uganda Ministry of Foreign Affairs, interview with author, August 2014.

82 National Vice Chairman of Youth League of NRM Kampala region, interview with author, Kampala Uganda, August 2014.

83 Ibid.

84 National Youth Chairman of NRM, interview with author, Kampala Uganda, September 2014.

85 Parliamentary Chair on Foreign Affairs, interview.

86 Joshua Rubongoya, Professor at Roanoke College Virginia, author of Regime Hegemony in Museveni's Uganda, interview with author, Kampala Uganda, September 2014.

87 Hickey, Sam, Badru Bukenya, Angelo Izama and William Kizito (2015) The political settlement and oil in Uganda, ESID Working Paper No. 48, March 2015.

88 Jowell, Marco (2014) Peacekeeping Country Profile: Uganda, Providing for Peacekeeping, February 2014, available at http://www.providingforpeacekeeping.org/2014/04/03/country-profile-uganda, accessed 13 May 2015; Shinn, David (2008) Military and Security Relations: China, Africa, and the Rest of the World, in Rotberg, Robert (Ed.) (2008) China into Africa: Trade, Aid, and Influence (Washington, D.C.: Brookings Institution Press), pp.155–96.

89 UPDF Lieutenant Colonel 1, interview.

90 UPDF Lieutenant Colonel 2, interview with author, Kampala Uganda, September 2014.

91 UPDF Colonel, Chief Political Commissar UPDF, interview with author, Kampala Uganda, August 2014.

92 UPDF Brigadier, interview.

93 Walsh, Barney (2015) Human Security in East Africa: The EAC's illusive quest for inclusive citizenship, Strategic Review for Southern Africa, 37: 1.

94 Constitution of Uganda, 1995, Objective XXVIII, Foreign policy objectives.

95 Constitution of the NRM, as amended in June 2010, Objective 7.k; 7.t.

96 Uganda representative of EALA, interview with author, Kampala Uganda, July 2014.

97 UPDF Colonel and Chief Political Commissar, interview.

98 NRM MP, Chairperson for Uganda Parliamentary Committee on EAC, interview with author, August 2014.

99 UPDF Brigadier, interview.

100 Keynote Address by H.E. Yoweri Kaguta Museveni, UN, New York, United Nations High-level Thematic Debate on Strengthening Co-operation between the United Nations and regional organisations in the maintenance of peace, security, human rights and development in their respective areas, available at Museveni calls for UN restructuring, New Vision, 5 May 2015.

101 Ugandan journalist/EAC expert, interview; see also Will Kadaga listen to the 'people's call' and run for presidency?, Daily Monitor, 6 January 2014.

102 Museveni calls NRM rebel MPs for talks, Daily Monitor, 29 June 2015; Court orders that rebel MPs be thrown out of parliament with immediate effect, Daily Monitor, 21 February 2014.

103 Joshua Rubongoya, interview; see also Kagoro (2013), p.31; Izama and Wilkerson (2011), p.71; FDC Party Structure Weak – Mafabi, URN, 24 September 2012; FDC struggles with weak youth league, Observer, 5 March 2009.

104 Bobi Wine: Uganda's 'ghetto president', BBC News, 22 February 2021, available at https://www.bbc.co.uk/news/world-africa-55572903 (accessed 20 May 2021).

105 Democratic Party MP, interview with author, Kampala Uganda, September 2014; see also MPs flock to China academy, Observer, 29 October 2013.

106 Independent MP, interview with author, Kampala Uganda, September 2014.

107 Ugandan journalist/consultant/oil expert, interview.

108 Money problems in Uganda's Parliament, Daily Monitor, 2 November 2014; Uganda: Museveni Says No to MPs' Loan Bailout Deal, Observer, 23 July 2013.

109 Kizza Besigye, interview.

110 Major General Kahinda Otefiire, Minister for Justice, interview with author, Kampala Uganda, August 2014.

111 Justice Kanyeihamba, Retired Uganda Supreme Court Judge, interview with author, Kampala Uganda, July 2014.

112 Ugandan journalist/consultant/oil expert, interview.

113 Ugandan journalist/consultant/oil expert, interview.

114 Kagenda, Patrick (2014) Behind the attacks in western Uganda, Daily Monitor, 28 July 2014.

115 Minister for Investments, Planning, and Development in Buganda Kingdom, interview with author, Kampala Uganda.

116 Chinese business person/ex-Secretary General of Ugandan Overseas China Association, interview; Zhang Ho, interview; see also CCS (2010), p.124.

117 Chinese influx into Uganda retail trade causes hostility among local businesses, East African, 25 January 2014; see also Uganda traders close shops in protest, BBC News, 6 July 2011; Kikuubo Traders Protest Unfair Competition by Chinese Retailers, Uganda Radio Network, 23 May 2009.

118 Kizza Besigye, interview.

119 Flavia Kabahandra, interview.

120 Roundtable discussion with author with KACITA representatives, Kampala Uganda, August 2014.

121 Roundtable KACITA.

122 Chinese business person/ex-Secretary General of Ugandan Overseas China Association, interview; Zhang Ho, interview.

123 Zhang Ho, interview.

124 Second Vice Chairperson of CAFAU, interview with author (via Skype), May 2014.

125 Xu Yuwei, quoted in Sserunjogi (2013).

126 Kenyan representative of EALA, former-Chair of the Regional Affairs and Conflict Resolution Committee, interview with author, Aruhsa Tanzania, January 2015.

127 Mugisha Muntu, interview.

128 Kizza Besigye, interview.

129 Ugandan journalist/EAC expert, interview.

130 Uganda import teargas trucks ahead of poll, East African, 17 January 2016; Amnesty International (2014) China's Trade in Tools of Torture and Repression, p.27.

131 China sees chance to woo Uganda as West mulls sanctions for bloody election, South China Morning Post, 22 February 2021, https://www.scmp.com/news/china/diplomacy/article/3122668/china-sees-chance-woo-uganda-west-mulls-sanctions-bloody.

132 Ugandan journalist/consultant/oil expert, interview.

133 Court Delivers a Judgement on Kaluma [sic] Hydro Power Project Dispute, EACJ, 28 November 2014; Firm petitions regional court over Karuma, Daily Monitor, 4 July 2013.

134 Robert Waggwa Nsibirwa, interview.

135 Vincent Bitature, UPDF Officer working on the Task Force of UPDF Doctrine writing, interview with author, August 2014; see also Why Kabaka Refused to Meet Museveni, Observer, 3 January 2008.

136 Chinese business person/ex-Secretary General of Ugandan Overseas China Association, interview; also discussed during Zhang Ho, interview; Fang Min, interview.

2 China and the East African Community: overarching and low-level impacts

1 Biswaro, J M (2012) The Quest for Regional Integration in Africa, Latin America and Beyond in the Twenty First Century: Experience, Progress and Prospects. Brasilia: Fernando Morais, p.92.

2 Aksum is described by the Periplus of the Erythraean Sea, an ancient Greco-Roman document discussing trade routes of the time written between the first and third centuries AD, as the major trading post for African ivory. The Periplus also describes trading centres in Opone in northern Somalia; Malao in northwestern Somalia; and Rhapta, thought to be South of modern Dar es Salaam in Tanzania, or possibly modern-day Quelimane in Mozambqiue; see Periplus of the Erythraean Sea translated by Schoff 1912.

3 Hull, Richard (1972) China in Africa, Issue: A Journal of Opinion, 2: 3, pp.49–50.

4 Kamata, Ng'wanza (2013) Perspectives on Sino-Tanzanian Relations, in Adem, Seifudein (ed) (2013) China's Diplomacy in Eastern and Southern Africa (Farnham: Ashgate), p.90; Mote, F.W (2003) Imperial China 900–1800 (Harvard University Press) p.614.

5 Kissinger, Henry (2012) On China (London: Penguin), p.18.

6 Crossley, Pamela (2010) The Wobbling Pivot: China Since 1800 (Sussex: Wiley-Blackwell), p.71.

7 Kamata (2013), p.87; Mazuri, Ali (2013) The Yellow Man's Burden: Race and Revolution in Sino-African Relations, in Adem, Seifudein (ed) (2013) China's Diplomacy in Eastern and Southern Africa (Farnham: Ashgate), pp.7–8.

8 Deng, Kent (2011) China's Political Economy in Modern times: Changes and Economic Consequences, 1800–2000 (London: Routledge), pp.74–80.

9 Walsh, Barney (2015) Human Security in East Africa: The EAC's illusive quest for inclusive citizenship, Strategic Review for Southern Africa, 37: 1), p.77.

10 Altorfer-Ong, Alicia (2009) Tanzanian 'Freedom' and Chinese 'Friendship' in 1965: laying the tracks for the TanZam rail link LSE Ideas.

11 Kannyo, Edward (2013) Sino-Ugandan Relations: Themes and Issues, in Adem (2013), p.110.

12 Mazuri (2013), pp.8–18.

13 Shinn, David and Eisenman, Joshua (2012) China and Africa (University of Pennsylvania Press), pp.294–5, 298–9.

14 Thomas, Darryl (2013) China's Foreign Policy Towards Africa, from Bandung Conference to the 21st Century (1955–2011), in Adem (2013), p.221.

15 EALA Hansard, 29 January 2013.

16 Chinese Senior Consultant for major international NGO, interview with author (via Skype), November 2015.

17 Nnaoli, Okwudibla (1990) The External Environment of Development in East Africa: An overview, in Chole, Eshetu, Wilfred Mlay and Walter Oyugi (eds.) (1990) The Crisis of Development Strategies in East Africa (OSSREA: Addis Ababa), pp.15–16; World Military Expenditure and Arms transfers, 1972–87, US Arms Control and Disarmament Agency.

18 Mazzeo, Domenico (1975) Foreign assistance and the East African common services, 1960–1970, with special reference to multilateral contributions (Münich: Weltforum Verlag), pp.46–7.

19 Siriar, Pabati Kuma (1990) Development through integration: Lessons from East Africa (Delhi: Kalinga Publishers), pp.142–3.

20 Shah, Anup (2013) Structural Adjustment – a Major Cause of Poverty, Global Issues, 24 March 2013; Schatz, Sayre (1994) Structural Adjustment in Africa: a Failing Grade So Far, The Journal of Modern African Studies, 32: 4, pp.679–92.

21 Thomas (2013), pp.222–4; Chai, Joseph (2011) An Economic History of Modern China (Cheltenham: Edward Elgar Publishing, Inc), pp.195–6.

22 Brautigam, Deborah (2009) The dragon's gift: the real story of China in Africa (OUP Oxford), pp.57–8.

23 Ndulu, B J and Mutalemwa, C (2002) Tanzania at the Turn of the Century: Background Papers and Statistics (Washington DC: World Bank), p.204.

24 EAC Senior Research Officer, interview with author, Arusha Tanzania, February 2015.

25 Tanzanian EALA representative, Chair of the Regional Affairs and Conflict Resolution Committee, interview with author, Arusha Tanzania, January 2015.

26 Expert and government advisor on EAC and Somalia, interview with author, Kampala Uganda, September 2014.

27 Ex-Director of Uganda External Security Organisation, interview with author, Kampala Uganda, July 2014.

28 UPDF Colonel, Directing Staff/Deputy Commandant at Senior Command and Staff Training College at Jinja, interview with author, September 2014.

29 Ibid.

30 Ugandan security expert/NRM MP, interview.

31 Peace and Security Expert at EAC Secretariat 1, interview with author, Arusha Tanzania, January 2015.

32 Senior member of EAC Secretariat, interview with author, Arusha Tanzania, February 2015.

33 Peace and Security Expert at EAC Secretariat 2, interview with author, Arusha Tanzania, January 2015.

34 EAC Peace and Security Expert 2, interview.

35 Kenyan representative of EALA, interview.

36 Senior member of EAC Secretariat, interview.

37 30th Meeting of the Council of Ministers, November 2014.

38 Shem Bageine, Ugandan Minister of State for EAC, interview with author, Kampala Uganda July 2014; 'Kenya, Rwanda, Uganda to establish a Mutual Defence Pact and Mutual Peace and Security Pact, Rwanda Ministry of Defence, 8 January 2014.

39 Assistant Commissioner in Charge of Planning in Uganda Ministry of Defence, interview with author, August 2014.

40 Tanzanian EALA representative, interview.

41 Ugandan security expert/NRM MP, interview; EAC to restart talks on expelled Rwandese, The Citizen (Arusha), 6 November 2015; Kagame publicly threatening to hit President Kikwete, The Rising Continent, 4 July 2013.

42 Ugandan security expert/NRM MP, interview.

43 27th EAC Council of Ministers report, 24 August 2013.

44 Kenyan representative of EALA, interview; South Sudan's Push to Join EAC Gains Momentum, East African, 7 November 2015.

45 East African Community Vision 2050, Draft, August 2050, p.24.

46 Ugandan journalist/consultant/oil expert, interview.

47 Onjala, Joseph (2013) Merchandise trading between Kenya and China: implications for the East African Community (EAC), in Adem (2013), pp.80–6, quote p.84.

48 EALA Hansard, 25 January 2002.

49 Ibid.

50 EALA Hansard, various.

51 EALA Hansard, 21 January 2013.

52 EALA Hansard, 30 January 2013, 23 September 2010, 12 August 2009; see also EU's push for MFN clause 'dangerous', East African, 5 May 2012.

53 Senior member of EAC Secretariat, interview.

54 Director of Infrastructure at the EAC Secretariat, interview with author, Arusha Tanzania, January 2015.

55 Uganda representative of EALA, interview.

56 EAC Director of Infrastructure interview.

57 15th EAC Summit of the Heads of State, 30 November 2013; and various others.

58 Chinese investors in EA seek double taxation relief, Daily Nation, 23 April 2015.

59 Senior member of EAC Secretariat, interview.

60 Manager of local Chinese Restaurant, interview with author, Arusha Tanzania, February 2015.

61 Kenyan economist and leading journalist, interview with author, February 2014.

62 EALA Hansard, 25 January 2002.

63 30th Meeting of the EAC Council of Ministers, 28 November 2014.

64 Justice Kanyeihamba, Retired Uganda Supreme Court Judge, interview with author, Kampala Uganda, July 2014.

65 Onjala (2013), p.84.

66 WikiLeaks cable 05NAIROBI3600_a, KENYA'S PRESIDENT GOES TO CHINA – AND WHAT IT MEANS, Kenya Nairobi, 5 September 2005, https://wikileaks.org/plusd/cables/05NAIROBI3600_a.html.

67 Kenyan representative of EALA, interview.

68 Uganda Ministry of Finance spokesperson, interview with author, July 2014.

69 Expert within EAC Conflict Early Warning office, Interview with author, January 2015.

70 Uhuru Kenyatta, 2013 speech to the AU, quoted in Manji (2015), p.4.

71 Kenyan economist/journalist, interview.

72 Kenya corruption watchdog makes allegations against 175 officials, Reuters, 1 April 2015.

73 Kenya's debt to China hits Sh101 billion as external loans pile, The Star (Nairobi), 28 March 2015.

74 Kenya boosts China ties with Sh7.9bn arms purchase deal, Daily Nation, 15 February 2016; China Step Closer to Exporting Reactors With Africa Agreement, Bloomberg.com, 9 September 2015.

75 Tullow rejects oil search deal with Chinese firm CNOOC, Daily Monitor, 21 February 2011.

76 Tanzanian EALA representative, interview.

77 Tanzania gas pipeline built, but not ready to start, Reuters, 31 March 2015.

78 SAIIA (2015); Alden and Sidiropoulos (2015); China Expands Investment in Tanzania, The New York Times-Sinosphere Blog, Briefing, 13 September 2014; China: Tanzania's biggest development partner Kampala, East African, 25 January 2014.

79 Kamata (2013), pp.95.

80 Tanzanian navy commissions new vessels, Defence Web, 8 May 2015; Kamata (2013), p.96.

81 Tanzanian EALA representative, interview.

82 Kamata (2013), p.102.

83 China influence seen as strong, positive in Tanzania, Afrobarometre News release, Dar es Salaam, Tanzania, 25 February 2015.

84 Various interviews, Kampala Uganda and Arusha Tanzania, 2014–15.

85 Dar ponders its fate in EAC, Citizen, 16 March 2013.

86 Shinn and Eisenman (2012), p.298.

87 Prunier (2009), p.27.

88 Abdul Karim Harelimana, Rwandan representative EALA Rwanda, interview with author, January 2015; see also China in Rwanda: Big projects, jobs and skills for the locals, East African, 25 January 2014; Shinn and Eisenman (2012), pp.298–9.

89 'Is China's Role in African Fragile States Exploitative or Developmental?', IDS Policy Briefing, Issue 91, March 2015.

90 Dowden, Richard (2011) Reconciliation for Kagame and Museveni, Huffington Post, 2 September 2011.

91 Former Rwandan Ambassador to the UN, and former Rwanda Minister, interview with author, Kigali Rwanda, January 2016.

92 Prominent Ugandan journalist and editor, interview.

93 Former Rwandan UN Ambassador, interview.

94 Kagame: China's donation to AU HQ symptom of Africa's bigger problems, East African, 2 February 2012.

95　Govt turns to Chinese to fast-track Nyabarongo II hydro-power project, New Times, 22 May 2015; Turkish firm wins contract to finish building Kigali centre, East African, 25 April 2015.

96　Shinn and Eisenman (2012), p.295.

97　Burundian working at EAC secretariat, interview with author, Arusha Tanzania, February 2015.

98　Shinn and Eisenman (2012), p.295.

99　EAC Conflict Early Warning expert, interview.

100　Burundian working at EAC secretariat, interview.

101　Parrin, Anjli (2015) Burundi crisis gets serious for regional leaders, IRIN, 14 July 2015.

102　Academic, leading Burundi expert, interview with author, Arusha Tanzania, January 2015.

103　Russia: U.N. Security Council should stay out of Burundi dispute, Reuters.com, 1 May 2015.

104　Will peacekeeper plan help end Burundi violence? IRIN News, 18 December 2015; Burundi: Conflict Alert, ICG, 5 November 2015; UNSC Resolution 2248 (2015) Adopted by the Security Council at its 7557th meeting, on 12 November 2015.

105　Guéhenno, Jean-Marie, Obe, Ayo and Adeola, Fola (2015) AU was set up for an explosive crisis like Burundi; it must act, East African, 14 November 2015; Burundi expels Rwandan diplomat for 'creating insecurity', BBC News, 7 October 2015.

106　EAC Conflict Early Warning expert, interview.

107　EAC Peace and Security Expert 2, interview.

108　Communiqué of the 12th Extra Ordinary Summit of EAC Heads of State, 28 April 2014, p.3; EAC leaders to continue war on terror, Daily Monitor, 1 May 2014.

109　Uganda representative of EALA, interview.

110　US warns against Burundi travel amid Al Shabaab threat, East African, 31 October 2014.

111　Al Shabaab could establish ties with DRC rebels, East African, 22 February 2014.

112　EAC Peace and Security Expert 2, interview.

113　Ibid.

114　EAC Conflict Early Warning expert, interview.

115　Environmental Investigation Agency (EIA) (2014) VANISHING POINT: Criminality, Corruption and the Devastation of Tanzania's Elephants, November 2014.

116　Hongxiang, Hunag (2013a) The Chinese ivory-smugglers in Africa, Chinadialogue.net, 27 November 2013; Zambia probes diplomats over ivory export, Xinhua News, 11 June 2013.

Notes

117 Bolton, Matthew (2015) Using the Arms Trade Treaty to Address Wildlife Poaching in East Africa: A Human Security Approach, ControlArms.org, Working Paper, Version 5.2, November 2015, p.9.

118 Tanzanian EALA representative, interview.

119 Representative of the Ugandan National Focal Point on SALW, Ministry of Internal Affairs, interview with author, Kampala Uganda, September 2014.

120 EAC Peace and Security Expert 2, interview.

121 Senior member of EAC Secretariat, interview.

122 Christy, Brian (2015) How Killing Elephants Finances Terror in Africa, National Geographic, 15 August 2015; see also Bolton (2015).

123 Kenyan representative of EALA, interview.

124 EAC Peace and Security Expert 2, interview.

125 EALA Hansard, 21 August 2013.

126 Ugandan National Focal Point representative, interview; see also Saferworld (2014) Tackling Illicit Small Arms and Light Weapons (SALW) and Ammunition in the Great Lakes and Horn of Africa, Final Working Paper, June 2014; EU Council Decision 2012/121/CFSP of 27 February 2012, in support of activities to promote EU–China–Africa dialogue and cooperation on conventional arms controls.

127 EAC Peace and Security Expert 1, interview.

128 FOCAC V Beijing Action Plan, 2.6.1.

129 EAC Peace and Security Expert 1, interview.

130 Senior member of EAC Secretariat, interview.

131 Dr Cobus van Staden, Lecturer, Media Studies of Wits University and Co-founder of the China Africa Project, speaking at FOCAC VI side-event on Wildlife conservation, 2 December 2015.

132 China Issues One Year Ban on Import of African Ivory Trophies, IFAW, 1 5 October 2015; China agrees to phase out its ivory industry to combat elephant poaching, The Guardian, 29 May 2015.

133 Successful operation highlights growing international cooperation to combat wildlife crime, CITES, 18 June 2015.

134 Honorable Yuxiao Zhou, former Chinese ambassador to Zambia, speaking at FOCAC VI side-event on Wildlife conservation, 2 December 2015.

135 Andrea Crosta, Executive Director and Co-Founder, Elephant Action League, speaking at FOCAC VI side-event on Wildlife conservation, 2 December 2015.

136 Kenyan representative of EALA, interview.

137 East African Countries Rise Defense Budgets On Increased Terrorism Threats, AFK Insider, 16 April 2014; Uganda, Burundi lead East Africa in military

spending, East African, 16 April 2014; Regional countries up security spending over terror and wars, East African, 14 June 2014.

138 The Eastern African Police Chiefs Cooperation Organisation (EAPCCO) provides a regional forum for the police. East African security specialist and government advisor, interview.

139 EAC Peace and Security Expert 1, interview.

140 EAC/Somalia expert, interview.

141 EAC Peace and Security Expert 1, interview.

142 5th Meeting of the EAC Sectoral Council on Tourism and Wildlife Management, 30 July 2013, pp.37–40.

143 4th Meeting of the EAC Sectoral Council on Tourism and Wildlife Management, 23 September 2011.

144 Alao, Abiodun Alao (2007) Natural Resources And Conflict In Africa The Tragedy Of Endowment (Rochester: University of Rochester Press), pp.157–206.

145 Ex-Director of Uganda's External Security Organisation, interview.

146 Kenyan representative of EALA, interview; see also Security: Al-Shabaab threaten Kenyan parliament, Turkana / West Pokot remains tense, Menas: Politics and Security, 4 March 2015.

147 EAC Conflict Early Warning expert, interview.

148 Massive military operation in Kenya's Turkana region to flush out bandits, Star Africa, 4 November 2014.

149 Zanzibar and Tanzania vie over oil reserves, Financial Times.com, 10 March 2015.

150 High risk, high reward: talking offshore oil security with Drum Cussac, OffshoreEnergyTechnology.com, 3 January 2013; Tanzania arrests 7 pirates after attack on oil vessel, Reuters.com, 4 October 2011.

151 DR Congo: 'FDLR rebels kidnap' Soco oil worker, BBC News, 15 February 2015.

152 Corporate Affairs Manager, Total E&P Uganda, interview with author, September 2014.

153 Shem Bageine, interview.

154 EAC Secretariat, Strategy for the Development of Regional Refineries Final Repot, February 2008; discussed during Ernest Rubondo, interview.

155 Tanzanian EALA representative, interview.

156 Uganda representative of EALA, interview.

157 EAC Director of Infrastructure interview.

158 EAC Ministers in China for Infrastructure Development Study Tour, Uganda Radio Network, 8 May 2008.

159 1st Retreat of the Heads of States of the EAC, June 2008.

160 Tanzanian EALA representative, interview.

161 Railway scandal: How the project slipped off, Daily Monitor, 31 August 2014; Why EA countries chose more costly route for standard gauge railway line, East African, 28 September 2013.

162 Uganda representative of EALA, interview.

163 EAC Director of Infrastructure interview.

164 NRM MP, Chairperson for Uganda Parliamentary Committee on EAC, interview with author, Kampala Uganda, August 2014.

165 EAC/Somalia expert, interview.

166 Tanzania to spend $14 bln on railways, eyes regional hub status, Reuters, 30 March 2015.

167 Tanzania awards $9 Bln Rail Projects to Chinese Companies, CNBCAfrica, 1 June 2015.

168 Uganda representative of EALA, interview.

169 EAC/Somalia expert, interview.

170 EAC Senior Research Officer, interview.

171 Report of the EAC Inter- Parliamentarians Relations Liaison Committee on Natural Resources on the site tour of Tanzanian Extractive Industries, Shinyanga – Kahama – Mwanza, 19th–23rd November 2008; Report of the EAC Inter-Parliamentary Relations Liaison Committee on Natural Resources on the site tour of Tullow Oil Industries in Hoima District, Uganda, 14th–19th June 2009.

172 EAC Senior Research Officer, interview; EAC expert working with Agriculture, Tourism and Natural Resources Committee, interview with author, February 2015.

173 Kenyan representative of EALA, interview.

174 Ibid.

175 EAC Director of Infrastructure interview.

176 Kenyan economist/journalist, interview; see also Kenya's railway levy collection exceeds target, CNBCAfrica, 16 June 2014.

177 Kenyan economist, interview; see also Ndii, David (2014) New railway is not value for money, Daily Nation, 14 February 2014.

178 EAC Director of Infrastructure, interview.

179 It's all about trade and pace of reforms, Daily Nation, 10 August 2015.

180 Tanzania to spend $14 bln on railways, eyes regional hub status, Reuters, 30 March 2015.

181 Full list of all LAPSSET projects can be found at http://www.lapsset.go.ke/home.

182 Kenyan economist/journalist, interview; Kenya says Chinese firm wins first tender for Lamu port project, Reuters, 11 April 2013.

183 Ugandan security expert/NRM MP, interview.

184 Will Uganda's oil wealth change LAPSSET into LAPSSEUT?, Indian Ocean Observatory, 31 August 2014 http://www.lapsset.go.ke/oilpipeline.

185 Kenyan economist/journalist, interview.

186 Tanzanian EALA representative, interview.

187 Kenya to acquire stake in Uganda's refinery, Oil in Uganda, 27 January 2015; Ernest Rubondo, interview.

188 Ex-Director of Uganda's External Security Organisation, interview.

189 EALA Hansard, 2 June 2010.

190 EALA Hansard, 29 May 2013.

3 China's role in regional security and the nature of Museveni's methods

1 Shem Bageine, Uganda Minister of State for the East African Community, Interview with author, Kampala Uganda, July 2014.

2 Titeca, Kristof and Vlassenroot, Koen (2012) Rebels without borders in the Rwenzori borderland? A biography of the Allied Democratic Forces, Journal of Eastern African Studies, 6:1, p.155.

3 Ugandan rebel leader's arrest a shot in the arm for justice, IRIN News, 30 April 2015; Walsh, Barney (2010) Uganda's Involvement in the DRC since 1998: Museveni and Regional Relations, ALC Monograph, Number 5, p.12.

4 Fisher, Jonathan (2014) Framing Kony: Uganda's war, Obama's advisers and the nature of 'influence' in Western foreign policy making, Third World Quarterly, 35:4, p.698; Economist Intelligence Unit (2002) Uganda Country Report, April 2002, p.15.

5 UGANDA: Museveni condemns terrorism in all its forms, IRIN, 12 September 2001.

6 Hansen, Stig Jarle (2014) Al-Shabaab in Somalia: the history and ideology of a militant Islamist group, 2005–2012 (Oxford: Oxford University Press).

7 UPDF Lieutenant Colonel 2, interview with author, Kampala Uganda, September 2014.

8 Fisher (2012), pp.418–19, referring to Parliament of Uganda proceedings (Hansard, 13 February 2007), and US praises Museveni for Somalia role, New Vision, 21 September 2009.

9 US Department of State (2012) The Lord's Resistance Army: Fact Sheet, 23 March 2012; UGANDA: LRA, ADF on American terrorist list, IRIN, 7 December 2001.

10 Various interviews with author, from UPDF officers, politicians, and officials, July–September 2014.

Notes

11 Fisher (2014).

12 Terrorism is alive in region, says CMI boss, Daily Monitor, 11 July 2011.

13 Museveni describes eastern DRC as terrorism conservation project, The Africa Report, 31 January 2013.

14 UPDF Lieutenant Colonel 2, interview.

15 UPDF must deal with indiscipline, Observer, 10 September 2014; 40 Uganda army officers face trial over thievery in Somalia, The Africa Review, 30 October 2013.

16 Expert and government advisor on EAC integration and Somalia, interview with author, September 2014.

17 Report of the Monitoring Group on Somalia and Eritrea pursuant to Security Council resolution 2111 (2013): Somalia, S/2014/726, 10 October 2014, pp.7, 8.

18 UPDF Brigadier, interview.

19 Joshua Rubongoya, Professor at Roanoke College Virginia, author of Regime Hegemony in Museveni's Uganda, interview with author, Kampala Uganda, September 2014.

20 Barkan, Joel D. (2011) Uganda: Assessing Risks to Stability, Centre for Strategic and International Studies (CSIS), A Report for the CSIS Africa Program, June 2011, p.9; Walsh (2010), pp.13–15.

21 Jowell (2014).

22 Prominent Ugandan journalist and editor, interview.

23 Kalinaki (2015), p.208.

24 Tough Times Ahead, Anti-Terrorism Bill Passed, Independent, 18 June 2015.

25 EALA Hansard, 21 May 2003; Kayunga (2005), pp.216–17.

26 Uganda Rejects Tanzanian and Kenyan Help Over Rebel War, Daily Nation, 2 March 2005.

27 Uhuru Kenyatta says terrorists are exploiting Kenya's expanded democratic space, Daily Nation, 26 September 2014.

28 Pierre Nkurunziza quoted in Stakeholders in Somalia's peacekeeping mission meet in Burundi, China People's Daily, 16 November 2010.

29 Burundi calls opposition protesters 'terrorists', BBC News, 2 May 2015.

30 Burundi's Nkurunziza: 'It's either me or al-Shabab', Al-Jazeera, 17 May 2015.

31 How Tanzania foiled terror attack on Kenya poll, Daily Nation, 19 April 2014.

32 Kikwete hints at possible terrorist operations in Tanzania, East African, 04 March 2015; Mohammed Emwazi went to Tanzania 'to commit terrorism', BBC News, 9 March 2015.

33 Kinana, Abdulrahman (2015), referred to in Koenings, Nathalie Arnold (2015) Tanzania cannot be allowed to be the new front for state-led Islamophobia, African Arguments, 2 October 2015.

34 Abdul Karim Harelimana, Rwandan representative EALA, interview with author, January 2015.

35 Attendee at October 2015 Nanyuki Series meeting, interview with author, December 2015; see also East African Legislative Assembly (2015) Report on the Eighth Inter-Parliamentary Relations Seminar (Nanyuki Viii) on the theme Insecurity and Terrorism as Threats to EAC Integration: How can EAC Develop a Common Position?, 30th October–2nd November, 2014, February 2015, pp.38–9.

36 Kagame declares 'shoot on sight' anti-terror policy, New Vision, 9 June 2014.

37 Peace and Security Expert at EAC Secretariat 2, interview with author, Arusha Tanzania, January 2015.

38 Final report of the Group of Experts on the Democratic Republic of the Congo, UN Report to the Security Council, S/2015/19, 12 January 2015.

39 Peace and Security Expert at EAC Secretariat 1, interview with author, Arusha Tanzania, January 2015.

40 UPDF Colonel, Chief Political Commissar, interview with author, Kampala Uganda, August 2014.

41 Tanzanian EALA representative, Chair of the Regional Affairs and Conflict Resolution Committee, Arusha Tanzania, interview with author, January 2015.

42 Uganda Minister for Security, interview with author, Kampala Uganda, July 2014.

43 Matsiko, Haggai (2014) Is it time for a China-Africa Command?, Independent, 16 November 2014; Chinese invasion, Independent, 16 January 2012; Report of the Monitoring Group on Somalia and Eritrea pursuant to Security Council resolution 2060 (2012): Somalia S/2013/413, 12 July 2013, p.161.

44 Statement by Ambassador Liu Jieyi at the Security Council Briefing on the Activities of the United Nations Regional Office for Central Africa and on the Lord's Resistance Army-Affected Areas, 20 November 2014; China urges LRA to cease violence, China Daily, 15 November 2011.

45 Cline, Lawrence (2013) The Lord's Resistance Army (Oxford: Praeger), p.65.

46 Representative of the Ugandan National Focal Point on SALW, Ministry of Internal Affairs, interview with author, Kampala Uganda, September 2014.

47 China and SALW expert, key participant in Saferworld dialogues, interview with author (via Skype), May 2015.

48 Henry Oryem Okello, interview.

49 Ibid.

50 Small Arms Survey, 2013 Year Book, Annex 8.1; see also SIPRI (2014) Fact Sheet, pp.4–5; SIPRI (2013) Policy Paper, p.46.

51 Ugandan National Focal Point representative, interview; see also Cakaj, Ledi (2010) The Lord's Resistance Army of Today, Enough Project, November 2010, p.17.

Notes 183

52 Small Arms Survey, 2014 Year Book, pp.200–1; see also Report of the UN Monitoring Group on Somalia and Eritrea, S/2011/433, 18 July 2011, pp.231–4; China Remains The Largest Supplier of Ammunitions to Al-Shabaab, Kenya Today Online, 26 September 2013; Shinn and Eisenman (2012), p.171.

53 Small Arms Survey, 2012 Year Book, p.152.

54 UPDF Lieutenant Colonel 2, interview.

55 UPDF Brigadier, interview.

56 Ugandan security expert, ex-Director of East African Standby Force, interview with author, Kampala Uganda, August 2014.

57 UPDF Brigadier, interview.

58 Small Arms Survey (2012) Sudan Issue Brief, Reaching for the gun: Arms flows and holding in South Sudan, Number 19, April 2012.

59 China Halts Arms Sales to South Sudan After Norinco Shipment, Bloomberg, 30 September 2014; China Sells South Sudan Arms as Its Government Talks Peace, Bloomberg, 9 July 2014.

60 UN: China arms firm sold $20M in weapons to South Sudan, Daily Mail, 25 August 2015; China's largest weapons manufacturer is allegedly selling arms to South Sudan – again, Quartz Africa, 26 August 2015.

61 Professor Daniel Large, China–Sudan/South Sudan expert, speaking at FOCAC VI side-event on China–Africa's maturing relationship, December 2015; China urges immediate end to conflict in South Sudan, The Guardian, 7 January 2014.

62 Without a soft landing for Kiir, the Igad-Plus peace proposal is doomed, East African, 8 August 2015; Matsiko (2014); Behind Museveni's defiance of US, Igad orders, East African, 15 February 2014.

63 Now Machar's men back UPDF stay in South Sudan, Daily Monitor, 27 September 2014.

64 Professor Daniel Large, FOCAC VI side, December 2015; U.N. Peacekeepers to Protect China's Oil Interests in South Sudan, Foreign Policy, 16 July 2014.

65 Museveni's visit to Sudan good for peace, Daily Monitor, 17 September 2015; President Museveni of Uganda Concludes Visit to Sudan, Sudan Now (Khartoum), 16 September 2015; Kasasira, Risdel (2015) What UPDF withdrawal means for Salva Kiir, Daily Monitor, 18 October 2015.

66 UPDF destroys over 200 tonnes of ammunition, Daily Monitor, 12 January 2014.

67 Bevan, James (2008) Crisis in Karamoja Armed Violence and the Failure of Disarmament in Uganda's Most Deprived Region, Small Arms Survey Occasional Paper 21, Geneva 2008, pp.47–8; see also Saferworld (2007) Mapping the small arms problem in Uganda: The development of Uganda's National Action Plan on Small Arms and Light Weapons, May 2007, p.8.

68 Museveni under fire over army, Independent, 6 October 2014.

69 Muggah, Robert and Sang, Francis (2013) The enemy within: rethinking arms availability in sub-Saharan Africa, Conflict, Security & Development, 13:4, p.422; Small Arms Survey, 2007 Year Book, pp.292–9; Saferworld (2007); Arms Crisis is Not Inherently African, Daily Nation, 13 August 2001; Uganda Army Destroying Mines, What About Rebels?, East African, 19 January 2000; see http://www.luweroindustries.com.

70 Jacqueline Susan Mbabazi, Profile, Agency for National Development, available at http://www.andug.org/JacquelineMbabazi.htm (accessed 20 December 2014).

71 Kizza Besigye, former leader of FDC, FDC Presidential candidate, interview with author, Kampala Uganda, July 2014; Wafula Oguttu, FDC MP, Leader of Opposition in Parliament, interview with author, Kampala Uganda, August 2014.

72 China/SALW expert, interview.

73 Saferworld (2014), p.30.

74 Ugandan National Focal Point representative, interview; China/SALW expert, interview.

75 China/SALW expert, interview.

76 Ibid.

77 Beijing meeting on African peace and security: combating illicit small arms and ammunition, Safer World, Seminar Report, Beijing, 18 March 2014, pp.2, 3.

78 Mr. Liu Jieyi, speaking at the UN Security Council 7036th meeting, 26 September 2013.

79 Beijing meeting on African peace and security: combating illicit small arms and ammunition, Safer World, Seminar Report, Beijing, 18 March 2014.

80 Arms Trade Treaty, UN, at https://thearmstradetreaty.org.

81 UPDF Lieutenant Colonel 2, interview.

82 Kalron, Nir and Crosta, Andrea (2014) Africa's White Gold of Jihad: al-Shabaab and Conflict Ivory, Elephant Action League, Special Report; Elephant Campaign: How Africa's 'white gold' funds the al-Shabaab militants, The Independent (London), 3 February 2014; Illegal ivory trade funds al-Shabaab's terrorist attacks, The Independent (London), 6 August 2013; Agger, Kasper and Hutson, Jonathan (2013) Kony's Ivory: How Elephant Poaching in Congo Helps Support the Lord's Resistance Army, Enough Project, June 2013, p.9; Lord's Resistance Army funded by elephant poaching, report finds, The Guardian, 4 June 2013.

83 Executive Director and Co-Founder Elephant Action League (EAL), interview with author (via email), December 2015.

84 Ssegawa, Mike (2014) How smuggling ivory limits tourists from streaming in, Special Report, Daily Monitor, 26 November 2014.

85 Bolton (2015), pp.6–7.

86 Missing Ivory: Mutagamba suspends UWA's executive director, Independent, 25 November 2015; Ivory scandal: UPDF colonel implicated as six are detained, Daily Monitor, 5 February 2015; Missing Ivory: Mutagamba suspends UWA's executive director, Independent, 25 November 2014.

87 Museveni doesn't make tracking ivory traffic any easier, Indian Ocean Newsletter, Uganda Politics & Power Brokers, N°1398, 27 February 2015.

88 Police seize tonnes of ivory, Daily Monitor, 15 June 2015.

89 UPDF Brigadier within UPDF Military Intelligence, interview with author, Kampala Uganda, July 2014.

90 Henry Oryem Okello, interview.

91 With the ivory burn, China can help save the elephant, East African, 18 January 2014; China increases prosecutions in response to illegal trade in elephant ivory, CITES, 29 November 2013.

92 Izama, Angelo (2013) Tracing Uganda's oil journey from 1913–2013, Daily Monitor, 31 December 2013; ex-Director of Uganda's External Security Organisation, interview; Ugandan journalist/consultant/oil expert, interview; Private Secretary in State House Uganda, interview.

93 Ex-Director of Uganda's External Security Organisation, interview.

94 Tullow's purchase from Heritage resulted in acrimonious court battles with each other and the Ugandan government over capital gains tax issues, which the Ugandan government ultimately won.

95 Henstridge, Mark and Page, John (2012) Managing a Modest Boom: Oil Revenues in Uganda, OxCarre Research Paper 90, June 2012. See also Hickey et al. (2015), p.9.

96 Izama (2012); see Government of Uganda (2012) Uganda Vision 2040.

97 Invest oil money in infrastructure, health-Survey, Oil in Uganda, 30 March 2015; Tough choices over oil, Independent, 22 September 2013; Uganda to use oil cash for infrastructure development, New Times, 30 August 2013.

98 David Bahati, Vice-Chair President of NRM and Deputy Chief Whip of NRM, interview with author, Kampala Uganda, August 2014.

99 Owners will lose rights over mineral-rich land – Museveni, Daily Monitor, 1 November 2014.

100 Felix Kulayigye, quoted in Grounds exist for a rebellion, Independent, 9 April 2012; and Albertine safe from rebel threat, police to take charge, Oil in Uganda, 15 May 2013; see also 'DRC-based Ugandan rebel group "recruiting, training"', IRIN, 11 July 2013.

101 Museveni (2010), quoted in Besigye is after oil money, says Museveni, Daily Monitor, 29 December 2010.

102 Opposition fire back at Museveni over oil control, Daily Monitor, 23 December 2015.

103 Muruuli Mukasa, Minister for Security, interview with author, Kampala Uganda, July 2014.

104 FDC shadow Minister for Water and Environment, interview; also discussed with Manager at the Democratic Governance Unit (Uganda), interview with author, Kampala Uganda, July 2014.

105 Aronda says army takeover possible, Daily Monitor, 24 January 2013.

106 Prominent Ugandan journalist and editor, interview; also discussed during various other interviews.

107 Ugandan president to approve all oil, gas deals, Reuters, 19 August 2010; Oil: Museveni takes over, Daily Monitor, 19 August 2014.

108 Global Witness (2014) A Good Deal Better? Uganda's Secret Oil Contracts Explained, September 2014; What do leaked oil contracts mean for Uganda's future?, Oil in Uganda, 12 December 2014; source within a Western donor organization, interview with author, August 2014.

109 Police Oil Unit gets new Commander, Oil in Uganda, 15 January 2014.

110 Various interview conducted in Kampala and in Hoima (oil region), July–September 2014.

111 Bunyoro leaders demand for more, Oil in Uganda, 15 June 2015; Uganda Public Finance Management Act, 2015, Section 74(8).

112 Bunyoro Kingdom in bloody land clashes, Oil in Uganda, 8 December 2014; Find lasting solution to land, tribal tensions, Daily Monitor, 24 July 2014.

113 Physical Planner Buliisa District, interview with author, Hoima Uganda, August 2014.

114 UPDF Lieutenant Colonel 2, interview.

115 Compensation remains messy, 'noisy' NGOs risk closure, Oil in Uganda, 7 October 2013.

116 Repressive NGO Act, Inter Press Service, 9 March 2016; Uganda: Bill Threatens Rights, Independent Groups, Human Rights Watch, 20 April 2015.

117 Ugandan journalist/consultant/oil expert, interview.

118 UPDF Brigadier, interview.

119 Speech by President Museveni on the 26th Anniversary (2011) of the National Resistance Movement in Kapchorwa, State House Uganda, 26 January 2012.

120 Ugandan journalist/consultant/oil expert, interview.

121 UPDF Lieutenant Colonel 2, interview.

122 Major General Kahinda Otefiire, Minister for Justice, interview with author, Kampala Uganda, August 2014.

123 The shifting river that is making Uganda smaller, The Guardian, 7 December 2010.

124 Government asked to name DRC looters, Daily Monitor, 2 September 2015.

125 Corporate Affairs Manager, Total E&P Uganda, interview.

126 EAC/Somalia expert, interview.

127 UPDF Brigadier, interview.

128 East Africa: Regional MPs Call for Joint Security Operations, New Times, 2 November 2014.

129 Uganda Ministry of Finance spokesperson, interview.

130 Wikileaks Cable 09KAMPALA1401_a, UGANDA: TULLOW SEES CORRUPTION IN OIL SALE, Uganda Kampala, 17 December 2009, https://wikileaks.org/plusd/cables/09KAMPALA1401_a.html ; Wikileaks Cable 10KAMPALA21_a, UGANDA: UK CONSIDERING CORRUPTION TRAVEL BANS, Uganda Kampala, 13 January 2010, https://wikileaks.org/plusd/cables/10KAMPALA21_a.html.

131 de Kock and Sturman (2012), p.45.

132 Museveni: I've never received oil bribes, The Daily Monitor, 13 October 2011.

133 Kiwanuka, Jenkins (2013) Is China promoting a new type of economic imperialism?, Daily Monitor, OpEd, 22 July 2013; China had role in oil deals signing, Observer, 12 February 2012.

134 Chinese oil expert working in Uganda, interview with author, September 2014.

135 Ugandan security expert/NRM MP, interview.

136 Manager at the Democratic Governance Unit (Uganda), interview; see also Museveni's 'bad language', oil and foreign interests, Daily Monitor, 16 December 2012.

137 Theodore Ssekikubo, NRM 'rebel' MP, former Chairperson of Parliamentary Committee on Oil and Gas, interview with author, Kampala Uganda, September 2014.

138 Chief Executive Officer for Africa Institute for Energy Governance, interview with author, Hoima Uganda, August 2014; Donor with expert knowledge of Ugandan oil sector, interview with author, Kampala Uganda, August 2014.

139 Municipal Planner for Hoima Municipality, interview with author, Hoima Uganda, August 2014.

140 Bunyoro Kingdom Minister of Culture, speaking during roundtable interview with author with Ministers from Bunyoro Kingdom, Hoima Uganda, August 2014.

141 Ugandan journalist/consultant/oil expert, interview.

142 Prominent Ugandan journalist and editor, interview.

143 Tullow Uganda Joint Venture Coordinator, interview with author, Kampala Uganda, August 2014; Corporate Affairs Manager, Total E&P Uganda, interview; Government to announce oil refinery investor, Daily Monitor, 25 February 2014;

Refinery for government, pipeline for the oil companies, Oil in Uganda, 7 July 2013.

144 Hickey et al. (2015); see also Vokes (2012), p.20.

145 Chief Executive Officer AFIEGO, interview.

146 A bonanza beckons, The Economist, 31 May 2010; also referred to in Shen and Taylor (2012), p.700.

147 Musisi, Frederic (2014) Financing questions lie ahead after MoU, Daily Monitor, Special Report, 11 February 2014; Museveni blasts oil companies over refinery, New Vision, 10 April 2013; Refinery could offer power push, Africa Energy Intelligence, Uganda Electricity, N°671, 14 March 2012.

148 Zongwei Xiao, referenced in Musisi (2014).

149 Uganda oil now for 2020, Independent, 8 February 2015.

150 Chief Executive Officer AFIEGO, interview.

151 Country Manager International Alert Uganda, Interview with author, Kampala Uganda, August 2014.

152 Uganda Wants Chinese-Built Infrastructure Paid for With Oil, Bloomberg, 9 July 2013.

153 EAC Director of Infrastructure interview.

154 UPDF Brigadier, interview.

155 Ugandan journalist, consultant and oil expert, interview with author, Kampala Uganda, September 2014.

156 Prominent member of the Uganda Overseas China Association, interview with author, Kampala Uganda, August 2014.

157 Uganda Ministry of Finance spokesperson, interview.

158 Source with close links to UPDF, interview with author, Kampala Uganda, July 2014.

159 Refinery contractor's military links raise eyebrows, Oil in Uganda, 23 February 2015; Russian, South Korean firms 'battle' for refinery contract, Oil in Uganda, 24 June 2014.

160 Ugandan journalist/consultant/oil expert, interview.

161 Imaka, Isaac and Musisi, Frederic (2013) Following the oil money: How much has it done?, Daily Monitor, Special Report, 3 December 2013.

162 Ugandan journalist/consultant/oil expert, interview.

163 Albertine Graben Consortium signs oil refinery pact with Uganda, Independent (Kampala), 18 April 2018; How Chinese firm DongSong lost lucrative refinery deal, East African, 21 August 2017.

164 Daily Monitor reporter on Oil and Gas, interview with author, Kampala Uganda, August 2014.

165 UPDF Lieutenant Colonel 2, interview.

166 Hydro-power Engineer and Ugandan government advisor, Interview with author, Kampala Uganda, August 2014.

167 Chief Executive Officer AFIEGO, interview; Funding queries over secrecy shrouded Karuma power project, East African, 21 June 2014.

168 Hydro-power Engineer, interview.

169 Quoted in Hickey et al. (2015).

170 All eyes on South Sudan as Kenya, Uganda push for Lapsset corridor project, East African, 26 October 2013.

171 Ugandan security expert/NRM MP, interview.

172 What's going on? Cracks appear in oil company partnership as pipeline saga drags on, Oil in Uganda, 28 December 2015; Museveni plays a wicked poker hand on Tanga, Africa Energy Intelligence, Uganda Oil N°756, 27 October 2015; Total brandishes Tanzanian card to thwart Lamu pipeline scheme, Africa Energy Intelligence, Uganda Oil N°752, 1 September 2015.

173 Ugandan oil sector expert, interview with author (via email), March 2016; Oil pipeline: Which way for Uganda?, Daily Monitor, 7 March 2016.

174 Anthony, Ross (2012) China's role in the East African oil and gas sector: a new model of engagement?, CCS Policy Briefing, August 2012.

175 Kenyan economist and leading journalist, interview with author, Nairobi Kenya, February 2015.

176 Wakabi, Michael (2015) Why Kenya and Uganda are racing to connect Juba to the SGR, Africa Review, 9 August 2015.

177 Why the Kampala-Kigali railway is off the track, Africa Intelligence, Uganda: Politics & Power Brokers N°1417, 18 December 2015; Wakabi (2015); Kampala-Kigali railway project derails, Independent, 19 July 2015.

178 Kampala-Kigali railway project derails, Independent, 19 July 2015; Why the Kampala-Kigali railway is off the track, Africa Intelligence, Uganda: Politics & Power Brokers N°1417, 18 December 2015.

Conclusion

1 Lib Quotes, referring to Global Briefing April 2021, at https://libquotes.com/yoweri-museveni/quote/lbe1h9o.

2 Reyntjens, Filip (2019) East Africa should intervene to defuse Rwanda-Uganda war of words, The Conversation, 25 March 2019, available at https://theconversation.com/east-africa-should-intervene-to-defuse-rwanda-uganda-war-of-words-114202 (accessed 10 January 2020).

3 Taylor, Ian (2020) Kenya's New Lunatic Express: The Standard Gauge Railway. African Studies Quarterly, 19.
4 Walsh, Barney and Kinkoh, Hubert (2020) COVID-19 and the Conundrum of China-Africa Relations, ALC COVID-19 OpEd Series, Vol 1 No 2, April 15.
5 Macron pushes East African oil pipeline as French banks shun project, Global Trade Review, 5 May 2021; Farmers, civil rights groups oppose Uganda's oil project, Mail and Guardian, 1 May 2021.
6 Bobi Wine: Uganda's 'ghetto president', BBC News, 22 February 2021.
7 FOCAC VI Johannesburg Declaration; FOCAC VI Johannesburg Action Plan.

Bibliography

15th EAC Summit of the Heads of State, 30 November 2013.

1st Retreat of the Heads of States of the EAC, June 2008.

20 years of explosive growth in China's trade ties with Kampala, East African, 30 January 2014.

27th EAC Council of Ministers report, 24 August 2013.

30th Meeting of the Council of Ministers, November 2014.

30th Meeting of the EAC Council of Ministers, 28 November 2014.

4th Meeting of the EAC Sectoral Council on Tourism and Wildlife Management, 23 September 2011.

5th Meeting of the EAC Sectoral Council on Tourism and Wildlife Management, 30 July 2013, pp.37–40.

A bonanza beckons, The Economist, 31 May 2010.

A dam nuisance, The Economist, 20 April 2011.

A'Zami, Darius (2015) 'China in Africa': From Under-researched to Under-theorised?, Millennium – Journal of International Studies, 43:2, pp.724–34.

Address by H.E. Xi Jinping at opening of FOCAC VI, 4 December 2015.

Agger, Kasper and Hutson, Jonathan (2013) Kony's Ivory: How Elephant Poaching in Congo Helps Support the Lord's Resistance Army, Enough Project, June 2013.

Al Shabaab could establish ties with DRC rebels, East African, 22 February 2014.

Alao, Abiodun Alao (2007) Natural Resources And Conflict In Africa The Tragedy Of Endowment (Rochester: University of Rochester Press).

Albertine Graben Consortium signs oil refinery pact with Uganda, Independent (Kampala), 18 April 2018.

Alden, Christopher (2007) China in Africa, (London: Zed Books).

Alden, Christopher (2014) Seeking security in Africa: China's evolving approach to the African Peace and Security Architecture, NOREF, March.

All eyes on South Sudan as Kenya, Uganda push for Lapsset corridor project, East African, 26 October 2013.

Allen, Kenneth W. and Baguma, Eva (2013) China-Uganda Relations: Closer is Not Necessarily Better, China Brief, Volume XIII, Issue 1, 4 January.

Altorfer-Ong, Alicia (2009) Tanzanian 'Freedom' and Chinese 'Friendship' in 1965: laying the tracks for the TanZam rail link LSE Ideas.

America plots to counter China in EAC with new pact, Business Daily (Nairobi), 20 May 2012.

Anthony, Ross (2012) China's role in the East African oil and gas sector: a new model of engagement?, CCS Policy Briefing, August 2012.

APSA 2010 Assessment Study, p.19, para. 48; Constitutive Act of the African Union, Article 3.l.

Arms Trade Treaty, UN, at http://www.un.org/disarmament/ATT.

Aronda says army takeover possible, Daily Monitor, 24 January 2013.

Ayangafac, Chrysantus and Cilliers, Jakkie (2011) African Solutions to African Problems, in Crocker, Chester A., Hamson, Fen Osler and Aall, Pamela (eds.) (2011) Rewiring Regional Security in a Fragmented World (Washington DC: US Institute of Peace), p.127.

Barkan, Joel D. (2011) Uganda: Assessing Risks to Stablity, Centre for Strategic and International Studies (CSIS), A Report for the CSIS Africa Program, June 2011.

Behind Museveni's defiance of US, Igad orders, East African, 15 February 2014.

Beijing meeting on African peace and security: combating illicit small arms and ammunition, Safer World, Seminar Report, Beijing, 18 March 2014.

Bevan, James (2008) Crisis in Karamoja Armed Violence and the Failure of Disarmament in Uganda's Most Deprived Region, Small Arms Survey Occasional Paper 21, Geneva 2008.

Biryabarema, Elias, Uganda says Chinese firm applies to build $1.4 bln power plant on the Nile, Reuters.com. 11 February 2020.

Biswaro, J M (2012) The Quest for Regional Integration in Africa, Latin America and Beyond in the Twenty First Century: Experience, Progress and Prospects. Brasilia: Fernando Morais.

Bobi Wine: Uganda's 'ghetto president', BBC News, 22 February 2021, available at https://www.bbc.co.uk/news/world-africa-55572903 (accessed 20 May 2021).

Bodomo, Adams (2015) Africans in China: Guangzhou and Beyond – Issues and Reviews, The Journal of Pan African Studies, 7: 10.

Bolton, Matthew (2015) Using the Arms Trade Treaty to Address Wildlife Poaching in East Africa: A Human Security Approach, ControlArms.org, Working Paper, Version 5.2, November 2015.

Brautigam, Deborah (2009) The dragon's gift: the real story of China in Africa (OUP Oxford).

Brautigam, Deborah and Xiaoyang, Tang (2011) African Shenzhen: China's Special Economic Zones in Africa, Journal of Modern African Studies, 49/1.

Brennan, Hugo (2013) North Africa: Are the Chinese Next On Al-Qaeda in the Islamic Maghreb's Hit List?, AllAfrica, 17 December 2013.

Bunyoro Kingdom in bloody land clashes, Oil in Uganda, 8 December 2014.

Bibliography

Bunyoro leaders demand for more, Oil in Uganda, 15 June 2015.

Burundi calls opposition protesters 'terrorists', BBC News, 2 May 2015.

Burundi expels Rwandan diplomat for 'creating insecurity', BBC News, 7 October 2015.

Burundi's Nkurunziza: 'It's either me or al-Shabab', Al-Jazeera, 17 May 2015.

Cáceres, Sigfrido Burgos and Ear, Sophal (2012) The Geopolitics of China's Global Resources Quest, Geopolitics, 17:1, p.62.

Cáceres, Sigfrido Burgos and Ear, Sophal (2013) The Hungry Dragon: How China's Quest for Resources is Reshaping the World (Oxon: Routledge), p.60.

Carmody, Pádraig and Taylor, Ian (2010) Flexigemony and Force in China's Resource Diplomacy in Africa: Sudan and Zambia Compared, Geopolitics, 15:3, pp.496–515.

Centre for Chinese Studies, Stellenbosch University (2007) China's Engagement of Africa: Preliminary Scoping of African case studies: Angola, Ethiopia, Gabon, Uganda, South Africa, Zambia.

Chakrabarty, Malancha (2015) Growth of Chinese trade and investment flows in DR Congo – blessing or curse?, Review of African Political Economy, DOI:10.1080/03 056244.2015.1048794, pp.8–9.

Chan, Stephen (2013) Afterword: The Future of China and Africa, in Chan, Stephen (ed.) (2013) The Morality of China in Africa: The Middle Kingdom and the Dark Continent (London: Zed Books).

Chau, Donovan C (2012) Historical island in a political volcano, African Security Review, 21:1, p.4.

China Expands Investment in Tanzania, The New York Times-Sinosphere Blog, Briefing, 13 September 2014.

China Halts Arms Sales to South Sudan After Norinco Shipment, Bloomberg, 30 September 2014.

China influence seen as strong, positive in Tanzania, Afrobarometre News release, Dar es Salaam, Tanzania, 25 February 2015.

China Issues One Year Ban on Import of African Ivory Trophies, IFAW, 15 October 2015; China agrees to phase out its ivory industry to combat elephant poaching, The Guardian, 29 May 2015; 4.

China negotiating Horn of Africa military base: Djibouti president, Times Live (Johannesburg), 9 May 2015.

China sees chance to woo Uganda as West mulls sanctions for bloody election, South China Morning Post, 22 February 2021, https://www.scmp.com/news/china/ diplomacy/article/3122668/china-sees-chance-woo-uganda-west-mulls-sanctions-bloody.

China Sells South Sudan Arms as Its Government Talks Peace, Bloomberg, 9 July 2014.

China signs deal with AU to connect Africa's big cities, Africa Report, 28 January 2015.

China Step Closer to Exporting Reactors With Africa Agreement, Bloomberg.com, 9 September 2015.

China urges immediate end to conflict in South Sudan, *The Guardian*, 7 January 2014.

China urges LRA to cease violence, China Daily, 15 November 2011.

China, EAC in new $500m trade, investment deal, East African, 27 November 2011.

China: Tanzania's biggest development partner Kampala, East African, 25 January 2014.

China's largest weapons manufacturer is allegedly selling arms to South Sudan – again, Quartz Africa, 26 August 2015.

China-Africa trade surpassed $200 billion in 2013, East African, 20 February 2014.

China's oil fears over South Sudan fighting, BBC News, 8 January 2014.

Chinese consortium to revive Uganda's once-vital copper mines, China-Africa Reporting Project, 9 May 2014.

Chinese influx into Uganda retail trade causes hostility among local businesses, East African, 25 January 2014.

Chinese invasion, Independent, 16 January 2012.

Chinese investors in EA seek double taxation relief, Daily Nation, 23 April 2015.

Christy, Brian (2015) How Killing Elephants Finances Terror in Africa, National Geographic, 15 August 2015.

Cline, Lawrence (2013) The Lord's Resistance Army (Oxford: Praeger), p.65.

Cohen, Herman J. (2012) Rwanda: Fifty Years of Ethnic Conflict on Steroids, American Foreign Policy Interests: The Journal of the National Committee on American Foreign Policy, 34:2, p.86.

Communiqué of the 12th Extra Ordinary Summit of EAC Heads of State, 28 April 2014.

Compensation remains messy, 'noisy' NGOs risk closure, Oil in Uganda, 7 October 2013.

Conroy-Krutz, J., & Logan, C. (2012). Museveni and the 2011 Ugandan election: Did the money matter? The Journal of Modern African Studies, 50(4), pp.625–55.

Court Delivers a Judgement on Kaluma [sic] Hydro Power Project Dispute, EACJ, 28 November 2014.

Court orders that rebel MPs be thrown out of parliament with immediate effect, Daily Monitor, 21 February 2014.

Crossley, Pamela (2010) The Wobbling Pivot: China Since 1800 (Sussex: Wiley-Blackwell).

Dar ponders its fate in EAC, Citizen, 16 March 2013.

de Oliveira, Ricardo Soares (2008) Making Sense of Chinese Oil Investment in Africa, in Alden, Christopher, Large, Daniel and Soares de Oliveira, Ricardo (eds.) (2008) China Returns to Africa: A Rising Power and a Continent Embrace (New York: Columbia University Press).

Deng, Kent (2011) China's Political Economy in Modern times: Changes and Economic Consequences, 1800–2000 (London: Routledge).

Djoumessi, Didier T. (2009) The Political Impacts of the Sino-US Oil Competition in Africa (London: Adonis & Abbey).

Dowden, Richard (2011) Reconciliation for Kagame and Museveni, Huffington Post, 2 September 2011.

DR Congo: 'FDLR rebels kidnap Soco oil worker', BBC News, 15 February 2015.

EAC leaders to continue war on terror, Daily Monitor, 1 May 2014.

EAC Ministers in China for Infrastructure Development Study Tour, Uganda Radio Network, 8 May 2008.

EAC Secretariat, Strategy for the Development of Regional Refineries Final Repot, February 2008.

East Africa: Regional MPs Call for Joint Security Operations, New Times, 2 November 2014.

East African Community Vision 2050, Draft, August 2015.

East African Countries Raise Defense Budgets on Increased Terrorism Threats, AFK Insider, 16 April 2014.

Economist Intelligence Unit (1998) Country Report: Uganda, Rwanda, Burundi, 1st quarter 1998, p.8.

Environmental Investigation Agency (EIA) (2014) VANISHING POINT: Criminality, Corruption and the Devastation of Tanzania's Elephants, November 2014.

Exclusive: U.S. to spend up to $550 million on African rapid response forces, Reuters, 6 August 2014.

Ezeanya, Chika (2012) Tragedy of the new AU headquarters, Pambazuka News, Issue 567.

Fabricius, Peter (2014) The elephant in the room, African Security Review, 23:4, p.415.

FACTBOX-Quotes from Uganda's Museveni, Reuters, available at https://www. reuters.com/article/uganda-museveni-quotes-idUKL2207523720080722 (accessed 21 June 2020).

Falling oil prices: Who are the winners and losers?, BBC News, 19 January 2015.

Farmers, civil rights groups oppose Uganda's oil project, Mail and Guardian, 1 May 2021.

Final report of the Group of Experts on the Democratic Republic of the Congo, UN Report to the Security Council, S/2015/19, 12 January 2015.

Find lasting solution to land, tribal tensions, Daily Monitor, 24 July 2014.

Fisher, Jonathan (2012) Managing donor perceptions: Contextualizing Uganda's 2007 intervention in Somalia, African Affairs 111, no. 444, pp.404–23.

Fisher, Jonathan (2013) Structure, agency and Africa in the international system: donor diplomacy and regional security policy in East Africa since the 1990s, Conflict, Security & Development, 13: 5, pp.537–67.

Fisher, Jonathan (2014) Framing Kony: Uganda's war, Obama's advisers and the nature of 'influence' in Western foreign policy making, Third World Quarterly, 35:4.

FOCAC VI Johannesburg Declaration; FOCAC VI Johannesburg Action Plan.

Global Witness (2014) A Good Deal Better? Uganda's Secret Oil Contracts Explained, September 2014.

Government asked to name DRC looters, Daily Monitor, 2 September 2015.

Government of Uganda (2012) Uganda Vision 2040.

Govt turns to Chinese to fast-track Nyabarongo II hydro-power project, New Times, 22 May 2015.

Grobler, John (2014) Chinese infrastructure lubricates outflow of Angolan and DRC resources, Pambazuka News, Issue 673, 10 April 2014.

Guéhenno, Jean-Marie, Obe, Ayo and Adeola, Fola (2015) AU was set up for an explosive crisis like Burundi; it must act, East African, 14 November 2015.

Hansen, Stig Jarle (2014) Al-Shabaab in Somalia: the history and ideology of a militant Islamist group, 2005–2012 (Oxford: Oxford University Press).

Henstridge, Mark and Page, John (2012) Managing a Modest Boom: Oil Revenues in Uganda, OxCarre Research Paper 90, June 2012.

Hickey, Sam, Badru Bukenya, Angelo Izama and William Kizito (2015) The political settlement and oil in Uganda, ESID Working Paper No. 48, March 2015.

High risk, high reward: talking offshore oil security with Drum Cussac, OffshoreEnergyTechnology.com, 3 January 2013.

Hongxiang, Hunag (2013) The Chinese ivory-smugglers in Africa, Chinadialogue.net, 27 November 2013.

How Chinese firm DongSong lost lucrative refinery deal, East African, 21 August 2017.

How Tanzania foiled terror attack on Kenya poll, Daily Nation, 19 April 2014.

How the US Can Help Kenya', Heritage Foundation Report, 25 March 2088, p.8.

Hull, Richard (1972) China in Africa, Issue: A Journal of Opinion, 2: 3.

I will leave power after East Africa is united – Museveni, Daily Monitor, 10 February 2016.

Illegal ivory trade funds al-Shabaab's terrorist attacks, The Independent (London), 6 August 2013.

Imaka, Isaac and Musisi, Frederic (2013) Following the oil money: How much has it done?, Daily Monitor, Special Report, 3 December 2013.

India and People's Republic of China, 29 April 1954, No. 4307 of UN Treaty Series, Vol. 299.

Invest oil money in infrastructure, health-Survey, Oil in Uganda, 30 March 2015.

Is China's Role in African Fragile States Exploitative or Developmental? IDS Policy Briefing, Issue 91, March 2015.

It's all about trade and pace of reforms, Daily Nation, 10 August 2015.

Ivory scandal: UPDF colonel implicated as six are detained, Daily Monitor, 5 February 2015.

Izama, Angelo (2013) Tracing Uganda's oil journey from 1913–2013, Daily Monitor, 31 December 2013.

Izama, Angelo and Wilkerson, Michael (2011) Uganda: Museveni's Triumph and Weakness, Journal of Democracy, 22: 3.

Jowell, Marco (2014) Peacekeeping Country Profile: Uganda, Providing for Peacekeeping, February 2014, available at http://www.providingforpeacekeeping. org/2014/04/03/country-profile-uganda, accessed 13 May 2015.

Kagame declares 'shoot on sight' anti-terror policy, New Vision, 9 June 2014.

Kagame: China's donation to AU HQ symptom of Africa's bigger problems, East African, 2 February 2012.

Kagenda, Patrick (2014) Behind the attacks in western Uganda, Daily Monitor, 28 July 2014.

Kagoro, Jude (2013) The Military Ethos in the Politics of Post-1986 Uganda, Social Sciences Directory, 2: 2, pp.31–46.

Kalinaki, Daniel (2015) Kizza Besigye and Uganda's Unfinished Revolution (Kampala: DominanetSeven).

Kalron, Nir and Crosta, Andrea (2014) Africa's White Gold of Jihad: al-Shabaab and Conflict Ivory, Elephant Action League, Special Report; Elephant Campaign: How Africa's 'white gold' funds the al-Shabaab militants, The Independent (London), 3 February 2014.

Kamata, Ng'wanza (2013) Perspectives on Sino-Tanzanian Relations, in Adem, Seifudein (ed) (2013) China's Diplomacy in Eastern and Southern Africa (Farnham: Ashgate).

Kampala-Kigali railway project derails, Independent, 19 July 2015; Why the Kampala-Kigali railway is off the track, Africa Intelligence, Uganda: Politics & Power Brokers N°1417, 18 December 2015.

Kannyo, Edward (2013) Sino-Ugandan Relations: Themes and Issues, in Adem, Seifudein (ed) (2013) China's Diplomacy in Eastern and Southern Africa (Farnham: Ashgate).

Kasasira, Risdel (2015) What UPDF withdrawal means for Salva Kiir, Daily Monitor, 18 October 2015.

Kayunga, Sallie Simba (2005) Deepening Political Integration of the EAC Countries: The Uganda Case, in Mohiddin, Ahmed (ed.) (2005) Deepening Regional Integration of the East African Community (Addis Ababa: DPMF).

Keating, Michael F. (2011) Can democratization undermine democracy? Economic and political reform in Uganda, Democratization, 18:2.

Kenya boosts China ties with Sh7.9bn arms purchase deal, Daily Nation (Nairobi), 15 February 2016.

Kenya corruption watchdog makes allegations against 175 officials, Reuters, 1 April 2015.

Kenya to acquire stake in Uganda's refinery, Oil in Uganda, 27 January 2015.

Kenya's debt to China hits Sh101 billion as external loans pile, The Star (Nairobi), 28 March 2015.

Keynote Address by H.E. Yoweri Kaguta Museveni, UN, New York, United Nations High-level Thematic Debate on Strengthening Co-operation between the United Nations and regional organisations in the maintenance of peace, security, human rights and development in their respective areas, available at Museveni calls for UN restructuring, New Vision, 5 May 2015.

Kikuubo Traders Protest Unfair Competition by Chinese Retailers, Uganda Radio Network, 23 May 2009.

Kikwete hints at possible terrorist operations in Tanzania, East African, 4 March 2015.

Kissinger, Henry (2012) On China (London: Penguin), p.18.

Kiwanuka, Jenkins (2013) Is China promoting a new type of economic imperialism?, Daily Monitor, OpEd, 22 July 2013.

Lanteigne, Marc (2013) Fire over water: China's strategic engagement of Somalia and the Gulf of Aden crisis, The Pacific Review, 26:3, pp.289–312.

Lee, Henry and Shalmon, Dan (2008) Searching for Oil: China's Oil Strategies in Africa, in Rotberg, Robert (Ed.) (2008) China into Africa: Trade, Aid, and Influence (Washington, D.C.: Brookings Institution Press).

Lemarchand, Rene (2000) The Crisis in the Great Lakes, in Harbeson, John and Rothchild, Donald (eds.) Africa in World Politics, (Boulder: West View Press), pp.327–31.

Litovsky, Alejandro (2014) Renegotiating the colonial-era treaty that gave Egypt a veto over any upstream Nile project is critical, Independent, 28 July 2014.

Lord's Resistance Army funded by elephant poaching, report finds, The Guardian, 4 June 2013.

Macron pushes East African oil pipeline as French banks shun project, Global Trade Review, 5 May 2021.

Bibliography

Madina et al. (2010) Impact of China-Africa Aid Relations: A Case Study of Uganda, Economic Policy Research Centre (EPRC), Final Report submitted to the African Economic Research Consortium (AERC) May, 2010.

Mariam, Alemayehu G. (2012) Ethiopia: African Beggars Union Hall? Nazret.com, 2 June 2012.

Massive military operation in Kenya's Turkana region to flush out bandits, Star Africa, 4 November 2014.

Matsiko, Haggai (2014) Is it time for a China-Africa Command?, Independent, 16 November 2014.

Mazzeo, Domenico (1975) Foreign assistance and the East African common services, 1960–1970, with special reference to multilateral contributions (Münich: Weltforum Verlag).

Mbabazi versus Museveni, Daily Monitor, 20 December 2013.

Mbabazi, Amama (2013) How China can propel Uganda's economic development, Daily Monitor, OpEd, 20 September 2013.

Missing Ivory: Mutagamba suspends UWA's executive director, Independent, 25 November 2015.

Mohan, Giles (2012) China in Africa: Impacts and prospects for accountable development, ESID Working Paper No. 12.

Mohan, Giles and Lampert, Ben (2012) Negotiating China: Reinserting African Agency into China–Africa Relations, African Affairs, 112: 446, pp.92–110.

Mohammed Emwazi went to Tanzania 'to commit terrorism', BBC News, 9 March 2015.

Money problems in Uganda's Parliament, Daily Monitor, 2 November 2014.

Mote, F.W (2003) Imperial China 900–1800 (Harvard University Press).

Muggah, Robert and Sang, Francis (2013) The enemy within: rethinking arms availability in sub-Saharan Africa, Conflict, Security & Development, 13:4.

Murithi, Tim (2009b) The African Union's Transition from Non-intervention to Non-Indifference: An Ad-hoc Approach to The Responsibility to Protect?; Constitutive Act of the African Union, Article 4.

Museveni blasts oil companies over refinery, New Vision, 10 April 2013.

Museveni calls NRM rebel MPs for talks, Daily Monitor, 29 June 2015.

Museveni comments overshadow London summit, East African, 1 November 2014.

Museveni describes eastern DRC as terrorism conservation project, The Africa Report, 31 January 2013.

Museveni distrusts Beijing and woos Seoul, Africa Intelligence, Uganda: Politics and Power Brokers, N°1413, 23 October 2015.

Museveni doesn't make tracking ivory traffic any easier, Indian Ocean Newsletter, Uganda Politics & Power Brokers, N°1398, 27 February 2015.

Museveni plays a wicked poker hand on Tanga, Africa Energy Intelligence, Uganda Oil N°756, 27 October 2015.

Museveni under fire over army, Independent, 6 October 2014.

Museveni: I've never received oil bribes, Daily Monitor, 13 October 2011.

Museveni's visit to Sudan good for peace, Daily Monitor, 17 September 2015.

Musisi, Frederic (2014) Financing questions lie ahead after MoU, Daily Monitor, Special Report, 11 February 2014.

Mutengesa, Sabiiti and Hendrickson, Dylan (2008) State Responsiveness to Public Security Needs: The Politics of Security Decision, Making Uganda Country Study and CSDG Papers, Number 16.

Mwenda, Andrew and Tangri, Roger (2008) Elite Corruption and Politics in Uganda, Commonwealth & Comparative Politics, 4:2, pp.177–94.

Ndulu, B J and Mutalemwa, C (2002) Tanzania at the Turn of the Century: Background Papers and Statistics (Washington DC: World Bank).

New twists in DR Congo's Inga 3 Dam saga, Pambazuka News, 13 March 2014.

Nnaoli, Okwudibla (1990) The External Environment of Development in East Africa: An overview, in Chole, Eshetu, Wilfred Mlay and Walter Oyugi (eds.) (1990) The Crisis of Development Strategies in East Africa (OSSREA: Addis Ababa).

Now Machar's men back UPDF stay in South Sudan, Daily Monitor, 27 September 2014.

Obore, Chris (2014) NRM delegates fooled as both Mbabazi and Museveni win, Daily Monitor, 21 December 2014.

Odgaard, Liselotte (2013) Peaceful Coexistence Strategy and China's Diplomatic Power, The Chinese Journal of International Politics, 6, p.235.

Oil: Museveni takes over, Daily Monitor, 19 August 2014.

Onjala, Joseph (2013) Merchandise trading between Kenya and China: implications for the East African Community (EAC), in Adem, Seifudein (ed) (2013) China's Diplomacy in Eastern and Southern Africa (Farnham: Ashgate), pp.63–8.

Opposition fire back at Museveni over oil control, Daily Monitor, 23 December 2015.

Owners will lose rights over mineral-rich land – Museveni, Daily Monitor, 1 November 2014.

Parliament okays $1.435 billion loan for Karuma, Daily Monitor, 25 March 2015.

Parrin, Anjli (2015) Burundi crisis gets serious for regional leaders, IRIN, 14 July 2015.

Peter, Melkunaite, Laura (2013) Research Note on the Energy Infrastructure Attack Database (EIAD), Perspectives on Terrorism, 7: 6.

Police Oil Unit gets new Commander, Oil in Uganda, 15 January 2014.

Police seize tonnes of ivory, Daily Monitor, 15 June 2015.

Power, Marcus and Mohan, Giles (2010) Towards a Critical Geopolitics of China's Engagement with African Development, Geopolitics, 15:3.

President Museveni of Uganda Concludes Visit to Sudan, Sudan Now (Khartoum), 16 September 2015.

Press Release – New Measures on Way for China-Africa Cooperation, Press & Public Affairs Section Embassy of the People's Republic of China in the Republic of South Africa, 26 November 2015.

Railway scandal: How the project slipped off, Daily Monitor, 31 August 2014.

Refinery contractor's military links raise eyebrows, Oil in Uganda, 23 February 2015.

Refinery could offer power push, Africa Energy Intelligence, Uganda Electricity, N°671, 14 March 2012.

Regional countries up security spending over terror and wars, East African, 14 June 2014.

Report of the EAC Inter- Parliamentarians Relations Liaison Committee on Natural Resources on the site tour of Tanzanian Extractive Industries, Shinyanga – Kahama – Mwanza, 19–23 November 2008.

Report of the EAC Inter- Parliamentary Relations Liaison Committee on Natural Resources on the site tour of Tullow Oil Industries in Hoima District, Uganda, 14th–19th June 2009.

Report of the Monitoring Group on Somalia and Eritrea pursuant to Security Council resolution 2060 (2012): Somalia S/2013/413, 12 July 2013.

Report of the Monitoring Group on Somalia and Eritrea pursuant to Security Council resolution 2111 (2013): Somalia, S/2014/726, 10 October 2014.

Repressive NGO Act, Inter Press Service, 9 March 2016.

Reyntjens, Filip (2019) East Africa should intervene to defuse Rwanda-Uganda war of words, The Conversation, 25 March 2019, available at https://theconversation.com/east-africa-should-intervene-to-defuse-rwanda-uganda-war-of-words-114202 (accessed 10 January 2020).

Rukandema, Mwita (2012) Uganda: Reflections of a Passing Generation (Fountain: Kampala).

Russia: U.N. Security Council should stay out of Burundi dispute, Reuters.com, 1 May 2015.

Russian, South Korean firms 'battle' for refinery contract, Oil in Uganda, 24 June 2014.

Saferworld (2007) Mapping the small arms problem in Uganda: The development of Uganda's National Action Plan on Small Arms and Light Weapons, May 2007.

Saferworld (2014) Tackling Illicit Small Arms and Light Weapons (SALW) and Ammunition in the Great Lakes and Horn of Africa, Final Working Paper, June 2014.

Sanusi, Lamido (2013) Africa must get real about Chinese ties, The Financial Times, 11 March 2013.

Schatz, Sayre (1994) Structural Adjustment in Africa: a Failing Grade So Far, The Journal of Modern African Studies, 32: 4, pp.679–92.

Schlichte, Klaus (2008) Uganda, Or: The Internationalisation of Rule, Civil Wars, 10: 4, pp.369–83.

Seyoum, Mebratu and Lin, Jihong (2014) Private Chinese Investment in Ethiopia: Determinants and Location Decisions, Journal of International Development, July 2014.

Shah, Anup (2013) Structural Adjustment – a Major Cause of Poverty, Global Issues, 24 March 2013.

Shinn, David (2008) Military and Security Relations: China, Africa, and the Rest of the World, in Rotberg, Robert (Ed.) (2008) China into Africa: Trade, Aid, and Influence (Washington, D.C.: Brookings Institution Press), pp.155–96.

Shinn, David and Eisenman, Joshua (2012) China and Africa (University of Pennsylvania Press).

Siriar, Pabati Kuma (1990) Development through integration: Lessons from East Africa (Delhi: Kalinga Publishers), pp.142–3.

Small Arms Survey (2012) Sudan Issue Brief, Reaching for the gun: Arms flows and holding in South Sudan, Number 19, April 2012.

Small Arms Survey, 2012 Year Book, p.152.

Small Arms Survey, 2013 Year Book, Annex 8.1.

Small Arms Survey, 2014 Year Book, pp.200–1.

Ssegawa, Mike (2014) How smuggling ivory limits tourists from streaming in, Special Report, Daily Monitor, 26 November 2014.

Stakeholders in Somalia's peacekeeping mission meet in Burundi, China People's Daily, 16 November 2010.

Statement by Ambassador Liu Jieyi at the Security Council Briefing on the Activities of the United Nations Regional Office for Central Africa and on the Lord's Resistance Army-Affected Areas, 20 November 2014.

Successful operation highlights growing international cooperation to combat wildlife crime, CITES, 18 June 2015.

Tanzania arrests 7 pirates after attack on oil vessel, Reuters.com, 4 October 2011.

Tanzania awards $9 Bln Rail Projects to Chinese Companies, CNBCAfrica, 1 June 2015.

Tanzania gas pipeline built, but not ready to start, Reuters, 31 March 2015.

Tanzania to spend $14 bln on railways, eyes regional hub status, Reuters, 30 March 2015.

Tatum, Dale C. (2002) Who Influenced Whom? Lessons from the Cold War (Maryland: University Press of America).

Taylor, Ian (2006) China and Africa: Engagement and compromise (Oxford: Routledge).

Taylor, Ian (2011) The Forum on China-Africa Cooperation (FOCAC) (London: Routledge).

Taylor, Ian (2020) Kenya's New Lunatic Express: The Standard Gauge Railway. African Studies Quarterly, 19.

Terrorism is alive in region, says CMI boss, Daily Monitor, 11 July 2011.

The shifting river that is making Uganda smaller, The Guardian, 7 December 2010.

Thomas, Darryl (2013) China's Foreign Policy Towards Africa, from Bandung Conference to the 21st Century (1955–2011), in Adem, Seifudein (ed) (2013) China's Diplomacy in Eastern and Southern Africa (Farnham: Ashgate).

Tisdell, Clem (2008) Thirty Years of Economic Reform and Openness in China: Retrospect and Prospect, Economic Theory, Applications and Issues, Working Paper No. 51, University of Queensland.

Titeca, Kristof and Vlassenroot, Koen (2012) Rebels without borders in the Rwenzori borderland? A biography of the Allied Democratic Forces, Journal of Eastern African Studies, 6:1, p.155.

Total brandishes Tanzanian card to thwart Lamu pipeline scheme, Africa Energy Intelligence, Uganda Oil N°752, 1 September 2015.

Tough choices over oil, Independent, 22 September 2013.

Tough Times Ahead, Anti-Terrorism Bill Passed, Independent, 18 June 2015.

Tripp, Aili Mari (2010) Museveni's Uganda: Paradoxes of Power in a Hybrid Regime, (Boulder: Lynne Reinner).

Tullow rejects oil search deal with Chinese firm CNOOC, Daily Monitor, 21 February 2011.

Turkish firm wins contract to finish building Kigali centre, East African, 25 April 2015.

Uganda faces tough choices as donors cut aid, East African, 8 March 2014.

Uganda import teargas trucks ahead of poll, East African, 17 January 2016.

Ugandan president tells Chinese construction boss: 'If you are not willing to co-operate, leave', Global Construction Review, 15 October 2014, available at https://www.globalconstructionreview.com/news/ugandan-pre3side8nt-tel0ls-chine6se-constr5uct2ion (accessed 20 April 2020).

Uganda to use oil cash for infrastructure development, New Times, 30 August 2013.

Uganda Wants Chinese-Built Infrastructure Paid for With Oil, Bloomberg, 9 July 2013.

Uganda, Burundi lead East Africa in military spending, East African, 16 April 2014.

Uganda: Bill Threatens Rights, Independent Groups, Human Rights Watch, 20 April 2015.

Uganda: Museveni condemns terrorism in all its forms, IRIN, 12 September 2001.

Uganda: Museveni Says No to MPs' Loan Bailout Deal, Observer, 23 July 2013.

Ugandan president to approve all oil, gas deals, Reuters, 19 August 2010.

Ugandan rebel leader's arrest a shot in the arm for justice, IRIN News, 30 April 2015.

Uhuru Kenyatta says terrorists are exploiting Kenya's expanded democratic space, Daily Nation, 26 September 2014.

UPDF destroys over 200 tonnes of ammunition, Daily Monitor, 12 January 2014.

UPDF must deal with indiscipline, Observer, 10 September 2014.

US Department of State (2012) The Lord's Resistance Army: Fact Sheet, 23 March 2012.

US warns against Burundi travel amid Al Shabaab threat, East African, 31 October 2014.

Wakabi, Michael (2015) Why Kenya and Uganda are racing to connect Juba to the SGR, Africa Review, 9 August 2015.

Walsh, Barney (2010) Uganda's Involvement in the DRC since 1998: Museveni and Regional Relations, ALC Monograph, Number 5.

Walsh, Barney (2015) Human Security in East Africa: The EAC's illusive quest for inclusive citizenship, Strategic Review for Southern Africa, 37: 1.

Walsh, Barney (2019) China's pervasive yet forgotten regional security role in Africa, Journal of Contemporary China 28, no. 120.

Walsh, Barney and Kinkoh, Hubert (2020) COVID-19 and the Conundrum of China-Africa Relations, ALC COVID-19 OpEd Series, Vol 1 No 2, April 15.

Walsh, Barney (2020) Revisiting Regional Security Complex Theory in Africa: Museveni's Uganda and Regional Security in East Africa, African Security, pp.300–24.

What do leaked oil contracts mean for Uganda's future?, Oil in Uganda, 12 December 2014.

What's going on? Cracks appear in oil company partnership as pipeline saga drags on, Oil in Uganda, 28 December 2015.

Why EA countries chose more costly route for standard gauge railway line, East African, 28 September 2013.

Why the Kampala-Kigali railway is off the track, Africa Intelligence, Uganda: Politics & Power Brokers N°1417, 18 December 2015; Wakabi (2015); Kampala-Kigali railway project derails, Independent, 19 July 2015.

WikiLeaks cable 05NAIROBI3600_a, KENYA'S PRESIDENT GOES TO CHINA – AND WHAT IT MEANS, Kenya Nairobi, 5 September 2005, https://wikileaks.org/plusd/cables/05NAIROBI3600_a.html.

Wikileaks cable 07KINSHASA1344, PRESIDENT KABILA DELIVERS UPBEAT 'STATE OF THE NATION' ADDRESS, Democratic Republic of the Congo Kinshasa, 7 December 2007, https://wikileaks.org/cable/2007 December 2007KINSHASA1344.html.

Wikileaks Cable 09KAMPALA1401_a, UGANDA: TULLOW SEES CORRUPTION IN OIL SALE, Uganda Kampala, 17 December 2009, https://wikileaks.org/plusd/cables/09KAMPALA1401_a.html.

Wikileaks Cable 10KAMPALA21_a, UGANDA: UK CONSIDERING CORRUPTION TRAVEL BANS, Uganda Kampala, 13 January 2010, https://wikileaks.org/plusd/cables/10KAMPALA21_a.html.

Will Kadaga listen to the 'people's call' and run for presidency?, Daily Monitor, 6 January 2014.

Will peacekeeper plan help end Burundi violence? IRIN News, 18 December 2015.

Will Uganda's oil wealth change LAPSSET into LAPSSEUT?, Indian Ocean Observatory, 31 August 2014; http://www.lapsset.go.ke/oilpipeline.

Williamson, Rachel (2014) Briefing: Somaliland, Oil and Security, IRIN News, 7 August 2014.

With the ivory burn, China can help save the elephant, East African, 18 January 2014; China increases prosecutions in response to illegal trade in elephant ivory, CITES, 29 November 2013.

Without a soft landing for Kiir, the Igad-Plus peace proposal is doomed, East African, 8 August 2015.

World Military Expenditure and Arms transfers, 1972–87, US Arms Control and Disarmament Agency.

Zambia probes diplomats over ivory export, Xinhua News, 11 June 2013.

Zanzibar and Tanzania vie over oil reserves, Financial Times.com, 10 March 2015.

Zaremba, By Haley (2020) China Is Rapidly Expanding Its Oil Resources In Africa, oilprice.com, available at https://oilprice.com/Energy/Crude-Oil/China-Is-Rapidly-Expanding-Its-Oil-Resources-In-Africa.html (accessed 10 January 2021).

Index

African Peace and Security Architecture
(APSA) 3, 8, 21, 71
African Standby Force (ASF) 8
African Union (AU)
    Agenda 2063 22
    China and 14–15, 151
    Mission to Somalia (AMISOM) 86, 90,
        108, 110, 111
    security, role in 8
    see also African Peace and Security
    Architecture (APSA)
Al-Qaeda 108
Al-Shabaab
    Chinese ammunition 116
    ivory poaching 91, 120–1
    regional links 112–13
    terrorism 86, 108, 109, 110
Allied Democratic Forces (ADF) 107, 109,
    113
Amin, Idi 29
Angola 18–19, 22
anti-terrorism laws 111
arms *see* small arms and light weapons
    (SALW)

Bandung Conference (1955) 13
Benguela Railway 22
Besigye, Kizza 29, 51, 53, 55, 119
Buganda 52–3, 56
Bunyoro 92, 127, 133
Burundi
    China and 65, 82–4, 103
    EAC and 32–3
    terrorism 86, 111–12

Cameroon 17
Central Africa 17–18
Chama Cha Mapinduzi (CCM)
    112
China
    pre-20th century history 13, 63–4

20th century relationships 13–14,
    29–30, 34, 64–8
21st century relationships 14–16, 37–8,
    101
academic research 23–4
Africa, relationship with 2–3, 5, 6–9
AU and 14–15, 151
EAC and 4, 10, 72–7, 94, 102, 148–9
EACJ and 55–6
East Africa, influence in 78–84
Five Principles of cooperation 13
infrastructure projects 22–3, 36, 75–6,
    80, 82, 98, 100, 134–5, 152 *see also*
    railways
investment in Uganda 38–9, 39–41
ivory poaching 86–91, 102, 122
Kingdoms and 52–3, 56, 58
MPs and 50–1, 54, 58
neutrality 117
non-interference policy 23, 24, 27, 58,
    67–8, 77, 84–5, 120, 147, 151, 152
NRM, relationship with 44–5, 55
oil 14, 93–4, 96, 102, 106, 131–5, 136,
    143–4
railways 94–5, 97–8, 137–8
regional involvement 16–20
role of 150–2
security 21–2, 24–5
small arms and light weapons (SALW)
    114–17, 118–20
sovereignty, promotion of 12–13, 15
strategy, improvisation of 24
and successors to Museveni 43–4
terrorism 122
trade with Africa 15, 18, 74
trade with Uganda 10, 38, 53, 56–7
Uganda and 10, 28–9, 35–7, 142–4,
    147–8
Uganda People's Defence Force and
    46–7, 48, 49
UN Security Council seat 66

Index

China Africa Friendship Association of Uganda (CAFAU) 53–4
China Civil Engineering Construction Corporation (CCECC) 138, 141
China–EAC Framework agreement 75–6, 94
China Harbour and Engineering Corporation (CHEC) 137–8
China International Fund (CIF) 22
China International Water and Electric Corporation (CWE) 56
China National Offshore Oil Corporation (CNOOC) 79, 124, 131–5, 140
China North Industries Group Corp (NORINCO) 117
Chinese local traders 53, 56–7
Coalition of the Willing (CoW) 69, 71, 81, 129, 154
Communist Party of China (CPC) 44
Confucian Institutes (CIs) 78
Continental Early Warning System (CEWS) 8
corruption 51–2, 54–5, 77, 79
Cultural Revolution 14

defence and security *see* security
Democratic Forces for the Liberation of Rwanda (FDLR) 72, 112
Democratic Republic of Congo (DRC) 17, 18, 22, 109, 129
Deng Xiaoping 14
development *see* infrastructure
developmental assistance *see* Forum on Africa-China Cooperation (FOCAC)

East African Community (EAC)
  20th century history 64, 65, 66
  21st century history 68–70
  China and 4, 10, 72–7, 94, 102, 148–9
  defence and security 70–1, 72, 88, 90, 91, 101
  definition of 3
  ivory poaching 88
  oil and natural resources 95–6, 97
  regional integration and 9–10, 32–4, 47, 101–2
  terrorism 112–13
East African Court of Justice (EACJ) 55–6

East African Legislative Assembly (EALA) 54–5, 74–5, 96–7, 111
economy 39–40, 74
Egypt 20, 22–3
elections 30, 51, 55
employment 39, 53–4
energy 39, 56, 138
Ethiopia 17
European Union (EU) 75
Export-Import Bank of China (EXIM) 138, 141

Fang Min 38, 41
Five Principles of cooperation 13
fixers 40
foreign investment *see* investment
foreign policy 35, 48
Forum for Democratic Change (FDC) 50
Forum on Africa-China Cooperation (FOCAC) 6, 21–2, 38, 88, 114

Global War on Terror (GWOT) 11, 108, 109
government 31–2

infrastructure
  China and 22–3, 36, 75–6, 80, 82, 100, 134–5, 152
  development and 124
  energy 39, 56, 138
  LAPSSET 98, 139, 140
  oil 98–9, 129–30, 133–4, 136–7
  railways 94–5, 97–8, 137–8
  regional integration and 141–2
Intergovernmental Authority on Development (IGAD) 10, 117, 118
investment
  in East Africa 76–7
  in Uganda 38–9, 39–41
  see also infrastructure; railways
ivory poaching 86–91, 102, 120–3

judiciary 51–2, 58
justice system *see* East African Court of Justice (EACJ)

Kabahandra, Flavia 39, 53
Kadaga, Rebecca 50
Kagame, Paul 81, 82, 103

Index

Kamba, Kate 99
Kampala City Traders Association (KACITA) 53
Kanyeihamba, George W. 51, 77
Karuma Dam 39, 56, 138
Kenya
    China and 64, 65, 103
    defence and security 70
    EAC and 66
    ivory poaching 121
    LAPSSET 98, 139, 140
    Museveni and 78–9, 139
    oil 79, 92
    railways 97–8, 141
    Somalia and 86, 90
    terrorism 111, 112
Kenyatta, Jomo 65
Kenyatta, Uhuru 79, 103, 139
Kibaki, Mwai 78
Kingdoms 52–3, 56, 58, 127–8
Kisembo, Charles 120

Lamu Port Southern Sudan–Ethiopia Transport (LAPSSET) 98, 139, 140
Libya 20
Lord's Resistance Army (LRA) 107–8, 109, 111, 113, 120–1
Luwero Industries 119

manufacturing 74, 78
Mao Tse-Tung 14, 64, 65
markets 53
Mbabazi, Amama 42–4, 136
Mbabazi, Jacqueline 119
Members of Parliament (MPs) 50–1, 54, 58
military activities 11, 90
military government 31–2
mineral exports 18
multi-party politics 30, 44
Muntu, Mugisha 41–2, 55
Museveni, Yoweri
    agency, summary of 153–6
    ambitions 33, 103
    authoritarianism of 32
    Burundi and 83–4
    challengers to 42–4
    China, comparison with 75

China, relationship with 38, 57, 138–9, 142–4, 146–7
China, use of 4–5, 27, 36–7, 140–2, 148, 150, 152
    conflicts, intervention in 72
    example of African agency 3, 150
    exile of 29
    influences on 30
    infrastructure and 124
    Kenya, influence in 78–9, 139
    oil and 123, 125–6, 127, 130, 131–2, 134, 135, 137, 141–2
    opposition to 31, 49–50, 55
    patronage of 32
    regional integration, role in 32–4, 49, 77, 98–9, 101–2, 141–2
    reputation 1, 2, 11, 30–1, 77
    Rwanda and 81–2
    South Sudan and 118
    Tanzania and 80–1, 139
    terrorism and 90, 91, 105–6, 107–8, 109, 110, 111, 113, 122–3, 130
    UPDF and 46, 121–2, 128
    West, support of 11
Mushega, Nuwe Amanya 74

National Army for the Liberation of Uganda (NALU) 107
National Resistance Movement (NRM) 30, 31–2, 44–5, 48, 55
Nigeria 19–20
Nile River Basin Cooperative Framework 22–3
Nkurunziza, Pierre 83–4, 103, 112
Non-Governmental Organizations (NGOs) 125, 127–8
non-interference policy 23, 24, 27, 58, 67–8, 77, 84–5, 120, 147, 151, 152
North Africa 20
Nyerere, Charles 66
Nyerere, Julius 64, 65, 80

Obote, Milton 28, 29, 64, 65
oil
    China and 14, 93–4, 96, 102, 106, 131–5, 136, 143–4
    infrastructure 98–9, 129–30, 133–4
    in Kenya 79, 92
    LAPSSET 98, 139, 140

210   *Index*

NGOs, threat of 125, 127–8
prices 7
refinery 133–4, 136–7
regionalization of 95–6, 98–9, 128–9,
    141–2
security asset 123–4
security threat 92–7, 100, 106,
    124–5
state control of 126–7
in Uganda 11, 39, 93, 98–9, 123–6,
    131–3
Okello, Henry 122
Onjala, Joseph 74

Pan-Africanism 16, 32, 48, 64, 66–7
'Panel of the Wise' 8
parliament 50
    see also Members of Parliament
    (MPs)
patronage 32, 40, 51
Peace and Security Council (PSC) 8
Petroleum Exploration and Production
    Department (PEPD) 126
piracy 17
poaching *see* ivory poaching
political control 34–5
Production Sharing Agreements (PSAs)
    136

railways 22, 94–5, 97–8, 137–8, 140–1
Regional Centre on Small Arms (RECSA)
    88
Regional Economic Communities (RECs)
    3, 8, 10, 24–5
regional integration
    development frameworks 95–7
    EAC and 9–10, 32–4, 101–2
    infrastructure and 141–2
    oil and 95–6, 98–9, 128–9, 141–2
    risks to 41–2, 54–6
    support for 47–9, 58–9
Russia 29, 136–7
Rwanda
    China and 65, 81, 82, 103
    EAC and 32–3
    genocide in 67
    military operations 72
    Museveni and 81–2
    terrorism 86, 112

Saferworld initiative 88, 119, 120
security 3, 8, 21–2, 24–5, 70–2, 88
security threats 85–97
    ivory poaching 86–91, 102, 120–3
    oil 92–7, 100, 106, 123–4, 124–5
    terrorism 85–6
Sezibera, Richard 99
small arms and light weapons (SALW) 87,
    88–9, 91, 102, 114–16, 118–20
Somalia 17, 21, 86, 90, 108–9, 110
South Africa 18, 69
South Korea 44, 136, 137
South Sudan 4, 17, 49, 69–70, 117–18, 139
Southern Africa 18–19
Southern African Development
    Community (SADC) 68–9
sovereignty, promotion of 12–13, 15
Staden, Cobus van 88
Standard Gauge Railway (SGR) 94–5,
    97–8, 137–8, 140–1
Structural Adjustment Programmes
    (SAPs) 67
Sudan 17, 21, 116–18

Tanganyika *see* Tanzania
Tanzania
    Amin, overthrow of 29
    China and 64–5, 65–6, 80–1, 87, 103
    EAC and 67, 68–9
    ivory poaching 87, 121
    Museveni and 80–1, 139
    oil 92–3, 139
    railways 95, 98
    Rwanda, military operations in 72
    terrorism 86, 112
terrorism 85–6, 105–14, 122–3, 130
trade
    China–Africa 15, 18, 74
    Uganda 10, 38, 53, 56–7
    see also ivory poaching; small arms
        and light weapons (SALW)
transport 39
    see also railways
Tullow Oil 79, 124, 131, 134

Uganda
    China and 10, 28–9, 35–7, 142–4,
        147–8
    economy 39–40

foreign policy 35, 48
investment in 38–9, 39–41 *see also* infrastructure
ivory poaching 121–2
oil 11, 39, 93, 98–9, 123–6, 131–3, 133–4, 136–7
political control in 34–5
regional integration, role in 48, 101
significance of 10–12
small arms and light weapons (SALW) 114–16, 118–20
terrorism 106–7, 108–9
trade 10, 38, 56–7
Vision 2040 124
West, relationship with 30, 36, 37, 58
Uganda People's Defence Force (UPDF)
China and 46–7, 48, 49
development and 128, 137, 138
infrastructure and 135
ivory poaching 121–2
oil and 127
South Sudan and 118
terrorism and 31, 109, 111, 113
use of 11
Ugandan Overseas China Association 53
Ugandan Wildlife Authority (UWA) 121
UN Arms Trade Treaty (ATT) 120

UN Organization Stabilization Mission in the Democratic Republic of the Congo (MONUSCO) 72, 109, 114
UN Security Council (UNSC) 66
United States of America
Global War on Terror (GWOT) 11, 108, 109
oil and 131–2

Wade, Abdoulaye 7
Wang Yi 7
Wapakabulo, James 74–5, 77
weapons 117, 119
see also small arms and light weapons (SALW)
West Africa 19–20
Wine, Bobi 50, 156

Xi Jinping 7, 21

youth leaders 45

Zambia 19
Zhang Dejiang 43
Zhang Ho 36, 38–9, 53
Zheng He 13
Zhou Enlai 13
Zimbabwe 19